Family Dynamics in China

Life Course Studies

David L. Featherman
David I. Kertzer
Series Editors

Nancy W. Denney
Thomas J. Espenshade
Dennis P. Hogan
Jennie Keith
Maris A. Vinovskis
Associate Series Editors

Family and the Female Life Course: The Women of Verviers, Belgium, 1849–1880
George Alter

The Ageless Self: Sources of Meaning in Late Life
Sharon R. Kaufman

Family, Political Economy, and Demographic Change: The Transformation of Life in Casalecchio, Italy, 1861–1921
David I. Kertzer and Dennis P. Hogan

Family, Class, and Ideology in Early Industrial France: Social Policy and the Working-Class Family, 1925–1848
Katherine A. Lynch

Event History Analysis in Life Course Research
Karl Ulrich Mayer and Nancy B. Tuma, eds.

Working Parents: Transformations in Gender Roles and Public Policies in Sweden
Phyllis Moen

Family Dynamics in China: A Life Table Analysis
Zeng Yi

Zeng Yi

Family Dynamics in China

A Life Table Analysis

The University of Wisconsin Press

The University of Wisconsin Press
114 North Murray Street
Madison, Wisconsin 53715

3 Henrietta Street
London WC2E 8LU, England

5   4   3   2   1

Printed in the United States of America

Library of Congress Cataloging-in-Publication Data
Zeng Yi.
   Family dynamics in China: a life table analysis / Zeng Yi.
      220 pp.   cm. — (Life course studies)
      Includes bibliographical references and index.
      1. Family demography—China.   2. Family size—China.
   3. China—Population.   4. Mortality—China—Tables.
   I. Title.   II. Series.
   HQ759.98.Z46   1991
   306.85'0951—dc20
   ISBN 0-299-12630-7   90-50102
   ISBN 0-299-12634-X (pbk.)   CIP

Contents

List of Figures

List of Tables

Preface

The effects of changing demographic conditions on family size, structure, and family life course has been of interest to demographers for a long time. However, until very recently, this topic received little attention in demographic research. Most past research has focused on the nuclear family, and it goes without saying that this does not suffice, since the extended family is an important family type in many Asian and other Third World countries.

The demographic situation in China was a mysterious issue until 1982, when the results of a well-conducted modern census were released. The relationship between recent demographic change and the dynamics of the family in China had not been carefully studied until that census because of a lack of proper models and data.

My first objective was to develop a model suitable for societies in which both nuclear and extended families are important; my second was to study the effect of dramatic demographic changes on Chinese family size, structure, and family life course. This book is based on my doctoral dissertation, which was submitted to Brussels Free University in March 1986, and on research continued and extended after that date.

The book consists of three parts. The first part presents an overview of the demographic profile (size, structure, and determinants) of families in China. The second part discusses the construction and validation of a general family status life table model, which is an extension of Bongaarts' nuclear family model. The third part deals with the application of the model and presents interesting new findings concerning family dynamics in China.

To supplement the book, I developed computer software for the family status life table analysis described in this book. The software is called FAMY. The fertility model schedule and the nuptiality and divorce model schedules as well as the model life tables have been included in FAMY. Use of the program does not require extensive background in mathematics and computer programming. The family simulations can be performed by just specifying some major demographic parameters. The interactive data imputation and checking procedures are also available. The simulations yield simple summarized tables and graphics as well as detailed tabulations.

I thank Frans Willekens, Thomas Pullum, and Thomas Espenshade for suggesting that I make a manual and diskette of FAMY available for wider application. I am also grateful to the Interuniversity Expertise Centre Pro-GAMMA and to Wang Zhenlian for helping me make my program user-friendly. FAMY is published and distributed by ProGAMMA. The price of the software and information on how to get a free copy of the manual and diskette for scholars from developing countries can also be obtained by writing to iec ProGAMMA, P.O. Box 841, 9700 AV Groningen, Netherlands (tel.: 050-636900, FAX: 050-636687).

I am indebted to many people for giving me academic and emotional support during the course of this study. First, I would like to express my gratitude to my teachers in China, who offered me a solid background, and to my teachers at the Interuniversity Programme in Demography in Brussels, who offered me sound formal demographic training at the postgraduate level.

I cannot find words to properly express my respect for and gratitude to Frans Willekens for his encouragement and invaluable advice. I am extremely appreciative of the profound concern of Ron Lesthaeghe and grateful for his invaluable advice. The suggestions provided by A. Rogers at a very early stage of the research and the discussions and recommendations provided by J. Bongaarts, Nico Keilman, S. Wijewickrema, Dirk J. Van de Kaa, Jenny de Jong-Gierveld, R. Cliquet, H. Page, E. Mandel, and H. Glejser are gratefully acknowledged. I benefited considerably from the comments by the referees and the editors and from the discussions with J. Vaupel, N. Keyfitz, A. Yashin, M. Stoto, Andrew Foster, William Hodges, John Wilmoth, R. Fernandos, and others. I am also grateful to Hu Huanyong, Yuan Fang, Zhang Chunyuan, Wu Cangping, Cai Wenmei, Shen Yimin, Zhao Xuan, Chen Lu, Guei Shixun, and Yian Zhenyuan for providing warm encouragement and updated information. I benefited a great deal from computational advice given by Yves de Roo. Of course, I am solely responsible for any errors that remain.

I am very grateful to the Netherlands Interdisciplinary Demographic Institute and The Institute of Population Research at Peking University for providing institutional support. Thanks are also due to Willemien Kneppelhout for editing the text and to Joan Vrind, Jacqueline van der Helm, and Tonny Nieuwstraten for patiently and skillfully typing the manuscript. I am particularly grateful to Ms. Joan Vrind, who put much effort into the realization of this book.

Most of the material in chapter 10 appeared as "Changing Demographic Characteristics and the Family Status of chinese Women" in *Population Studies* 42(2) (1988): 183–203. Most of chapter 11 appeared as "Changes in Family Structure in China: A Simulation Study" in *Population and Development Review* 12(4) (1986): 675–703. Figures 2.6, 3.3, and 3.4 and the related discussions are drawn from Zeng Yi, J. Vaupel, and A. Yashin, "Marriage and Fertility in China: A Graphical Analysis" in *Population and Development Review* 11(4) (1985): 721–36. I would like to acknowledge both *Population Studies* and *Population and Development Review* for permitting me to include these materials in this book.

Finally I would like to express my gratitude to my parents and my wife. Without their continuous contributions, this book would not have been completed.

Introduction

The family is the most fundamental unit of social organization and has long been a subject of study by social scientists. In common usage, *family* has at least two clearly distinct meanings: the set of blood relatives and the coresident domestic group (Brass 1983:38). The term *family* in this study refers to a group of coresidential persons who are related through marriage, blood, or adoption.

The strongest relations between people are relations of marriage, blood, and adoption. Many activities take place within a family context and many decisions affecting people's lives are made within the family unit.

In most societies, the family maintains its position as the unit of social activity and decision making. In some Western societies, relations of marriage, blood, and adoption are becoming weaker, and their significance as an organizing principle of social structure and social processes is waning. Some of the functions of the family have been taken over by alternative living arrangements economic relations, such as cohabitation without marriage.

This study, however, deals with the People's Republic of China, a typical non-Western society in which the family, based on marriage, blood, or adoption, is still the fundamental unit of social organization and will remain so for the foreseeable future.

The concept of the family used in this study includes both the nuclear family and the extended family. The characteristics of the family that are considered here are demographic characteristics, such as size and composition. The creation of a family, a change in family size, and the dissolution of a family as well as changes in family characteristics can be called *family dynamics*. It is directly associated with the occurrence of demographic events. The events that are important in the study of family demography are marriage, childbearing, death of child, death of spouse, death of parent(s), divorce, remarriage, children leaving parental home, and so on.

Family characteristics influence population change to a considerable extent, both directly through the effect of family size and indirectly through the effect of fertility, mortality, and migration. They also affect the socioeconomic status of the family (e.g., the amount of care given to the young and old, labor force participation, housing demand, demand for other consumer goods). The factors that affect the size and composition of the family may be grouped into two categories: demographic and socioeconomic determinants. Demographic variables such as nuptiality, fertility, and mortality are the direct determinants of family dynamics and family characteristics. Socioeconomic factors such as income, education, and occupation do not directly affect the size and composition of the family. Instead, they must operate through demographic determinants (Bongaarts 1983a). We have, therefore, the following relations:

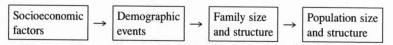

Brass calls the demographic factors "proximate determinants" of the family in order to distinguish the more "intermediate" operational factors from the deeper, underlying social and economic effects. Brass also argues that formal demography of the family is the investigation of how demographic factors control the size and composition of families in a given population (Brass 1983).

A dominant feature of past demographic studies on the relation between family characteristics and demographic processes has been the inclusion of one or more variables without much attention given to the interdependence between the variables. Relatively little research has been devoted to the formal demography of the family, which deals with the quantitative aspects of family size, composition, and changes therein (Bongaarts 1983a). Recently, however, there have been a number of attempts to combine the variables related to the status and characteristics of the family in an integrated framework. This has resulted in models of family demography.

In this study I adopt a multistate demographic approach to examine family dynamics and the demographic processes that take place within a family context. The processes considered are fertility, nuptiality, mortality, and children leaving the parental home. In the multistate approach, different family states are distinguished, each exhibiting a distinct type of demographic behavior. Due to events resulting from demographic processes, persons may move from one family status to another. The distinct demographic behavioral variables of the family simultaneously relate to fertility, mortality (child mortality and widowhood), and nuptiality (first marriage, marriage dissolution, and remarriage). Therefore, an integrated analysis of these demographic processes is needed.

The conventional multistate demographic approach deals with an age dimension and another dimension having several states, such as the region of residence in the multiregional life table model, marital status in the marital status life table model, and labor force status in the working life table model. In this study, we deal with age and several other dimensions simultaneously, such as fertility, marriage, and mortality. Each of these can have a number of states.

An integrated analysis of demographic processes and family dynamics raises several methodological problems. One of the two purposes of this study is to specify and clarify methodological problems associated with the study of family dynamics within the context of a multistate demographic analysis. The other purpose is to apply the integrated framework to gain a better understanding of the interdependence between family dynamics and demographic processes in China.

The aim of the study is therefore twofold. The first aim is to develop a model for the multistate integrated analysis of family dynamics that takes into account fertility, mortality, nuptiality, and children leaving the parental home. The second aim is to obtain a better understanding of the relation between family dynamics and demographic variables in China.

The first part of this volume deals with substantive aspects of the demographic situation and demographic family characteristics and their determinants, such as marriage, fertility, mortality, widowhood, and divorce as well as the rural-urban, ethnic, and regional differences of the determinants in China. It gives a general overview and serves as a base for the mathematical model and framework. The methodological issues of the mathematical modeling of a multistate analysis of family dynamics are treated in Part II. Part III presents applications to a time dimension (a comparison of the periods 1950–70 and 1981) and to a spatial dimension (a comparison of Chinese rural and urban areas).

Part One
Overview:
A Demographic Profile

The following three chapters discuss demographic family characteristics and their determinants in China. We will see that the average size of the Chinese family is much smaller than before the foundation of the People's Republic in 1949. The nuclear family has become a major family form, whereas the large family with married brothers living together has become rare. But the three-generation family is still one of the important family types in Chinese society.

Mortality has declined remarkably since 1949. Marriage in China has always been universal and very stable. A relatively late marriage pattern has emerged. Fertility declined dramatically after 1970. Current fertility in China is not only age-dependent but mainly parity-dependent. Also, any attempt to summarize the demographic situation in China should take into account the significant rural-urban and ethnic differences in demographic variables.

Chapter 1 briefly reviews the population trends and the major data sources, such as the 1982 census, the nationwide one-per-thousand fertility survey, and other demographic surveys. A demographic profile of the Chinese family and its determinants is described in chapter 2. Chapter 3 deals with the rural-urban, ethnic, and regional differences in demographic determinants of family dynamics.

1
A Brief Review of Population Trends in China and the Major Demographic Data Sources

1.1. Population Trends and Family Planning

China is a country with a total population of more than 1.1 billion (April 1989), about 22% of the world's population. The total territory of about 9.6 million square kilometers consists of 22 provinces (including Taiwan), 3 municipalities (Beijing, Shanghai, Tianjin), and 5 autonomous regions (figure 1.1).

Before 1949, China's population growth was characterized by a high birth rate, a high death rate, and a low rate of natural increase. It was estimated that in 1936 the birth rate was about 38 per thousand, the death rate was 28 per thousand, and the natural growth rate was only around 10 per thousand. In the 109 years from 1840 to 1949, the average annual growth rate stood at only 2.5 per thousand (Qian 1983a:295).

There have been five stages in China's population growth since the founding of the People's Republic (see figure 1.2).

a. 1949–57. The birth rates were fairly high (32–38 per thousand). The death rates were remarkably reduced due to a more egalitarian distribution of food and universal, albeit rudimentary, medical care. Consequently, the natural growth rates were high (16–25‰). This was the first baby boom in China. The results of the first census, in 1953, spurred the Chinese government to launch the first birth-planning campaign. Premier Zhou Enlai officially endorsed birth control in 1956. The government started to train birth-planning personnel and launched a large-scale publicity campaign.

b. 1958–61. With the Great Leap Forward in 1958, the first birth-planning phase came to an end. Some Chinese social scientists who warned against the potential economic problems of continued rapid population growth were criticized. Chief among them was Professor Ma Yinchu, who was removed from his position as president of Peking University and was not rehabilitated until 1978. The Great Leap Forward and the natural disasters that befell China in the three years that followed the launching of its policies damaged industrial

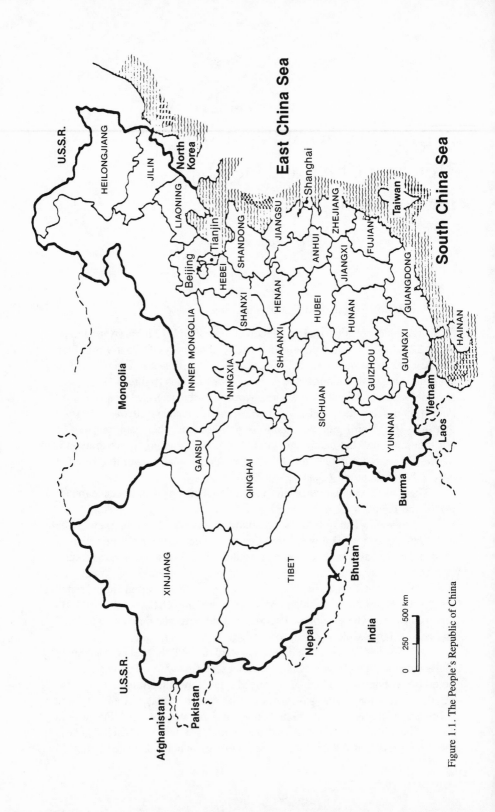

Figure 1.1. The People's Republic of China

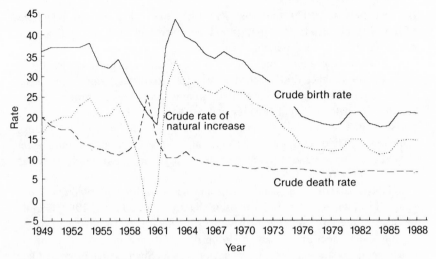

Figure 1.2. Crude rates per 1,000 people per year
Source: SSB 1988a:222.

and agricultural productivity and led to a decline in living standards. This, in turn, caused the death rate to increase remarkably during the years 1959–61 (the death rate was as high as 25.4 per thousand in 1960) and the birth rate and the natural growth rate to decrease substantially (the growth rate was as low as −4.57 per thousand in 1960).

   c. 1962–70. The death rate fell to 10 per thousand in 1962 as normal conditions were restored. The postcrisis peak birth rate was very high: 43.4 births per thousand in 1963. The reinstitution of the family-planning program took place in 1962. The State Council began a birth-planning campaign. Nationwide birth-planning measures, promoting contraceptives and late marriage, quickly followed. Just when this birth-planning campaign might have started to show results, the so-called Cultural Revolution, begun in 1966, disrupted the new program. Red Guard activities shut down factories and distribution networks, cutting off supplies of contraceptives. Also, government controls on birth planning were lifted. The birth rates during 1962–70 were very high (33.4–43.4 per thousand). Natural growth rates were also very high (25.5–33.3 per thousand). This was the second baby boom in China.

   d. 1971–79. An efficient family-planning campaign was initiated that emphasized three elements:

Wan: late marriage (midtwenties for women, late twenties for men);

Xi: long birth intervals (3–4 years);

Shao: fewer children (no more than two children per couple in the cities and three in the rural areas).

Between 1970 and 1979, the "Wan Xi Shao" policies led to rapid reductions of the birth rate from 33.4 to 17.8 per thousand and of the natural growth rate from 25.8 to 11.6 per thousand.

   e. 1979 to present. The large cohorts of children born in the 1960s and early 1970s have now reached or are close to marriageable age. Consequently, even limiting families to two children each would result in a considerable growth in population for at least half a century. As a preventive measure, in 1979 the Chinese government launched the famous birth control campaign of advocating one child per couple. The Chinese government regarded population control to be of strategic importance and family planning a basic policy (Qian 1983b).

   Notwithstanding the widespread and successful family-planning campaign, birth rates in China have risen slightly from 1980 to 1982, mainly because of the large number of newlyweds, which may be attributed to the demographic effect of the baby boom in the 1960s and the relaxation of the marriage-age restriction (i.e., the policy of Wan Xi Shao, which promoted late marriage) by the New Marriage Law, which took effect in early 1981. The birth rate again decreased in the period 1982–84.

   Birth rates have significantly increased from 17.5 per thousand in 1984 to 21.0 per thousand in 1987 and 20.78 per thousand in 1988, according to data released by the State Statistical Bureau. The birth rate derived from the two-per-thousand fertility and contraceptive survey conducted in 1988 is even higher, namely, 23.2 per thousand in 1987. The total fertility rate, which removes the effects of age structure, rose from 2.35 children per woman in 1984 to 2.59 in 1987 and 2.31 in 1988, according to the two-per-thousand fertility and contraceptive survey.

   Four reasons may be given for the recent rise in birth rates. First, the young people who were born in China's second baby boom in the 1960s are reaching marriageable age. The number of women of childbearing age (15–49 years old) increased from 269 million in 1984 to 285 million in 1986 and 299 million in 1988 and will increase up to 310 and 339 million in 1990 and 2000, respectively. The number of women of age 20–29, who have the highest potential for childbearing,[1] increased from 91 million in 1984 to 102 million in 1988. This has consequently resulted in a new baby boom, which will last for about 10 more years. My demographic analysis of standardization shows that if the age-specific fertility rate in 1987 were applied to the age structure in 1982, the birth rate would be 20.3 per thousand, in contrast to the observed birth rate of 23.2 per thousand in 1987. In other words, the influence of changes in age structure in 1987 (i.e., the people born in the baby boom in the 1960s reaching childbearing age) resulted in an increase in the birth rate of 14.8%. The

---

1. Births by women aged 20–29 currently account for about 80% of all births in China.

second reason for the rise in birth rate is that the new responsibility system[2] in rural areas has reinforced, at least to some extent, the economic value of children and the economic incentives of having a larger family. Third, the administrative decentralization, which forms part of the large-scale economic and political reforms, lessens government control over birth planning and the age at first marriage. My demographic analysis has shown that if a cohort of women followed age-specific rates of first marriage for rural Chinese women in 1986, one-fourth of them would get married before age 20, the minimum legal age for first marriage for women (see chapter 12). Fourth, birth control regulations have actually been relaxed to some extent in some rural areas.

In sum, although one may regret that strategic mistakes resulted in two baby booms in the 1950s and 1960s, family planning in China has been the most successful of all such programs of developing countries in reducing mortality since 1949 and in reducing fertility since 1970.

1.2. Availability of Demographic Data

From the 1950s through the 1970s, the supply of demographic data for the People's Republic of China was limited. For instance, in 1953, China's census asked for only the name, sex, age, and nationality (ethnic origin) of the head of the household and for a list of the members of the household and their relationship to the respondent. The census also determined whether the location of the household was urban or rural. The 1964 census added three more items to the questionnaire (level of education, occupation, and social "class"). But the detailed information of the 1964 census was not published, due to the disturbances caused by the Cultural Revolution.

A household registration system has been in force since 1955. Theoretically, the data quality from household registration ought to be good, because registration is closely linked to many aspects of daily life, such as food rationing, employment, and education, and because individuals know their exact date of birth due to the traditional Chinese belief in astrology. The prerequisites for obtaining accurate data are present. However, because of the disruptions during the Great Leap Forward and the Cultural Revolution, as well as for a number of other reasons, the registration data were neither complete nor properly compiled and published in the 1950s, 1960s, and 1970s.

Since the late 1970s, with the rapid development of the field of demogra-

2. In the Chinese collective mode in the 1950s, 1960s and 1970s, the farmers worked in production teams under unified direction and with collective income distribution. Starting at the beginning of the 1980s, the new responsibility system spread all over the country. Under the new system, the land is assigned to each peasant household and the peasant households have been replacing the production team as the unit of production.

phy in China, the Chinese government has realized that improving the statistical system could be of great value to the "four modernizations" (industry, agriculture, science and technology, and defence). Data availability and data quality have improved remarkably in recent years. I will now briefly describe the main current sources of demographic data.

1.2.1. The 1982 National Census

The preparation of the 1982 National Census began toward the end of 1979. The census itself took place on July 1, 1982. The questionnaire included 5 categories concerning household topics and 13 categories concerned with the individual. Each person was asked his or her name, sex, age, ethnic origin, place of residence, and place of registration. Those above the age of 6 were asked about their level of education, and those aged 15 and over were asked four specific questions related to their occupation, employment status, and marital status. Women aged 15–64 were asked the number of children they had borne and the number of those children still living, and women between 15 and 49 were asked to report any children born in 1981 and the birth order of those children.

The 1982 census of China was carried out in collaboration with the United Nations. Twenty-nine computers were installed (21 IBM computers contributed by the United Nations and 8 Wang computers purchased by China). A postenumeration sampling check gives the following indicators regarding the enumeration work:

Coverage: overcount 0.71 per thousand
           undercount 0.56 per thousand
           net overcount 0.15 per thousand
Error rate in reporting sex: 0.03 per thousand
Error rate in reporting age: 6.15 per thousand

According to the research results presented in the international seminar on China's 1982 population census (Beijing, China, March 1984), we can be sure that the data quality of China's 1982 census had reached an advanced level. Vaino Kannisto, former interregional adviser of the United Nations, pointed out, "The quality of these data, as far as head counts are concerned, is equal to that of the best European census" (Kannisto 1984:19). Apart from the post-

---

3. For the sake of comparison, I list the Whipple's index and the Meyer's index of a few countries (Ma An 1984: 259–60):

Whipple's Index	Meyer's Index
USA (1960): 100.9	USA (1970): 1.1
Philippines (1960): 156.0	Sweden (1970): 0.6
Soviet Union (1926): 159.1	Peru (1970): 13.0
Turkey (1945): 219.0 (male)	Nicaragua (1970): 27.9
342.0 (female)	

Table 1.1. Comparison of births in 1981 reported from China's 1982
census and the 1982 one-per-thousand fertility survey

	First birth	Second birth	Third and higher births	Total
1982 census	47.3	25.7	27.0	100
1982 one-per-thousand fertility survey	46.6	25.4	28.1	100

enumeration sampling check mentioned above, the high quality of China's 1982 census can be demonstrated by three facts: (1) The survival ratios are plausible from each census to the next. (2) The age distribution shows no digit preference. The Whipple's index is 102.1 for the male population and 101.9 for the female population. The Meyer's index gives both males and females a value of 3.0 (Yu 1984:2).[3] The United Nations index developed to test the accuracy of enumeration indicates an acceptable accuracy for the 1953 and 1964 census and an even better one for 1982 (Caldwell et al. 1984:19). (3) The fertility measures obtained from the 1982 one-per-thousand fertility survey and the 1982 census are also consistent. The birth rate for 1981 found in the 1982 census is 20.6 per thousand, and in the 1982 fertility survey, it is 20.9 per thousand. The proportions of births by birth-order from these two totally different statistical sources are quite similar (see, e.g., table 1.1).

At the special session on China's 1982 census of the 20th General Conference of the International Union for the Scientific Study of Population held in June 1985, demographers from all over the world interested in the population of China reached the same general conclusion as in the Beijing international seminar of March 1984, namely, that the data of China's 1982 census are of an advanced level and that the census contributed significantly to the knowledge of the world's population (see Liu Zheng 1985a; Li Chengrui 1985b; Wu 1985a; Banister 1985; Calot 1985). It was also pointed out that several adjustments should be made for the sake of greater accuracy, such as adjusting the age-sex distribution to be able to take into account the enumerated persons whose age is unknown or unstated and adjusting the annual evaluations of population changes to allow for the undercoverage of vital registration (see, e.g., Calot 1985). The previously unreported age and sex of 4.24 million military personnel have been published recently (SSB 1985), and the age-sex distribution of China's population has been adjusted too (Liu Zheng 1985b).

1.2.2. The One-per-Thousand Fertility Survey

Using the addresses of the 1982 census, a well-designed sample survey of 1,017,574 people (sampling fraction of 1‰), covering 28 provinces, municipalities, and autonomous regions (except Taiwan and Tibet), was conducted by 3,676 investigators between September and November 1982. A total of 310,462 women aged 15–67 were questioned in person on age, ethnic origin, place of residence, marital status, occupation, education, birth control measures, abortion, birth history (such as the number of children ever born, number of living children, and birth-order and date of birth of each child), and marital status and date of first marriage. The total error rate in recording the data from the questionnaires was a negligible 1.07 per thousand. We have mentioned above that the results from this nationwide one-per-thousand fertility survey and the 1982 census are quite consistent. This shows that the quality of China's 1982 one-per-thousand fertility survey is rather good. Twenty-six preliminary analytical articles with extensive data were published in a special issue of *Population and Economics* in 1983. An English translation of this issue was published (entitled *Analysis of China's National One-per-Thousand-Population Fertility Survey*) by the China Population Information Centre in 1984 (CPIC 1984).

Coale (1984) combined and masterfully analyzed the one-per-thousand fertility survey data and the census data for 1953, 1964, and 1982 on numbers of persons by sex and single years of age. He concluded that the survey data have passed a series of stringent tests of accuracy and consistency. He also argued that the same analysis reveals that official data (household registration data) and death rates have understated the true numbers by a considerable margin. Chinese and American researchers have been analyzing the data tapes from the survey at the East-West Centre's Population Institute over the past years and 25 papers were presented by Chinese and American demographers at a mid-October conference in Beijing in 1985.

1.2.3. The In-Depth Fertility Surveys

The first phase of a large survey project called the In-Depth Fertility Surveys was conducted in April 1985 by the State Statistical Bureau of China, with the technical assistance of the Research Centre of the International Statistical Institute. The new fertility surveys cover three provinces and the municipalities Hebei, Shaanxi, and Shanghai, with a total population of 93 million (SSB 1986:3). The second phase of the In-Depth Fertility Surveys was conducted in April 1987 in Beijing Municipality and Liaoning, Shandong, Guangdong, Guizhou, and Gansu provinces, covering a total population of 236 million (SSB 1988b). Based on the standard of the World Fertility Survey, the questionnaire of this new fertility survey covers six demographic aspects: background, marriage history, detailed birth and pregnancy history, contraceptive knowledge and history of contraceptive use, fertility preference, and background of current or last spouse. These Chinese fertility surveys have provided a very rich set of demographic data.

1.2.4. The 1987 national one-percent population survey

In 1987, the State Statistical Bureau conducted the one-percent population survey. The standard enumeration time of the survey was July 1, 1987. With a sampling probability of 1%, 10,711,652 persons were surveyed, covering all provinces, autonomous regions, and municipalities in mainland China. In addition to the questions asked in the 1982 census, three important questions on migration were incorporated in the survey. As announced by the State Statistical Bureau, the intervals for the Crude Birth Rate (CBR) and Crude Death Rate (CDR) are CBR$\pm$0.11 per-thousand and CDR$\pm$0.06 per-thousand, respectively (confidence probability of 95%) (SSB, 1988d). Detailed tabulations have been published and a sampling of 5% of the data from the survey is available on tape for researchers.

1.2.5. The two-per-thousand fertility and contraceptive survey

The State Family Planning Commission organized the two-per-thousand fertility and contraceptive survey in July 1988: 2.15 million people were actually surveyed, of whom 459,269 ever-married women aged 15–57 were interviewed in detail on 67 items such as background, marriage, pregnancy history, contraception, breast-feeding, childbearing, and mobility. The survey covered all provinces, autonomous regions, and municipalities in mainland China. With a confidence probability of 95%, the intervals for the CBR and CDR at the national level are CBR$\pm$0.11 per-thousand and CDR$\pm$0.06 per-thousand, respectively. The intervals at the provincial level range from CBR$\pm$0.99 to CBR$\pm$2.03 per-thousand and CDR$\pm$0.56 to CDR$\pm$1.02 per-thousand, respectively (SDSFPC 1989).

1.2.6. Household registration data

In China, seven statistical items are required in urban household registration: usual residence, temporary residence, births, deaths, immigration, outmigration, and any changes in and corrections to these items. There are five statistical items in rural household registration: usual residence, births, deaths, immigration, and outmigration. Both urban and rural areas have annual statistical tabulations, from brigade (or village) and neighborhood committees to the national level. A nationwide thorough household registration check was conducted just before the 1982 census. In recent years, the government has also tried to increase the number and improve the quality of statistical agencies from the central to the local level. It has emphasized the independence of the agency's work from that of the local authorities, uniformization of statistical indices, development of automatic data processing, and so on. It is generally expected that the household registration system will become more complete and accurate, although it has been found that births were seriously underreported.

1.2.7. 1972–75 Nationwide Cancer Epidemiology Survey and other
nationwide and local surveys

The Nationwide Cancer Epidemiology Survey was a monumental undertaking
and included an attempt to record every death in China for a period of three
years; an extra effort was made to achieve an acceptable level of reporting infant deaths. Over 18 million deaths were thus documented. For the first time
in China's history, reasonably accurate life tables applicable to the whole of
China became available.

In recent years, many surveys have been conducted at the local level by
local family-planning workers, health service agencies, universities, and social
science institutes. These local surveys are obviously good data sources for regional demographic research. Other nationwide surveys, such as household
income and expenditure surveys, a 1987 national survey of people over the age
of 60, a migration survey of 74 cities and towns, and annual population change
surveys can also provide a considerable number of demographic data.

2

The Chinese Family and Its Demographic Determinants

Family characteristics and their determinants can be classified into two categories:

1. Demographic factors, such as average family size and composition, and their determinants, such as fertility, nuptiality, and mortality.

2. Socioeconomic factors, such as average income and expenditure per family, occupation and educational level of family members, and philosophy and ideology regarding family.

This chapter deals mainly with demographic characteristics of the family and their determinants in China. Section 2.1 focuses on family size and composition, and section 2.2 discusses the demographic determinants of family dynamics. Section 2.3 describes how government policies affect family dynamics.

2.1. Family Size and Structure

2.1.1. The Chinese feedback model versus the Western continued linear model

In most Western societies, children leave the parental home either when they get married or when they enter college. The older parents depend financially on a pension or on social security. Children are not responsible for the financial support of their parents (of course, they may still have emotional and possibly financial connections with their parents, even if they no longer live with their parents).

In Chinese society, however, the philosophy regarding the support of one's older parents is quite different from that of modern Western societies. Filiation has been one of the cornerstones of Chinese society for thousands of years and it is still highly valued. The philosophical ideas of filiation include not only respect for older generations but also the responsibility of children to take care of

13

their parents. Both current marriage law and the current constitution of China state clearly that children should take care of their parents.

Professor Fei Xiaotong, the well-known Chinese sociologist, recently called the Chinese family model a "feedback model," which can be formulated as $F1 \leftrightarrow F2 \leftrightarrow F3 \leftrightarrow Fn$ (F stands for generation). It means that generation $F1$ fosters generation $F2$, and generation $F2$ takes care of generation $F1$ when $F1$ is old; the same relation holds between generations $F2$ and $F3$, and so on. In comparison, Professor Fei called the Western model a "continued linear model," which can be formulated as $F1 \rightarrow F2 \rightarrow F3 \rightarrow Fn$. That is, generation $F1$ fosters generation $F2$ without financial feedback from $F2$ to $F1$, and generation $F2$ fosters generation $F3$, again without financial feedback from $F3$ to $F2$, and so on (Fei 1983:7).

Consequently, the typical family pattern of Western society is the so-called nuclear family consisting of husband, wife, and unmarried children. Nuclear families may be simply divided into husband-wife families and one-parent families. One-parent families can be divided further, according to the sex and marital status of the parent (Bongaarts 1983). However, the Chinese family structure is not as simple, since married children do not necessarily leave the parental home.

The difference between the Chinese feedback model and the Western continued linear model implies that the average Chinese family size is much bigger than the Western family size and that the proportion of families consisting of more than two generations in China is much higher than in Western society.

2.1.2. Family size

Table 2.1 and figure 2.1 show that the average family size in China before the establishment of the People's Republic (1949) was around 5.3. The average family size in 1953 (census figure) was 4.3, which is considerably lower than the figures before 1949. This sharp decline was mainly due to the increase in the number of families by the breaking up of some extended families, especially those of more than three generations and extended families in which married brothers lived together.

However, the family size increased significantly to 4.78 in 1978. This might be due to the housing shortage (building construction was seriously disrupted during the Cultural Revolution from 1966 to 1976), as a result of which some married brothers had to live together. The average family size found in the 1982 census was 4.43, which is higher than in the 1953 and 1964 censuses.

As stated in the note accompanying the figures from the 1982 census published by the State Statistical Bureau the census might underestimate average family size because of the overcount of the number of families. There are two main causes. First, in so-called urban-rural households, that is, in families in which one or more members are state employees and are eligible for com-

Table 2.1. Average size of Chinese families

Period	Source	Average family size
1911	*1934 Economic Year Book of China*	5.17
1912	Statistics of the Former Ministry of Interior Affairs	5.31
1928	Statistics of the Former Ministry of Internal Affairs	5.27
1933	*Statistical Abstracts*	5.29
1936	Reports of the Former Ministry of Internal Affairs	5.38
1947	Statistics of the Former Ministry of Internal Affairs	5.35
1930	A survey by Prof. Li Jing Han in Ding County	5.80
1931	A survey of a vast area of 22 provinces by Prof. J. L. Buck	5.21
1933	Review of data from surveys of 10 regions by Prof. Chen Da	4.84
1930–40	A survey of birth history covering 7 regions by the Population Research Centre of the Chinese Academy of Social Sciences	5.58
1953	1953 census	4.30
1964	1964 census	4.29
1978	Household registration statistics	4.78
1982	1982 census	4.43
1987	National one-percent population survey	4.30

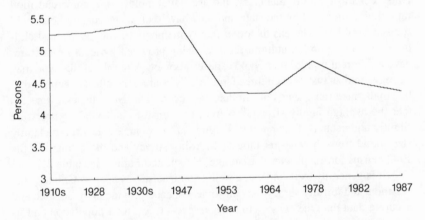

Figure 2.1. Average sizes of Chinese families

Source: See table 2.1. Family sizes in the 1910s and 1930s are averages of the available data from the years shown in table 2.1.

mercial food rationing provided by the state, whereas the other members are peasants, the same family may have two household register booklets and may thus be registered as two families. Second, some towns give a better supply of grain and foodstuffs to collective households; this encourages members of certain families who actually reside at home to register separately in the collective household where they work. Therefore, the State Statistical Bureau adjusted

Table 2.2. Family size in the 1982 census and in the
one-per-thousand fertility survey for three provinces

Province	Average family size from 1982 census[a]	Average family size from one-per-thousand fertility survey[b]
Liaoning	4.1	4.22
Hebei	4.1	4.28
Fujian	4.8	5.02

[a] SSB 1982.
[b] Lavely and Li 1985.

the average urban family size from 3.84 to 3.95 through a postcensus sample check. The average rural family size was not adjusted. The second reason for underestimating family size does not apply to rural areas since there are no collective households there. But the first factor might play a role. In some rural families, some members may work in the town; they may be state employees such as local administrative personnel, teachers, doctors, or local shop assistants. For those family members who are state employees, commercial food rationing is provided by the state and they have their own separate household register booklets, whereas the other family members (mainly wives and children), who rely on agricultural food rationing provided by local production, have a different type of household register booklet. A family of this type may be registered as two or even three families. Of course, the effect is expected to be small since these kinds of families are uncommon. Nevertheless, it seems that the average family sizes taken from the censuses and vital registers are slightly understated. To support this argument, we compare the average family size found from the one-per-thousand fertility survey and those found in the 1982 census for the provinces Liaoning, Hebei, and Fujian (see table 2.2).

It is generally expected that a well-organized survey such as China's one-per-thousand fertility survey may, in some respects, provide more detailed and accurate data than the census. In other respects (e.g., total population and its age structure), this may not be the case. The average family size found in the one-per-thousand fertility survey is consistently higher than that found in the census for all three provinces compared. We suppose that the survey figures are more reliable because the survey interviewers were well trained and were able to correctly follow instructions and thus would probably record the true membership of each family.

Whatever the interpretation of the fluctuating figures on average family size presented in table 2.1 may be, one point is clear: the current average Chinese family is much smaller compared with the 1910s, 1920s, 1930s, and 1940s. The remarkable reduction in family size in the 1950s and 1960s com-

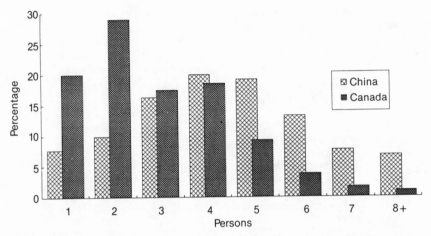

Figure 2.2. Percentage distribution of family sizes in China in 1982 and in Canada in 1981
Sources: China, SSB 1983a; Canada, Priest and Pryor 1984.

pared with the 1940s and earlier was obviously due to far-reaching social structural changes that caused an increase in the proportion of nuclear families rather than a decline in birth rates since the fertility level in the 1950s and 1960s did not decrease (the average total fertility rate was 5.44 in the 1940s, 5.88 in the 1950s, and 5.68 in the 1960s). It is somewhat puzzling, however, that the average family size found in the 1982 census was higher than that recorded by the 1953 and 1964 censuses, given that fertility was dramatically reduced in 1982 (the total fertility rate was 2.48 in 1982; see Zhao Xuan 1985:32). This result will be discussed in the next section.

Although the average family sizes found in the 1953, 1964, and 1982 censuses were significantly smaller than those from before 1949, the Chinese family is still much larger than the Western family. For example, the average family size in Canada was 3.9 in 1961, 3.5 in 1971, and 2.9 in 1981. The percentage distribution of family households by number of persons in China is also quite different from that in Canada (figure 2.2).

The enormous difference between the average family size in China and in Western countries is probably due to the difference between the Chinese feedback model (which has led to an important proportion of three-generation families in Chinese society) and the Western continued linear model, as well as a number of other factors such as lower fertility, higher marriage discontinuity, a better housing supply, and the high value placed upon privacy in contemporary Western society.

Table 2.3. Percentage distribution of family types in 1930, 1982, and 1987

Period	Source	Nuclear (including one-person) families	Three-generation and other extended families	Total
1930	A survey by Prof. Li Jing Han in Ding County in Hebei province[a]	51.47	48.53	100.0
1982	Census[b]	81.19	18.81	100.0
1982	One-per-thousand fertility survey data from Liaoning province[c]	80.55	19.45	100.0
1982	One-per-thousand fertility survey data from Hebei province[c]	76.51	23.49	100.0
1982	One-per-thousand fertility survey data from Fujian province[c]	70.03	29.97	100.0
1987	National one-percent population survey[d]	80.00	20.00	100.0

[a]Quoted from Ma 1984.   [c]Lavely and Li 1985.
[b]SSB 1983b.   [d]SSB 1988c.

2.1.3. Family structure

Table 2.3 shows that in 1982 the proportion of nuclear families had increased by about 30 percentage points and multigeneration families and joint families with married brothers living together had sharply declined, compared with 1930. Such changes in family structure have a deeply rooted socioeconomic background. In old China (before the foundation of the People's Republic), well-to-do families made every effort to preserve their large joint multigeneration families so as to safeguard the land and property they had accumulated over generations. The parents did not want their children to live separately, because they did not want to break up their land and property. The poorer families owned very little land and scanty means of production, which were not subdividable. Under the individual ownership system and extremely low productivity levels, it appeared profitable to maintain large multigeneration families and families in which married brothers lived together.

Following the establishment of the People's Republic of China in 1949, feudal land ownership was abolished and the land was reallocated. The former large well-to-do families were consequently split up, because they no longer owned large amounts of land and property, which had previously prevented them from disintegrating. The former poorer families received more land and property, as a result of which married brothers were able to live apart, and unmarried brothers were able to get married and leave the large family. Furthermore, as a result of the cooperative movement, members of families no longer worked only on their own land; instead, they worked in a production team under unified direction and with a collective income distributed among the workers.

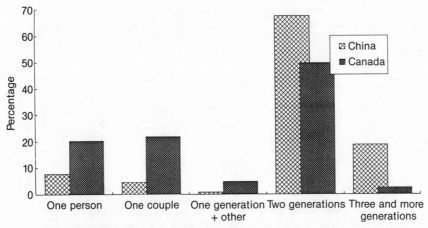

Figure 2.3. Percentage distribution of family types in China in 1982 and in Canada in 1981
Sources: China, SSB 1983a; Canada, Priest and Pryor 1984.

The advantages of maintaining a large family in which married brothers lived together and worked at private production were suppressed. Besides, the possible disputes between mothers and daughters-in-law or among sisters-in-law might have encouraged the division of large families.

Clearly, the Chinese family has become a smaller unit and there are fewer extended families than in the 1930s. However, the three-generation family is still an important family type in China. The China 1982 census data and other data sources indicate that around 20% of Chinese families are some form of extended family, which is about 7 times as large as the proportion in Canada in 1981 (see figure 2.3).

Other recent surveys also confirm the above argument. For example, according to a recent sample survey of 2,035 peasant families in Sichuan Province, families of more than three generations accounted for only 0.98%, but three-generation families accounted for 22.26% of the total (Zhao Xishun 1985). A family survey in the five largest cities (Beijing, Shanghai, Tianjin, Nanjing, and Chengdu) indicates that three-generation families in these cities accounted for about 20% of the total from the 1930s until 1982. (GRFFC, 1985). The increase in the proportion of nuclear families was mainly due to the significant decrease in the proportion of joint families in which married brothers live together (see table 2.4).

2.1.4. Coresidence

The In-Depth Fertility Surveys (conducted in 1985 and 1987 in eight provinces and four municipalities by the State Statistical Bureau of China, see section 1.2.3) show that a large majority of women surveyed were living or had lived

Table 2.4. Family types of the five largest Chinese cities in different years

Period	Nuclear (including one-person) families	Three-generation families	Joint families with married brothers living together	Other	Total
1937	64.0	21.7	8.8	5.5	100.0
1938–45	66.0	19.7	7.2	7.1	100.0
1946–49	64.0	21.5	8.8	5.7	100.0
1950–53	64.6	22.9	5.4	7.1	100.0
1954–57	64.2	20.4	7.9	7.5	100.0
1958–65	69.0	20.4	5.1	5.5	100.0
1966–76	74.1	18.3	3.9	3.7	100.0
1977–82	72.4	20.2	3.1	4.4	100.0

Note: These data are from a family survey conducted in late 1982 and early 1983 by the Sociology Institute of the Chinese Academy of Social Sciences, and scholars from other research institutes. The survey covers the five largest cities in China: Beijing, Shanghai, Tianjin, Nanjing, and Chengdu. The sample size is 5,057 (ever-married women, from 4,385 different families). The above percentage distribution of family types was obtained by asking questions about the structure of the respondent's own family and the husband's family at the time of marriage. The number of families actually inquired about in this way was 9,859. The survey data and the preliminary analysis have been compiled in GRFFC 1985. Table 2.4 is a summary of two tables in this book: table 102 (p. 484) "Type of respondent's own family at the time of marriage" and table 110 (p. 508) "Type of respondent's husband's family at the time of marriage."

with their husbands' parents (60%–81%) and a small proportion of women were living or had lived with their own parents after marriage (3%–12%) (see tables 2.5 and 2.6). Note that these surveys did not collect data on whether the parents of the woman's husband and her own parents were alive at the time of her marriage. In fact, the proportion of women whose parents were alive when the women were married and who ever coresided with their parents is higher than what is shown in tables 2.5 and 2.6.

According to a life table analysis by Dankert et al., (Dankert et al. 1989; Dankert and Hu Yu 1989) the highest average median durations of the coresidence (months, since marriage, at which 50% of the couples are still coresiding with parents) were found in Shaanxi (87 months), Gansu (86 months), and Guangdong (83 months); the lowest was in Liaoning (35 months); and the other provinces were between 41 and 62 months. Among those couples who coresided or had coresided with parents, more than 90% did so for at least 1 year, and one-third to two-thirds continued to live with parents for at least 5 years. For the youngest marriage cohorts (0–5 years since marriage) and the next youngest (6–10 years since marriage), tables 2.5 and 2.6 show a tendency for shorter duration of the coresidence in four provinces and a

Table 2.5. Percentage distribution of women who coresided with parents after marriage and duration of the coresidence by marriage cohort, according to the first phase of the In-Depth Fertility Surveys, conducted in 1985

	Years since first marriage					All marriage cohorts
	0–5	6–10	11–15	16–20	21+	
Hebei						
% with husband's parents	78	77	79	77	71	77
% with wife's parents	3	2	2	2	3	3
Median duration (months)	37	43	54	75	103	53
% coresiding ≥ 1 year	84	89	93	94	95	90
% coresiding ≥ 5 years	31	37	46	57	63	46
Shaanxi						
% with husband's parents	80	79	83	81	78	80
% with wife's parents	4	5	5	8	5	5
Median duration (months)	49	62	83	116	131	87
% coresiding ≥ 1 year	90	91	96	97	96	94
% coresiding ≥ 5 years	43	51	61	71	68	60
Shanghai						
% with husband's parents	62	59	55	52	48	57
% with wife's parents	10	10	14	13	15	12
Median duration (months)	57	45	66	81	81	62
% coresiding ≥ 1 year	86	80	86	89	91	86
% coresiding ≥ 5 years	49	42	53	58	56	51

Source: Dankert, Qian, and Xu 1989.
Notes:
% with husband's parents: percentage who ever coresided with husband's parents after marriage.

% with wife's parents: percentage who ever coresided with her own parents after marriage.

Median duration (months): months (since marriage) at which 50% of the couples are still coresiding with parents, derived by life table technique.

% coresiding ≥ 1 year: percentage of couples who coresided with parents for at least 1 year, derived by life table technique.

% coresiding ≥ 5 year: percentage of couples who coresided with parents for at least 5 years, derived by life table technique.

reverse tendency in the other four provinces. However, these two groups of marriage cohorts generally coresided with parents for a shorter period of time compared with the older cohorts.

The one-per-thousand fertility survey conducted in 1982 indicated that 25.9%, 31.6%, and 40.9% of all persons were living in families composed of three or more than three generations in Liaoning, Hebei, and Fujian provinces, respectively (Lavely and Li 1985:14).

In a 1981 survey of 709 older people (males over 60, females over 55)

Table 2.6. Percentage distribution of women who coresided with parents after marriage and duration of the coresidence by marriage cohort, according to the second phase of the In-Depth Fertility Surveys, conducted in 1987

	Years since first marriage					All marriage cohorts
	0–5	6–10	11–15	16–20	21+	
Beijing						
% with husband's parents	63	61	60	52	57	60
% with wife's parents	10	7	7	9	7	8
Median duration (months)	51	47	53	72	84	57
% coresiding ≥ 1 year	85	84	89	92	93	88
% coresiding ≥ 5 years	45	49	53	57	58	48
Shandong						
% with husband's parents	79	79	84	84	82	81
% with wife's parents	4	3	2	2	2	3
Median duration (months)	29	28	39	54	66	41
% coresiding ≥ 1 year	78	80	87	92	95	85
% coresiding ≥ 5 years	33	28	33	47	53	38
Guangdong						
% with husband's parents	78	78	77	73	69	76
% with wife's parents	6	5	5	4	4	6
Median duration (months)	72	68	83	86	120	83
% coresiding ≥ 1 year	93	93	94	94	95	94
% coresiding ≥ 5 years	56	54	63	63	69	60
Guizhou						
% with husband's parents	81	74	76	70	73	75
% with wife's parents	3	2	4	4	4	4
Median duration (months)	30	37	45	65	80	52
% coresiding ≥ 1 year	80	82	89	94	95	88
% coresiding ≥ 5 years	35	37	42	53	60	46
Gansu						
% with husband's parents	85	78	76	80	78	80
% with wife's parents	3	3	4	4	3	4
Median duration (months)	67	70	83	101	102	86
% coresiding ≥ 1 year	95	96	96	95	97	96
% coresiding ≥ 5 years	55	56	65	69	68	64
Liaoning						
% with husband's parents	72	70	74	75	67	71
% with wife's parents	4	3	3	4	4	4
Median duration (months)	37	25	29	38	62	35
% coresiding ≥ 1 year	80	76	84	88	91	83
% coresiding ≥ 5 years	39	27	34	35	51	35

Source: Dankert and Hu 1989.
Note: See note to table 2.5.

in Lanchou, a city with about 2.3 million inhabitants, 63.5% of the respondents report that they would prefer to live with a married child. Note that most of the parents express this preference even when they are still physically capable of living alone.

At a national level, did the 1981 preference of parents for living with one of their married children reflect a change in attitudes between the 1950s and 1980s? The data in table 2.4 shows that the proportion of three-generation families remained stable from the 1950s to 1982, but the proportion of joint families with married brothers living together significantly decreased, which led to the increase in the proportion of nuclear families in the five largest cities. Direct observed data on family structure in the 1950s and 1960s at a national level are not available. We have only the census observations of national average family sizes: 4.30 in 1953, 4.29 in 1964, and 4.43 in 1982. The total fertility rate in 1982 (2.48) was less than half of that found in 1950–70 (5.78). The reduction in fertility certainly decreases the family size if other factors remain unchanged. Reduced mortality, on the contrary, may increase family size. It seems unlikely, however, that the effects of the mortality decline between 1950 and 1982 exceed the effects of such a remarkable fertility decline. Therefore, the average family size in 1982 would have been reduced if the proportion of parents and one of their married children wishing to live together had significantly decreased by 1982, compared with the 1950s and 1960s. Because this was not the case, we may reasonably say that the prevalence of coresidence between parents and one of the married children remained stable from the 1950s until the early 1980s (whereas the proportion of families with married brothers living together decreased). The following explanations may be given.

First, the complete abolition of feudal land ownership occurred in the early 1950s. The collective mode of production was introduced in the early 1950s, and the transition was complete by the late 1950s. This revolutionary change in land ownership led to the disintegration of many multigeneration families, especially families in which married brothers lived together. After these revolutionary social changes, land ownership and the collective mode of production remained unchanged until the 1982 census. It is therefore reasonable to believe that dramatic changes in living arrangements would not occur from the mid-1950s to the early 1980s, because no dramatic change in land ownership or mode of production took place during this period. Second, the ethical tradition of respecting and caring for the elderly has remained important; almost all old parents in rural areas depend economically on their children. This holds true for more than 80% of the total population of China. Third, in three-generation families, the grandparents may perform the housework and take care of grandchildren, or they may work in the fields or in business if they are still active, whereas the middle-generation couples usually work outside the home. The mutual care in work and in daily life compensates for problems that may arise between the mother-in-law and the daughter-in-law. The two generations could cooperate well through their rational division of labor. Fourth, housing construction in the cities and towns had not received proper attention and was not well organized during the Cultural Revolution (from the mid-1960s to the late 1970s). The severe housing shortage may counteract, to a large extent, some urban parents' desire to live apart from their married children.

2.1.5. Three-generation families

It is even more interesting to note that in 1987 the proportion of families of three or more generations had been increased by 1.2 percentage points compared with that in 1982 (see table 2.7). How can we interpret this phenomenon, which deviates from the classical theory that states the family will tend to become nuclear as modernization proceeds? Three preliminary explanations may be given. First, the young people who were born in China's second baby boom in the 1960s (mainly in rural areas) are reaching marriageable and childbearing ages, so that the number of newly married couples in 1987 was much larger than that in 1982. Given the fact that a large majority of newly married couples do not leave their parental home immediately after marriage, and that almost every couple would like to have a baby as soon as possible, more three-generation families may thus be formed in 1987 than in 1982. Second, the function of rural family households has changed from a consumer unit under the previous collective mode into both a consumer and a production unit under the current responsibility system. This radical change may enhance the economic value of the three-generation family since the collaboration of members from different generations may increase the efficiency of household production activities. Third, the fertility of Chinese urban populations started to decline beginning in 1959 (with the exception of 1963, which had a high fertility rate, seemingly compensating for the famine period of 1960–62). The urban total fertility rate declined from about 5.4 in the 1950s to 2.9 in 1967. Given that the desire of most Chinese parents to live with one of their married children has not rapidly changed, the probability of moving out of the parental home to form a nuclear family for the children born in the 1960s has declined because they have a much smaller number of brothers and sisters than the previous generation. The fact that the proportions of three-generation families in 1987 in the three largest cities—Beijing, Tianjin, and Shanghai—in which fertility declined even earlier and quicker, have all significantly increased compared with 1982 supports this speculation (see table 2.7; this speculation on the impact of fertility reduction on family structure will be verified through simulations in the third part of this book).

In summary, compared with the 1930s, the proportion of extended families has decreased sharply—in particular, large families of more than three generations or married brothers living together. But both in the countryside

Table 2.7. Percentage distribution of family types in 1982 and 1987

	Nuclear (including one-person) families		Three-generation and other extended families		Total	
	1982	1987	1982	1987	1982	1987
All China	81.19	80.00	18.81	20.00	100	100
Beijing	83.29	80.74	16.71	19.26	100	100
Tianjin	84.81	82.00	15.19	18.00	100	100
Shanghai	78.75	77.92	21.25	22.08	100	100

Sources: SSB 1983b, 1988c.

and in the cities, there is not only a desire for three-generation families but also a necessity (Ma Xia 1984:15). The three-generation family is still an important family type in China, as in many other Asian countries. For instance, the proportion of families of three or more generations and of other types of extended families in Japan was 25.4% in 1970. In 1975 and 1980 the proportions were 22.8% and 22.1%, respectively (census figures, Bureau of Statistics of Japan, cited from Kobayashi and Tanaka 1984). The proportion of extended families was 49.0% in a simple random sample of 405 families near Jodhpur, western Rajasthan, India; 32.4% for 467 towns and 19.9% for 153 villages in Java; 19.6% in the 1968 national demographic survey in the Philippines; 33.2% in a sample of 4,900 families from the South Korean 1966 census; 33.9% in the rural areas, 25.3% in the provincial urban areas, and 28.3% for Bangkok-Dhonburi, according to a national longitudinal study of the social, economic, and demographic changes in Thailand from 1968 to 1972 (Concepción and Landa-Jocano 1974:254).

Therefore, the model which will be constructed in the second part of this volume, and which is expected to be applicable to China and other Asian countries, must take into account both nuclear families and three-generation families.

2.2. Demographic Determinants of Family Dynamics

2.2.1. Marriage

Marriage is a particularly important variable in Chinese families since births occur almost exclusively within marriage (Tien 1983:20), and almost all women eventually get married (the percentages of single women aged 45–49 in 1982 and 1987 were 0.2% and 0.1%, respectively; see table 2.8).

The near universality of marriage in China is also demonstrated by the cohort data from the 1982 one-per-thousand fertility survey. For every cohort,

Table 2.8. Percentage distribution of women by marital status in 1982 and 1987

Age	Single		Married		Widowed		Divorced		Total	
	1982	1987	1982	1987	1982	1987	1982	1987	1982	1987
15–19	95.6	95.8	4.3	4.2	0.0	0.0	0.0	0.0	100	100
20	75.1	70.7	24.7	29.1	0.0	0.0	0.1	0.1	100	100
21	62.5	55.7	37.2	44.1	0.0	0.0	0.1	0.1	100	100
22	48.6	39.3	51.2	60.5	0.0	0.1	0.2	0.2	100	100
23	33.2	24.7	66.6	75.1	0.1	0.1	0.2	0.2	100	100
24	21.0	14.8	78.8	84.9	0.1	0.1	0.2	0.2	100	100
25	12.0	8.7	87.7	90.8	0.1	0.2	0.2	0.3	100	100
26	6.8	5.5	92.9	94.0	0.1	0.1	0.2	0.3	100	100
27	3.7	3.3	95.9	96.1	0.2	0.2	0.2	0.3	100	100
28	2.2	1.9	97.4	97.6	0.2	0.2	0.3	0.3	100	100
29	1.4	1.2	98.1	98.3	0.3	0.2	0.3	0.2	100	100
30–34	0.7	0.6	98.6	98.7	0.5	0.4	0.3	0.3	100	100
35–39	0.3	0.3	98.2	98.4	1.2	1.0	0.3	0.3	100	100
40–44	0.2	0.2	96.7	97.1	2.9	2.4	0.3	0.3	100	100
45–49	0.2	0.1	93.3	94.5	6.2	5.1	0.4	0.3	100	100

Sources: SSB 1983a, 1988c.

more than 97.5% of the women were married by age 35, and for most of the cohorts the total exceeded 99%. The cohorts for which more than 1% (but less than 2.5%) of the women were unmarried by age 35 were the cohorts who were 20 years old in 1955–56, 1958–59, 1962, and 1975; these cohorts may have been particularly severely affected by the disturbances of the Great Leap Forward in 1959–61, the Cultural Revolution, and the mobilization of many school graduates to go to mountain and rural areas in the late 1960s and early 1970s. It is somewhat puzzling, however, that adjacent cohorts were not similarly affected. Detailed examination of the impact of external events on cohorts may shed light on this, but the explanation may lie in stochastic fluctuations or sampling errors. What is perhaps most remarkable is that despite various disturbances from 1957 until the early 1970s, which disrupted many young people's marriage and career plans, nearly all Chinese females still got married.

The average age at first marriage of Chinese women increased gradually between 1949 and 1970 and increased rapidly from 1970 to 1979, due to the Wan Xi Shao (late marriage, longer birth intervals, fewer children) family-planning campaign and to delayed marriages among urban school graduates who went to work in the countryside and mountain areas. In 1950, more than half of the Chinese women were married by age 18 and 90% by age 22. In 1982, the median age at first marriage had risen to age 22; the 90% level was not reached until age 26. The 1982 survey also shows the continuing concentration of marriage within a short age bracket. In 1950, half of all first marriages occurred at ages 17–19; in 1982, half occurred at ages 20–23.

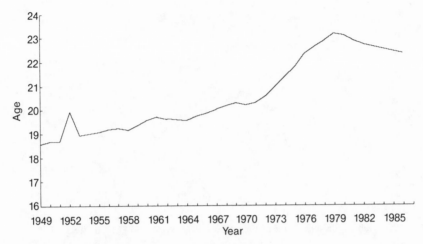

Figure 2.4. Mean age of Chinese women at first marriage

Sources: For 1949–81, see Zhao Weigang and Yu Huilin 1984. For 1982, see Zhao Xuan 1985. The figures for 1983, 1984, and 1985 are derived though linear interpolation. For 1986, see SSB 1988c.

Since 1980, the age at marriage has fallen (see figure 2.4). The percentage distribution of marital status in 1982 and 1987 shown in table 2.8 also indicates a significant earlier marriage pattern in 1987 than in 1982. This trend is mainly a result of administrative decentralization, which has lessened governmental control over age at marriage.

According to the 1982 fertility survey, China had three marriage booms, defined as periods with a total period first-marriage rate (TPFMR) exceeding 1.0. The first marriage boom immediately followed the foundation of the People's Republic in 1949 (TPFMR = 1.02). The second marriage boom was in 1962 and 1963 (TPFMR = 1.19 and 1.01, respectively) after the Great Leap Forward and three years of natural calamity. The third marriage boom was in 1980, 1981, and 1982 (TPFMR = 1.137, 1.303, and 1.340, respectively) due to the relaxation of the restriction on age at first marriage by the New Marriage Law, which took effect officially on January 1, 1981. The years in which the TPFMRs were lowest were 1971–77 (between 0.641 and 0.749), because of the restriction on age at marriage in the Wan Xi Shao family-planning period and the relatively late marriage of urban school graduates who went to work in the countryside and mountain areas.

2.2.2. Fertility

The fertility level in China has fluctuated from a fairly high level (average TFR = 6.06 in 1950–58) via an accidental decrease (average TFR = 3.87 in 1959–61) to a fairly high level again (average TFR = 6.12 in 1962–70) and to a re-

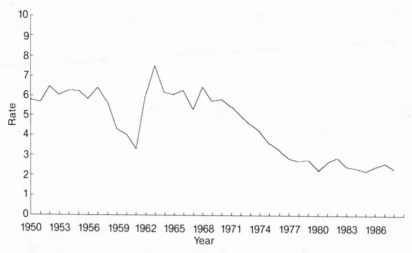

Figure 2.5. Total fertility rates for China
Sources: For 1950–81, see CPIC 1984. For 1982–88, two-per-thousand fertility and contraceptive survey by the leading group of the survey (in Chinese).

markable decline after 1970 (TFR was as low as 2.24 in 1980, increased to 2.86 in 1982, and decreased again to 2.20 in 1985). As explained earlier, a recent increase in fertility level was observed in 1986 and 1987 (see figure 2.5).

Figure 2.6 presents a contour map of Chinese fertility rates by single year of age from 15 to 49 years old and for single year of time from 1940 to 1981.[1] The fertility rates are defined as the number of women who gave birth at age *a* in year *t* divided by the total number of women of that age at that time. The most striking feature of the map is the rapid decline in fertility after 1970. This decline is well known and often summarized by the dramatic drop in TFR: in 1970, TFR = 5.8; by 1981, it had fallen by 55% to 2.6. The map reveals graphically the age pattern of decline. Consider the ages where the fertility rate exceeds 20%. In 1968, this period of high fertility stretched from ages 20 to 37. By 1981, in contrast, the period of high fertility was concentrated from age 23 to 27. In 1968, more than 20% of all 20-year-olds and more than 10% of all 40-year-olds gave birth. By 1981, the fertility rate of 20-year-olds had fallen under 10%, and the fertility rate of 40-year-olds had fallen under 2%. The precipitous decline in the fertility contours at older ages and the marked increase in the contours at younger ages reflect the success of the Chinese birth con-

1. The computer program used to produce the contour map was written by Bradley A. Gambill and J. W. Vaupel (Gambill and Vaupel 1985; see also Vaupel, Gambill, and Yashin 1985). For a more detailed graphical analysis of marriage and fertility in China, see Zeng, Vaupel, and Yashin 1985.

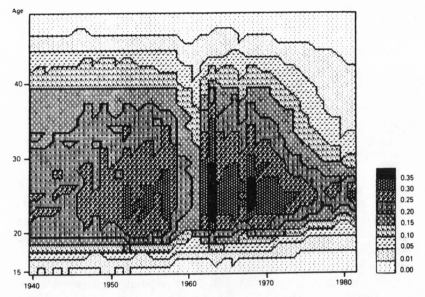

Figure 2.6. Fertility rates among Chinese women aged 15–49
  Source: Zeng, Vaupel, and Yashin 1985:728.

trol program, including the increase in age at first marriage and, even more importantly, the widespread use of contraceptives.

The radical narrowing of the period of high fertility was slightly reversed in 1981, and there is some evidence of an increase in births among 25- and 26-year-old women. This is undoubtedly the result of the New Marriage Law, announced in 1980, and the concomitant boom in marriages, especially among women in their midtwenties.

The most conspicuous period disruption on the map is the trough in fertility in 1959–61. This coincides with the Great Leap Forward. The recovery of fertility rates from their depressed level was dramatic: for ages between 23 and 29, fertility rates rose from under 20% per year in 1961 to over 30% per year in 1962 and over 35% per year in 1962.

The fertility data pertaining to earlier years, especially the years before 1950, have to be interpreted with caution since they are reconstructed from interviews taken in 1982. The general patterns seem reassuringly plausible: during the course of the 1940s and 1950s, fertility rates were fairly stable, with a slight tendency to rise. This is consistent with trends of improving living standards and the absence of widespread contraception during this period.

Obviously, the remarkable reduction of the fertility level in China since 1971 is the result of the successful family-planning program. According to the

Table 2.9. Percentage distribution of births by parity

Year	First birth	Second birth	Third and higher births	Total
1970	20.73	17.06	62.21	100.00
1977	30.86	24.59	44.55	100.00
1981	46.57	25.35	28.08	100.00
1986	52.15	30.35	17.49	100.00
1987	52.55	32.08	15.37	100.00

Sources: Song, Shi, and Zhan 1984; SSB 1988c; SDSFPC 1989.

one-per-thousand fertility survey, 69.5% of all ever-married women aged 15–49 were using contraceptives in 1982 (Qiu, Wu Shutao, and Wang 1984:131). China's current national fertility policy is the advocacy of one child per couple, control of second births, and resolute prevention of third births. Of course, we must keep in mind that events do not always occur as planned. The violation of birth-planning norms, in particular, is not uncommon in the rural areas and in some small towns and cities. The proportion of third and higher-parity births has decreased remarkably, but it still accounts for a considerable percentage (see table 2.9).

The fertility of women in China is not only dependent on their age and marriage duration but depends mainly on the age-parity distribution. The parity status of women is therefore essential for the demographic analysis of family formation and population change in China.

Sexual activities outside marriage are culturally taboo. Illegal births are negligible in China. Illegitimacy does occur, but the extent of this phenomenon cannot be documented.

2.2.3. Mortality

It is well known that mortality in China has been greatly reduced during the past 40 years. The mortality rate was above 20 per thousand in the pre-1949 period. It dropped to 10–18 per thousand in the 1950s and further decreased to slightly more than 7 per thousand in the early 1970s (Qian 1983b). It decreased further to 6.6 per thousand in 1985.

The infant mortality rate went from 200 per thousand of live births before 1949 down to 70.9 per thousand in 1957 (Qian 1983a). According to China's one-per-thousand fertility survey, the infant mortality rates in 1980 and 1981 were 36.5 and 36.9 per thousand, respectively (Yang and Dodd 1985). Life expectancy of China's population increased from 47 years in 1950 to 67.9 years in 1981 (66.4 years for males, 69.35 for females) (Jiang, Zhang, and Zhu 1984:5).

Mortality affects fertility, since a reduction of mortality allows more women to survive into childbearing age (enlarging the number of births) and increases the insurance of surviving children (reduces people's motivation to have more children to guarantee the desired number of surviving children).

2.2.4. Widowhood, divorce, and remarriage

China's 1982 national census shows that the proportions of widowed and divorced women are very low (see table 2.8). The proportions of widowed and divorced women of childbearing age were 1.05% and 0.20%, respectively, and the proportions of women in the high-potential-fertility age-group 15–34 were even smaller (0.15% and 0.16%, respectively). The In-Depth Fertility Surveys conducted in 1985 show that the proportions of divorced or separated women were low: 0.1%, 0.3%, and 0.4% among all ever-married women of childbearing age in Hebei and Shaanxi provinces and in Shanghai Municipality, respectively. The proportions of widows among all ever-married women of childbearing age were 0.5%, 0.6%, 1.0% in Hebei, Shaanxi, and Shanghai, respectively. The 1987 one-percent population survey also shows a similar pattern of very low proportions of widowhood and divorce.

It is well known that divorce has long been culturally out of favor in China. During the 10-year turmoil of the Cultural Revolution, the legal system in China was seriously undermined, and political life was entirely disrupted. Some lower-level courts did not even accept divorce cases. Hence, the number of divorces dwindled (Li Ning 1985:18). The restrictive policy on granting divorce has been relaxed by the New Marriage Law, which took effect officially on January 1, 1981 and places more emphasis on the emotional basis for a happy marriage. The number of divorces granted jumped from about 113,600 in 1979 to 187,000 in 1981 (Li Ning 1985:18; *Encyclopedic Yearbook of China* 1982:644) to 427,000 in 1982 (SSB 1983a:5). The number of divorces granted in 1982 was 4 times as great as in 1979. However, if we take into account the population increase, the divorce level in 1982 was not above the average level found for the years between 1950 and 1980, although the total number of divorces granted in 1982 (427,000) was higher than the average number of divorces granted between 1950 and 1980 (400,000) (Li Ning 1985:18).

Although the divorce level is still low compared with many other countries, the annual crude divorce rate increased from about one divorce per thousand married couples in 1981 to about two and a half divorces per thousand married couples in 1986.

Officially published remarriage rates for Chinese women are not yet available. Nevertheless, some relevant information from censuses or surveys indicated indirectly that remarriage rates in China are relatively high.

First, we know that the proportions currently widowed are very low, whereas mortality in China is (relatively) low compared with other developing countries but is not low compared with developed countries. Thus a logical inference is that remarriage rates must be high.

Second, as found by Coale (1984:55), the difference between the ratios

Table 2.10. Ratios of currently married to ever-married women by age

Year	Age				
	20–24	25–29	30–34	35–39	40–44
1982	0.986	0.977	0.960	0.933	0.888
1929–31	0.981	0.968	0.953	0.916	0.860

Source: Coale 1984: 55.

of currently married to ever-married women aged 20–45 in 1982 and in 1929–31 is very small (see table 2.10). The surprisingly small difference in these ratios, despite the very substantial difference in mortality, implies that the higher incidence of widowhood in 1929–31 must have been offset by a high rate of remarriage by widows. It also implies that remarriage rates have been more or less stable.

Why are remarriage rates high and stable? The absence of strong religious beliefs prohibiting remarriage is probably one of the explanations. Although Confucianism opposed remarriage, economic constraints—both for themselves and for their small children—prevented most poor widows and divorcees from living up to the Confucian ideal. After the founding of the People's Republic, remarriage was encouraged by the Chinese authorities in an effort to undermine the feudal ideal of preventing widows and divorcees from remarrying. Remarriage, however, may be on the decline, due to the increased economic independence of women. The above-mentioned effects are usually very gradual; also, they may partially cancel each other out.

2.3. The Impact of Population Policies on Family Dynamics

In the former sections we referred to population policies. In this section we would like to emphasize that population policies are one of the major factors influencing family dynamics in China.

As Professor Keyfitz pointed out, the political structure of Chinese society is such that policy decisions can be quickly implemented (Keyfitz 1984:22), so that population policies exert a big influence on the determinants of family dynamics and population change in China. We may probably say that demographic determinants such as current nuptiality and fertility are to a considerable extent the outcome of population policies. For instance, Wan Xi Shao policies increased the average age at first marriage and reduced total first-marriage rates remarkably, particularly in urban areas. When the restriction on age at first marriage of the Wan Xi Shao family-planning campaign during the 1970s was relaxed by the New Marriage Law around 1980, the average age at first marriage rose and the total first-marriage rate increased from 0.922

in 1979 to 1.303 in 1981. The strictly parity-dependent fertility pattern is also mainly the result of birth policies.

China's current national fertility policy is to advocate one child per couple, control of second births, and resolute prevention of third births. It does not mean, of course, that all Chinese couples of childbearing age can have only one child. In fact, according to the 1982 fertility survey, only 21.2% of all couples who have children are one-child couples. What is the meaning, therefore, of the control of second births? Under what circumstances can a couple have a second child? In 1983, Dr. Qian Xinzhong, former minister in charge of the State Family Planning Commission of China, stated three conditions that entitle a couple to have a second child: when the first child is disabled; when one party (especially the wife) is married for the first time and the other party is remarried and has one child from a previous marriage; and when a couple has adopted a child because one party is sterile, but later the illness is cured.

Despite the fact that Chinese government has emphasized from the very beginning that the policy of promoting one child per couple should be carried out voluntarily with state guidance and that it should enjoy the full support and participation of the Chinese people, some local cadres did not focus on education and propaganda but simply used administrative authority to achieve the local birth control targets. To correct this unfair situation and to strengthen the family-planning efforts, the government issued Document Number 7 in 1984. Document Number 7 denounced the use of force in family planning and instead advocated the use of propaganda and education and the improvement of relations between family-planning workers and the people. At the same time, the document demanded the continuance of the policy of promoting one child per couple. Document Number 7 is more permissive toward second children among rural couples with "real difficulties." From early 1984, revisions of provincial family-planning regulations generally expanded the categories of couples who qualified for approval of a second child. Some provinces started to officially allow rural couples whose first child was a girl to have a second child. With the approval of the central government, some rural areas even started to test a policy of universally allowing two children per couple with appropriate spacing. In accordance with the general principles expressed in Document Number 7, the target of keeping China's population under 1.2 billion in the year 2000 was replaced by "about 1.2 billion." The interpretation of the Chinese expression "about 1.2 billion" is "not exceeding 1.25 billion."

In the face of the recent increase in birth rates and a large group of young people who are reaching marriageable and childbearing ages, the Chinese leadership has reemphasized on public occasions the importance of controlling population growth and the promotion of one-child families. Nevertheless, the messages from several very important meetings for policy-making, evaluation, and implementation conducted in 1988 and early 1989 by the State Family Planning Commission tell us that the leadership wanted to continue existing family-planning policies, including the revisions, since 1984, of provincial regulations expanding the categories of couples who qualified for approval of a second child. In the rural areas, couples whose first child is a daughter are allowed to have a second birth with spacing. This regulation was practiced by a considerable number of provinces before 1988 but was officially granted to most rural areas of the country in 1988.[2] Until February 1989, six provinces or autonomous regions (Guangdong, Hainan, Yunnan, Ningxia, Qinghai, and Xinjiang) even practiced a policy of universally allowing two children per couple with spacing in rural areas. Thus, taken together, all the categories for allowing a second child in the rural areas result in somewhere between a 1.6- and a 2-child policy. Chinese demographers (including the author) who participated in the policy meetings were told that the leadership did not reject the idea of a policy of two children with spacing, but it could only be introduced gradually. Based on cumulative experiences in some testing areas, they realize that any sudden declaration of large changes in the current population policy would, in such a big country of about 1.1 billion people, create a sudden rush of births.

Differential population policies were implemented in different areas based on the local situation, such that control of second, third, or more children is stricter in urban areas and for the Han nationality than in rural areas and for ethnic minorities. These differential policies are one of the reasons why there are such big differences in fertility levels between rural and urban areas and between minorities and the Han majority.

Since the political structure of Chinese society allows policy decisions to be quickly implemented, population policies had and will continue to have a large effect on family dynamics and population change in China. The evaluation of the impact of population policies on demographic trends and the investigation of the possible optimal population policies are important tasks for demographers interested in China's population problems.

---

2. A few rural areas where the level of economic development is high and population density is also very high have not yet officially adopted the policy of allowing the farmers whose first child is a girl to have a second child with spacing. These areas are the suburban areas of Beijing, Tianjing, and Shanghai and most rural areas of Jiangsu and Sichuan provinces.

3
Rural-Urban, Ethnic, and Regional Differences

3.1. Rural-Urban Composition

In 1982, roughly four-fifths of the Chinese population could be classified as rural; the remaining one-fifth is urban. The reported proportion of the urban population jumped from 20.8% in mid-1982 to 31.9% at the end of 1984, and to 36.9% in 1987. This extraordinarily rapid change can be partially attributed to movements of people from rural to urban areas. Massive urbanization is now under way (Banister 1986; S. Goldstein 1985; S. Goldstein and A. Goldstein 1985). This shift has resulted from China's impressive economic reforms. Agricultural production is now managed through household initiative rather than by production teams under communal command. Food production has more than doubled. This success has, on the one hand, stimulated the development of various kinds of businesses in urban areas and, on the other hand, reduced the size of the labor force required on farms. The need for surplus rural workers to find new employment and the labor demands of the growing urban businesses are the driving forces of the urbanization occurring today.

However, a substantial part of the increase in urban population is due to administrative changes in the classification of areas as urban or rural. To promote the development of the towns, in 1984, the State Council of China modified the regulations for establishing a township. In 1986, the State Council officially encouraged the cities to include the adjacent counties into the administrative boundaries of the cities and relaxed the criteria for the establishment of a city. These two important policy adjustments resulted in a tremendous increase in the number of towns and cities in China. The number of towns increased from 3,547 in 1982 to 9,121 in 1987, 2.6 times as many as in 1982; and the number of cities increased from 239 in 1982 to 347 in 1987. Even more important, the administrative boundaries of the towns and cities were significantly enlarged, resulting in the misclassification of farmers as urbanites.

Table 3.1. Average family sizes in rural and
urban areas of China

Year	Whole country	Rural	Urban
1953	4.30	4.26	4.66
1964	4.29	4.35	4.11
1982	4.43	4.57	3.95
1987	4.30	4.44	4.07

Sources: 1953, 1964, 1982: Ma Xia 1984: 12.
1987: SSB 1988c.

In almost half of the 347 cities in 1987, the majority of the population were mainly engaged in agriculture (Ma Xia 1988; Bai 1986).

3.2. Rural-Urban Differences in Family Size and Structure

In rural areas, the average family size is larger than in urban areas, except in 1953 (table 3.1). The smaller family sizes found in rural areas in 1953 may be explained by the effects of the dramatic change from feudal ownership (land and other property) patterns in the early 1950s (discussed in section 2.1.3). As a result, large families—particularly in the rural areas—were broken up. If we compare rural and urban family sizes in 1982 with those in 1953, we find a slight increase in rural family size and a significant decrease in urban family size. This is due to a more abrupt decline in fertility in urban areas than in rural areas and to the fact that the parental preference for living with one married child is more persistent in rural than in urban areas.

Table 3.2 gives a comparison of family types in rural areas, towns, and cities in 1982 and 1987. In both 1982 and 1987, the proportions of two-generation families in rural areas, towns, and cities were more or less equal. The 1982 proportion of families with three or more generations was much higher in rural areas than in towns and cities, accompanied by a much lower proportion of one-person and one-couple households in rural areas. The large rural-urban differences in family types seem to have largely diminished by 1987, which may be partially attributed to the misclassification of farmers as urbanites described in the previous section. However, the family types of elderly in rural areas, towns, and cities in 1987, shown in table 3.3, differ substantially. How can we explain the fact that much smaller proportions of urban elderly live in the three or more generation households than their rural counterparts, while the overall proportions of three or more generation families in rural and urban areas were similar in 1987? One interpretation may be that as a result of the substantially reduced fertility in Chinese urban areas in the early and mid-1960s, young couples in urban areas nowadays have a much smaller number

Table 3.2. Comparison of family types in Chinese rural areas, towns, and cities

Family type	1982				1987			
	Total	Rural	Town	City	Total	Rural	Town	City
One person	8.0	7.5	11.3	9.3	5.5	5.4	5.8	5.7
One couple	4.8	4.5	5.7	5.7	5.5	5.0	5.8	6.8
One generation and other relatives or nonrelatives	1.2	1.1	1.8	1.7	0.7	0.7	0.7	1.0
Two generations and other relatives or nonrelatives	67.3	67.3	67.7	67.2	68.3	68.0	68.5	68.8
Three generations or more	18.7	19.7	13.5	16.1	20.0	21.0	19.2	17.7
Total	100	100	100	100	100	100	100	100

Sources: 1982: SSB 1988a. 1987: China 1% Population Sample survey, SSB, 1988c.

Table 3.3. Comparison of family types of the elderly aged 60 and over in Chinese rural areas, towns, and cities in 1987

Family type	Rural		Town		City	
	Male	Female	Male	Female	Male	Female
One person	2.95	2.07	4.75	8.46	3.41	7.76
One couple	8.00	6.97	26.45	19.07	24.90	17.40
Two generations	31.56	19.21	35.89	19.56	36.73	23.77
Two generations, with grandparents and grandchildren[a]	1.61	2.03	3.48	4.25	4.27	5.17
Three generations or more	54.61	68.30	29.10	48.37	30.56	45.46
Other	1.25	1.43	0.33	0.29	0.41	0.43
Total	100	100	100	100	100	100

Source: CASS 1988.

[a] Middle generation is absent.

of siblings. Therefore, they have a much slighter chance of moving out of the parental home to establish a nuclear family, given the fact that most elderly parents still prefer to live with one married child. This speculation will be further explored through simulations in part three of this book.

3.3. Rural-Urban Differences in Nuptiality and Fertility

Rural women get married significantly earlier than urban women: there is an average difference of about 2.8 years for the period 1964–86 (see figure 3.1).

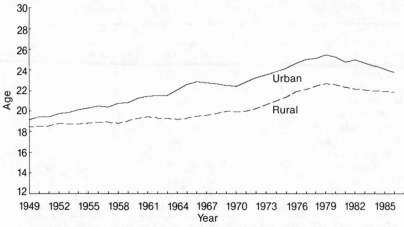

Figure 3.1. Mean age at first marriage in rural and urban areas of China
Sources: For 1949–81, see Zhao Weigang and Yu Huilin 1984. For 1982, see Zhao Xuan 1985. The figures for 1983, 1984, and 1985 are derived through linear interpolation. For 1986, see SSB 1988c.

Table 3.4. Percentage distribution of women by marital status: Comparison between rural and urban areas, China, 1982

Age	Area	Never married	Married for first time	Remarried	Divorced	Widowed	Total
15–19	Rural	94.8	5.1	0.1	0.0	0.0	100.0
	Urban	99.4	0.6	0.0	0.0	0.0	100.0
20–24	Rural	39.2	59.9	0.6	0.1	0.1	100.0
	Urban	72.9	76.9	0.0	0.1	0.0	100.0
25–29	Rural	2.9	94.9	1.9	0.1	0.2	100.0
	Urban	17.4	81.8	0.3	0.3	0.1	100.0
30–34	Rural	0.4	95.6	3.4	0.2	0.4	100.0
	Urban	3.6	94.0	1.1	0.8	0.5	100.0
35–39	Rural	0.2	93.1	5.4	0.2	1.1	100.0
	Urban	0.7	94.9	2.1	1.0	1.2	100.0
55–59	Rural	0.2	69.3	14.2	0.3	15.9	100.0
	Urban	0.5	74.7	9.2	0.8	14.8	100.0
65–69	Rural	0.2	53.0	11.9	0.3	34.6	100.0
	Urban	1.1	50.8	7.9	1.2	38.9	100.0

Source: State Family Planning Commission 1983.
Note: Because information on remarriage was not collected in 1987, we use only the marital status distribution in 1982 here.

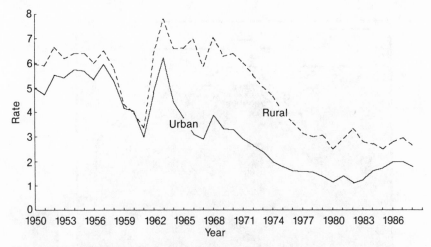

Figure 3.2. Total fertility rates in rural and urban areas of China

Sources: For 1950–81, see CPIC 1984. For 1982–88, see two-per-thousand fertility and contraceptive survey conducted in 1988, a report on the two-per-thousand fertility and contraceptive survey by the leading group of the survey of State Family Planning Commission (in Chinese).

Note: Given the fact that the definition of rural areas in the two-per-thousand survey is the same as used by the State Statistical Bureau (SSB), we used the TFR of rural areas from the two-per-thousand survey report directly. However, the report listed the urban TFR classified by urban proper, suburban, and state-owned agricultural enterprises, etc., which are not the same statistical categories used by SSB and by us in this book. We therefore estimated the 1982–88 urban TFR using the method of proportion allocation and the TFR data for the whole country and for rural areas from the two-per-thousand survey as well as the proportions of urban population published by SSB.

Table 3.4 tabulates the percentage distribution of marital status (including remarriage status) of rural and urban populations in 1982. A considerable proportion (17.4%) of urban women were still single at age 25–29, which is 6 times as large as that for their rural counterparts. The proportion of divorced women in urban areas was higher than in rural areas, but the proportions of widows in rural and urban areas were more or less the same. It is very interesting to note that the proportion of remarried women in rural China was much higher than that in urban areas. This may be explained in two different ways. One explanation is that although the feudal idea of preventing widows from remarrying is more influential in rural areas, urban women are economically more independent so that they are more likely to remain unmarried after widowhood or divorce. Another explanation is that the higher mortality plus earlier marriage in rural areas might produce more widows, who are the population at risk for remarriage.

The rural and urban total fertility rates (TFR) for the period 1950–88 are shown in figure 3.2. The data show that there were modest differences in fertility between rural and urban areas in the 1950s and that the difference

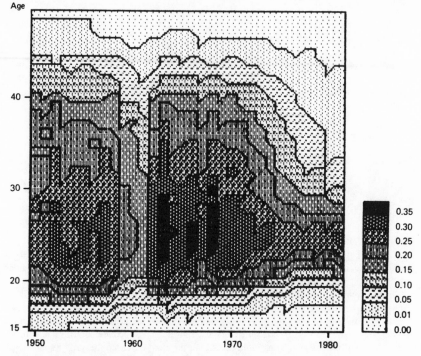

Figure 3.3. Age-specific fertility rates in rural China
Source: Zeng, Vaupel, and Yashin 1985:732.

has become very large since 1964. In 1981, the rural TFR (2.9) was more than twice the urban TFR (1.4). More recent data show that this very large difference still exists. The significant increase of urban fertility in the 1980s revealed by figure 3.2 is largely due to the misclassification of farmers in the suburban areas as urbanites.

As shown by the maps in figures 3.3 and 3.4, patterns of fertility in the urban and rural areas of China were roughly the same in the 1950s. Indeed, during this decade total urban fertility fluctuated between 80% and 100% of total rural fertility. After 1960, the patterns sharply diverge, with urban fertility falling further and more rapidly than rural fertility. In the 1970s and early 1980s, total urban fertility was just under half of total rural fertility.

The biggest difference between urban and rural age patterns of fertility lies in the tendency of urban women to have children in their late twenties, whereas rural women have children throughout their twenties. Since 1975, fertility rates of more than 10% per year have been concentrated in urban areas between ages 25 and 28, whereas similarly high rates of rural fertility have

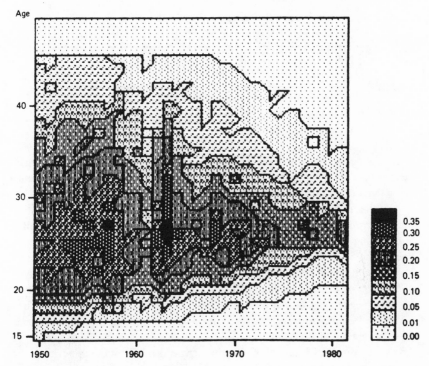

Figure 3.4. Age-specific fertility rates in urban China
  Source: Zeng, Vaupel, and Yashin 1985:733.

been concentrated between ages 21 and 29. In both urban and rural areas there
has been a radical decrease in childbearing above age 30 and a substantial decrease before age 20, although such patterns were apparent earlier and have
proceeded further in urban areas.

3.4. Ethnic and Regional Differences

According to the results of three national censuses taken in 1953, 1964, and
1982, China's regional population distribution was as unbalanced in 1982 as
in 1953 or 1964. Professor Hu Huanyong, a well-known Chinese population
geographer, drew a famous fictitious line from Aihui (a town in the north-
ern part of Helongjiang Province) to Tengchong (a town in the western part
of Yunnan Province). About 94.4% of China's population lives southeast of
this fictitious line, occupying only 42.9% of the country's territory. By contrast, 5.6% of the population of China is sparsely distributed in 57.1% of the
country, that is, northwest of the Aihui-Tengchong line. The big differences be-

Table 3.5. Percentage distribution of births by birth order among minority and Han women in rural areas of China, 1981

| | Parity | | | | | |
	1	2	3	4	5+	Total
Minorities	22.99	18.76	15.40	13.64	29.21	100
Han	44.12	27.91	14.21	6.82	6.94	100

Source: Li Hechang, Song Tingyou, and Li Cheng 1984:104.

tween the population distribution on each side of the Aihui-Tengchong line may be explained by the different ecological conditions and economic development. For a detailed discussion of this topic, the reader is referred to Hu 1983.

China is a united multinational country, integrating various nationalities (ethnic groups) for thousands of years. The Han is the biggest nationality, constituting 93.3% and 92.0% of the population in 1982 and 1987, respectively. The 55 minority nationalities accounted for 6.7% in 1982 and increased to 8% in 1987. Although the minorities are fewer in number, they inhabit 50%–60% of China's territory (Hu 1982:15). The cultural tradition, level of economic development, population density, and birth control policies differ between the Han majority and the minorities. Consequently, fertility and marriage patterns are quite different too.

According to China's 1982 fertility survey, the TFR of the minorities was almost twice the TFR of the Han majority (TFR = 5.05 for the rural minorities and TFR = 2.76 for rural Han in 1981). The distribution by parity of the Han majority and the minorities in rural areas is shown in table 3.5. The average childbearing age and the average age at first birth of minority and Han females in rural areas are shown in table 3.6. We can see clearly that the women of China's minorities have a higher fertility level, younger age at first birth, and longer childbearing life span than the Han female population. The increase of the minorities' share in the total population in 1987 compared with 1982 is due to the higher fertility level among minority groups, which is

Table 3.6. Average age at childbearing and average age at first birth among minority and Han women in rural areas of China, 1981

	Average age at childbearing	Average age at first birth
Minorities	28.56	22.78
Han	26.40	24.03

Source: Li Hechang, Song Tingyou, and Li Cheng 1984:105.

Table 3.7. Percentage distribution of marital status among minority and Han women of child-bearing ages in rural areas of China, 1981

	Single	First marriage	Remarried	Divorced	Widowed	Total
Minorities	28.79	59.72	9.02	0.83	1.64	100
Han	30.66	65.59	2.79	0.08	0.88	100

Source: Shen and Ma Qingping 1984:131.

an outcome of the much less strict birth control policies and the lower level of socioeconomic development.

The average age at first marriage is 20.53 years for minority women and 22.38 years for Han women (Shen and Ma Qingping 1984:123). The differences in marital status between minorities and Han are shown in table 3.7. The minority women get married at a younger age and their marriages are less stable than those of the Han women.

Because of the large demographic differences between minorities and Han, we grouped China's 30 provinces, municipalities, and autonomous regions into two demographic regions. The minority-dominant region (the regions in which the minorities are numerically important) comprises 5 autonomous regions (Inner Mongolia, Ningxia, Xinjiang, Guangxi, Tibet) and 3 provinces (Qinghai, Guizhou, and Yunnan). All the other municipalities and provinces are Han-dominant regions. The provincial demographic statistics and the weighted average of the demographic statistics of the Han-dominant region and the minority-dominant region are shown in table 3.8 on the following pages.

Table 3.8. Provincial demographic statistics for China, 1981 and 1982

Province	Total population	Territory (km²)	Density	TFR	CBR (%)	CDR (%)	NGR (%)	MBR (%)	FS	PM (%)	RR	Sex ratio
Whole country (except Taiwan)	1,003,937,078	9,600,000	104	2.584	2.091	6.36	1.455	27.03	4.4	6.7	0.79	106.3
Han-Dominant Region												
Shanghai	11,859,748	6,200	1,913	1.316	1.64	0.64	0.97	0.9	3.6	0.4	0.41	99.3
Beijing	9,230,687	16,814	549	1.588	1.75	0.58	1.18	2.9	3.7	3.3	0.35	102.4
Tianjin	7,764,141	11,302	687	1.645	1.86	0.61	1.25	5.3	3.9	2.0	0.31	103.1
Liaoning	35,721,693	145,803	245	1.773	1.85	0.53	1.32	9.3	4.1	8.3	0.58	104.2
Jilin	22,560,053	188,000	120	1.842	1.77	0.53	1.24	14.6	4.4	8.2	0.60	105.0
Heilongjiang	32,665,546	473,414	69	2.061	1.98	0.49	1.48	19.2	4.5	4.9	0.39	104.9
Hebei	53,005,875	187,964	282	2.650	2.40	0.61	1.79	20.2	4.1	1.6	0.86	104.8
Shanxi	25,291,389	156,120	162	2.385	2.03	0.65	1.38	24.5	4.1	0.2	0.79	108.5
Jiangsu	60,521,114	102,578	590	2.075	1.85	0.61	1.24	12.8	3.9	0.2	0.84	103.4
Zhejiang	38,884,603	101,792	383	1.982	1.79	0.63	1.17	19.1	4.0	0.4	0.74	107.7
Anhui	49,665,724	139,510	356	2.799	1.87	0.52	1.35	34.0	4.6	0.5	0.86	107.8
Fujian	25,873,259	121,471	213	2.717	2.21	0.59	1.62	29.1	4.8	1.0	0.79	105.9
Jiangxi	33,184,827	166,758	199	2.790	2.04	0.65	1.39	35.2	4.9	0.05	0.81	106.5
Shandong	74,419,054	153,126	486	2.104	1.88	0.63	1.26	14.9	4.2	0.5	0.81	102.9
Henan	74,422,739	166,867	446	2.631	2.06	0.60	1.46	27.6	4.7	1.1	0.86	104.1
Hubei	47,804,150	187,467	255	2.445	2.02	0.73	1.28	22.0	4.5	3.8	0.83	105.5
Hunan	54,008,851	210,151	257	2.833	2.11	0.70	1.41	25.9	4.2	4.0	0.86	108.1
Guangdong	59,299,220	211,783	280	3.283	2.50	0.55	1.95	35.1	4.8	1.8	0.81	104.6

	Area	Density	TFR	CBR	CDR	NGR	MBR	FS	PM	RR	Sex ratio
Sichuan	99,713,310	566,553	176	2.434	1.80	0.70	1.09	19.3	4.2	3.7	0.86	106.6
Shaanxl	28,904,423	204,996	141	2.394	2.04	0.71	1.33	24.1	4.5	0.5	0.81	107.4
Gansu	19,569,261	455,099	43	2.728	2.01	0.57	1.44	31.8	5.1	8.0	0.85	107.2
Total or average	864,369,667	3,973,763	217	2.437	2.00	0.62	1.38	22.6	4.3	2.4	0.79	105.4
Minority-Dominant Region											
Inner Mongolia	19,274,279	1,204,642	16	2.621	2.31	0.58	1.73	29.4	4.5	15.4	0.71	109.0
Qinghai	3,895,706	779,141	5	3.927	2.67	0.75	1.92	53.6	5.2	39.9	0.80	106.0
Ningxia	3,895,578	66,027	59	4.120	2.96	0.61	2.36	49.1	5.1	32.4	0.78	106.2
Xinjiang	13,081,681	1,635,210	8	3.883	2.91	0.84	2.07	54.7	4.3	59.8	0.72	106.0
Tibet	1,892,393	1,182,746	2	—	3.11	0.99	2.11	—	5.1	96.1	0.91	97.8
Guangxi	36,420,960	230,512	158	4.103	2.72	0.56	2.16	45.0	5.1	38.5	0.88	107.3
Guizhou	28,552,997	176,253	162	4.355	2.79	0.85	1.94	55.7	4.9	26.1	0.80	105.2
Yunnan	32,553,817	392,215	83	3.814	2.54	0.86	1.68	49.0	5.2	31.7	0.87	102.8
Total or average	139,567,411	5,666,744	25	3.80	2.66	0.73	1.93	46.6	4.9	33.8	0.82	105.7

Key: Density Population density, persons/km²

TFR Total fertility rate

CBR Crude birth rate

CDR Crude death rate

NGR Natural growth rate

MBR Multiple birth rate (ratio of third and higher order births to the total number of births in a given year)

FS Average family size

PM Proportion of minority population

RR Ratio of rural population to total population

Sources: The figures for total population, FS, RR, and sex ratio are for 1982 (1982 census data): SSB 1982. The figures for TFR, CBR, DCR, NGR, and MBR are for 1981 (1982 census data): Beijing Review 11, March 19, 1984, p. 29. The figures for population density and proportion of minority population are based on the 1982 census. For Tibet, data on TFR and MBR are not available.

Part Two
The Model: An Extension of the Bongaarts Life Table Methods

Family formation, growth, "decline," and dissolution are together known as family dynamics. Family dynamics is related to various demographic events, such as first marriage and remarriage (formation or reorganization of the family), childbearing (growth of the family), deaths of children and children leaving the parental home (decline of the family), and widowhood and divorce (dissolution or decomposition of the family). An integrated analysis of these demographic processes is therefore needed.

The impact of demographic processes on family size and composition has been a subject of demographic research for many years. An extensive bibliographic review of existing literature on family and household demography can be found in Burch 1979 and in Bongaarts 1983. Recent contributions to the field have been compiled in two proceedings, CICRED 1984 and OPCS 1983, and in two books, Bongaarts, Burch, and Wachter 1987 and Keilman, Kuijsten, and Vossen 1988.

Bongaarts points out that prominent among different approaches which describe and analyze the size and structure of families is the multistate life table (1987:1). The multistate marital status life table and the parity-fertility table have both been developed in the past decade. The marital status life table provides a detailed description of marital status transitions and of the distribution over the life course of members of a cohort (see, e.g., Schoen and Urton 1979; Schoen and Baj 1984; Willekens et al. 1982; Willekens 1987; Zeng 1985b). Hoem (1970) discusses fertility models of the life table type. Oechsli (1975) considers the age and parity (the never-married status being parity -1) of women by means of multistate parity life tables. Suchindran, Namboodiri, and West (1979) use life table methods to study increments and decrements in human reproduction. Rodriguez and Hobcraft (1980) analyze birth intervals using the life table. Chiang and van den Berg (1982) and Chiang (1984) propose a fertility table using parity instead of the woman's age as the basic variable for studying the reproductive experience of a given population. Nour and Suchindran (1984b) and Lutz and Feichtinger (1985) present applications of the multistate marital-parity status life table. Kuijsten (1984) develops a population projection model which classifies the population according to age, marital status, and parity status. And Hofferth (1985) studies the family structure from the children's family experience by means of the multistate life table technique.

Willekens (1983) extended the marital status life table model to accommodate fertility and thus to yield estimates of average nuclear family size. Bongaarts developed a nuclear family status life table model which takes the multistate marital status life table to the next logical step by adding a variety of maternal (or paternal) states (Bongaarts 1987). Watkins, Menken, and Bongaarts (1984) and Menken (1985) applied Bongaarts' model to investigate the implications of a set of demographic rates on the family status of American females.

Some of the above-mentioned models focus on nuptiality only. Some focus on fertility only. Some look at both. Most of them treat the individual, instead of a group of people, as the unit of analysis. Family characteristics are inferred from the life course or family status (such as marital, parity, and maternal states) of the individual cohort members. How can the individual unit be made to represent the family? Brass generalizes the idea of the head of household into the "marker" of the family. The marker is the reference person of a family. Brass argues that on the whole it is better to take the senior female as the marker, because females get married at an earlier age and live longer (1983).

Our multistate family status life table model treats the individual as the unit of analysis too and follows Brass's concept of the marker to study how demographic rates of nuptiality, fertility, and coresidence may affect family size and structure. The model is, in fact, an extension of Bongaarts' model (Bongaarts 1987). We will therefore briefly review his model in chapter 4.

Chapter 5 identifies a general family status system including both nuclear families and three-generation families. Chapter 6 discusses the procedures for estimating transition probabilities. The methods for constructing a multistate family status life table will be presented in chapter 7. Chapter 8 presents a stable population, classified by family states. An illustrative application to China's data for a family system including both nuclear families and three-generation families is presented in Part III.

4

The Bongaarts Nuclear Family Model

A Review and Discussion

4.1. The Marital-Parity-Fecundity Life Table

Bongaarts (1987) first defines a marital-parity-fecundity status life table population. Let $l_{mpf}(x)$ denote the size of the life table population in marital status m, parity status p, and fecundity status f at exact age x; where $m = 1, 2, 3, 4$ refers to never-married, currently married, widowed, and divorced, respectively; $p = 0, 1, 2 \ldots N$ refers to parity $0, 1, 2 \ldots N$; $f = 1, 2$ refers to fecund and sterile, respectively.

Starting from a birth cohort, the life table population $l_{mpf}(x)$ is calculated for each single age x from $x = 0$ to $x = 90$, say. Bongaarts argues that the calculation of the life table can be greatly simplified by assuming that particular events take place at one point in time rather than throughout the age interval between x and $x + 1$. He assumes that women make transfers from the fecund to the sterile state at the beginning of an age interval, that transfers between marital states as well as deaths take place exactly in the middle of each age interval, and that parity transitions occur during the first half and second half of the age intervals.

Define:

$l_{mpf}(x1)$ = life table population at the beginning of the age interval but *after* the transfers between fecundity states have been made;

$l_{mpf}(x2)$ = life table population in the middle of the age interval *before* marital status transfers and deaths are taken into account (but after the parity status transfers during the first half of the age interval);

$l_{mpf}(x3)$ = life table population in the middle of the age interval *after* marital status transfers and deaths have occurred.

The procedure for calculating $l_{mpf}(x + 1)$ from $l_{mpf}(x)$ consists of four steps.

49

1. *Fecundity status transitions*. Only transfers from the fecund to the sterile state (assuming no transfers from the sterile state to the fecund state) are taken into account in this step, so that

$$l_{mp1}(x1) = l_{mp1}(x)[1 - S_{mp}(x)],\tag{4.1}$$

$$l_{mp2}(x1) = l_{mp2}(x) + S_{mp}(x)l_{mp1}(x),\tag{4.2}$$

where $S_{mp}(x)$ = proportion of fecund women in marital status m and parity status p who become sterile at age x.

2. *Parity status transitions in the first half-year interval*. During the first half-year interval, only transfers of parity states are made, giving

$$l_{mp1}(x2) = l_{mp1}(x1) - \tfrac{1}{2}b_p(x,m)l_{mp1}(x1)$$
$$+ \tfrac{1}{2}b_{p-1}(x,m)l_{m,p-1,1}(x1),\tag{4.3}$$

$$l_{mp2}(x2) = l_{mp2}(x1),\tag{4.4}$$

where $b_p(x,m)$ = probability of transferring from parity p at exact age x to parity $p+1$ at exact age $x+1$ among women of marital status m.

3. *Marital status transition*. This step is very similar to the calculation of a marital status life table because it involves only transfers between marital states and deaths. The relevant equations in Bongaarts' paper (1987) were taken directly from Schoen 1975.

4. *Parity status transitions in the second half-year interval*. The equations are similar to equations (4.3) and (4.4):

$$l_{mp1}(x+1) = l_{mp1}(x3) - \tfrac{1}{2}b_p(x,m)l_{mp1}(x3)$$
$$+ \tfrac{1}{2}b_{p-1}(x,m)l_{m,p-1,1}(x3),\tag{4.5}$$

$$l_{mp2}(x+1) = l_{mp2}(x3).\tag{4.6}$$

This four-step procedure is repeated for each single age, yielding a complete life table population $l_{mpf}(x)$.

Note that in equations (4.3) and (4.5), Bongaarts assumes that the parity transition probabilities in the first half and second half of a single age interval are equal to half of the probability for the whole age interval. We will comment on this treatment in section 4.4 and suggest a refinement in section 6.2.

4.2. The Family Status Life Table

The marital-parity-fecundity status life table cannot be considered a true family status life table, because it makes no reference to the characteristics of children. To describe the family composition of women at a given age, it is necessary to keep track not only of marital, parity, and fecundity states but also of the number and residential status of living children.

Bongaarts denotes $l_{mpfc}(x)$ as the size of the family status life table population of marital status m, parity status p, fecundity status f, and number of living children c. If the probability of dying for a child were independent of the child's age, the transitions from one c state to the next could be calculated relatively easily. However, a child's mortality varies greatly with age, a fact which cannot be ignored. In order to take into account the variation with age in child mortality, Bongaarts developed a partial family status life table technique.

Without taking into consideration the number of surviving children, the status distribution at age $x + 1$ can be calculated directly from the status distribution at age x, which is described in section 4.1. When the number of living children is taken into account, the usual calculation does not work. For instance, the number of living children a woman will have at age 40 cannot be calculated from the number of living children at age 39, because we do not keep track of the children's ages and we are not able to properly estimate the children's probability of dying between the mother's age of 39 and 40.

The partial life table technique is particularly designed to solve this problem. The basic idea is that for each age, the calculation is carried out from age 0 to that age and is always connected to that age. For instance, when we compute the number of living children at mother's age 40, we apply observed birth rates, death rates, marital status change rates, and so on, from age 0 to 40. When a woman gives birth at age 20, the child will be $40 - 20 = 20$ years old when the mother reaches age 40. Multiplying the probability of surviving up to age 20, we obtain the fraction of children born when the mother is 20 who will be alive when the mother is 40. When a woman gives birth at age 25, a proportion of $P(40 - 25) = p(15)$ children born when the mother is 25 will survive when the mother reaches age 40, and so on. Of course, with the calculation of the number of living children, the cohort member's other status changes are also calculated. The calculation from age 0–40 is called a partial life table; 40 is the highest age in this partial life table. Only the status distribution for the highest age 40 is used for the completed table. Because of the truncation at age 40, it is called a partial life table. For each of the other ages we need a partial life table, and only the status distribution at the highest age in each partial table will be used for the family status life table.

In general, let x denote the highest age of the partial life table. Denote the ages in the partial table as a $(a = 0, 1, 2, \ldots, x)$. Let $l_{mpfc}(x, a)$ denote the partial family status life table population in marital status m, parity status p, fecundity status f at exact age a $(a \leq x)$, where c refers to the number of children born before the mother's age a who will be alive at the mother's exact age x. Note the difference between this number and the number of children alive at the mother's age a; some of the children who survive at the mother's age a may die before their mother reaches age x. From each partial table, only the results at age x are used for the family status life table. In a partial table, a transition from state c to state $c + 1$ takes place at the birth of a child that will survive to age x of the mother. The probability of such an event is estimated by multiplying the parity-specific fertility probability at age a by the probability that the child will survive $x - a - \frac{1}{2}$ years from its birth to the mother's age x. If $p(x - a - \frac{1}{2})$ denotes the probability that a child survives to age $x - a - \frac{1}{2}$, then a proportion $p(x - a - \frac{1}{2})$ of women, who have parity p and c living children and give a birth of order $p + 1$ at age a, will advance from maternal state c to $c + 1$. The remaining proportion $1 - p(x - a - \frac{1}{2})$ of women, who give a birth of order $p + 1$ at age a, will not change their c status but do change their parity status from p to $p + 1$. The probability $p(x - a - \frac{1}{2})$ is easily obtained from a standard mortality life table (average of $p(x - a - 1)$ and $p(x - a)$).

By modifying parity transition probabilities and survival probabilities of children $p(x - a - \frac{1}{2})$, the partial life table technique for the estimation of $l_{mpfc}(x)$ can be extended to calculate family status life tables that include other characteristics of children, such as the number of surviving sons and surviving daughters, sons and daughters living at home, and the age structure of children. If we are interested in knowing the number of surviving children by sex, we multiply the birth rate by the proportion of boys or girls among all births. If we are investigating the number of children living at home, we use the probability of surviving and living at the parental home instead of the probability of surviving. If we want to know the age structure of children—for example, how many children younger than 18 a woman may have—we simply set $p(a)$ equal to 0, except when $a < 18$.

4.3. Simplifying Assumptions for an Illustrative Numerical Application

In addition to the Markovian assumption (assuming that status transitions depend on the status occupied at the beginning of the interval but not on the person's past history), Bongaarts assumes that particular events occur at one point in time rather than throughout the year. He made a number of simplifying assumptions and used model schedules to construct an illustrative example. His assumptions are:

Only currently married fecund women bear children.

Mortality risks are a function of age and sex only.

Mortality is independent of other status changes.

The risks of first marriage, remarriage, divorce, and widowhood are functions only of age and marital status.

At the time of a marital disruption, all children present in the family stay
with their mother.

The rates of children departing from their mother's home are a function of
the children's age and sex only.

The sex ratio at birth is a constant equal to 1.05 males per female birth.

Multiple births are counted as single births.

The risk of the onset of sterility is a function of age only.

Bongaarts pointed out that each of these assumptions can be changed or elimi-
nated in future studies because they are not an intrinsic requirement of the
model itself.

4.4. Discussion of the Model and the Objectives of an Extension

According to our view, Bongaarts' model of the family status life table is a significant step forward in family demography. The model allows us to estimate the
number, size, and age structure of nuclear families in a stationary population.
The proportion of women in different family states and the average duration in
each state can also be estimated. Since these output variables are a direct function of the input, the model can be used to make detailed analyses of the effects
of various proximate determinants (fertility, mortality, marriage, divorce, remarriage, children leaving the parental home, etc.) on family composition and
on the timing and quantity of life course events.

By assuming that particular events take place at one point in time rather
than throughout the year between x and $x + 1$, Bongaarts' method greatly sim-
plifies the calculation. He assumes that marital status changes and deaths occur
in the middle of the age interval and parity status changes occur in the first half
and the second half of the year, depending on the marital status at the beginning of each half-year. This implies that in the second half of the age interval the
women who newly married have the same birth probability as those women who
married before the age interval. This is only an approximation, because newly
married women differ from previously married women with regards to the nine-
month pregnancy period and the extent of premarital pregnancy. A refinement
on this approximation will be proposed in section 7.2.

Bongaarts assumes in equations (4.3) and (4.5) that the parity transition
probabilities for the first half and the second half of a single age interval are
equal to half of the age, parity, and marital status-specific fertility probabilities for the whole age interval. This is naturally the simplest approximation
to implement. However, for the purpose of further developing his original,
innovative model, we would like to comment on this approach.

For the sake of illustration, we take the simplest case in which parity progression does not vary with parity. Denote the parity progression probability between exact age x and $x + 1$ by b, between exact age x and $x + \frac{1}{2}$ by $b1$, and between exact age $x + \frac{1}{2}$ and $x + 1$ by $b2$. Since the observed data with half-year intervals are usually not available, we have to estimate $b1$ and $b2$ based on the knowledge of b for one whole age interval. Therefore, a natural criterion is that the sum of parity transitions in the first and second half of the year estimated by $b1$ and $b2$ should be equal to the parity transitions estimated by b.

If there is no division of the whole age interval and if one uses observed b directly, a proportion b of women at risk will experience parity progression and a proportion $1 - b$ of women will not. In Bongaarts' approach, he assumes that women who give birth in the first half of the year will have the same probability $(b2)$ of bearing a child in the second half of the year as do women who do not give birth in the first half of the year. He made a further simplifying assumption: $b1 = b2 = \frac{1}{2}b$. In that case, during the course of one year, a proportion $(1 - \frac{1}{2}b)^2 = 1 - b + \frac{1}{4}b^2$ of women at risk will experience no parity progression, which is more than what should be $(1 - b)$ by a margin of $\frac{1}{4}b^2$; a proportion of $b(1 - \frac{1}{2}b)$ will have one birth and a proportion of $\frac{1}{4}b^2$ will have two births within a single year; the proportion of women who bear at least one child in the year is $b(1 - \frac{1}{2}b) + \frac{1}{4}b^2 = b - \frac{1}{4}b^2$, which is less than what should be (b) by a margin of $\frac{1}{4}b^2$.

Note that in the conventional calculation, using data of whole single age intervals, multiple births are counted as single births. The number of women who make parity progression from parity p to $p + 1$ between exact age x and $x + 1$, as stated earlier, is equal to the number of women of parity p at exact age x multiplied by the parity progression probability b. In other words, one ignores the very small proportion of women who make multiple parity transitions within a single year. A very small proportion of women do in fact complete two successive pregnancies in one year and a very small proportion (about 1%) of pregnancies end in multiple births. However, Bongaarts' approach does not seem to give a proper estimation of multiple parity transitions. We know that ovulation is not resumed until one month after childbirth. Therefore, only women who give birth in the first two months of the year, who do not breast-feed their babies, and who resume ovulation and sexual relations one month after delivery have a chance of giving birth to a second child within one year. This chance is definitely very small. Let's now take some hypothetical values of b to determine the magnitude of estimated multiple parity transitions within a single year using Bongaarts' approach.

The calculation in table 4.1 shows that the estimated proportions of multiple births and multiple deliveries among all births are too large, especially when the birth probability is high. This is due to the unrealistic assumption that women who give birth in the first half of the year will have the same probability of bearing a child in the second half of the year as do women who have

Table 4.1. Hypothetical calculation of multiple parity transitions

Parity progression probability for age interval $(x, x + 1)$: b	Probability of multiple parity transitions: $\frac{1}{4}b^2$	Percentage of multiple deliveries or multiple births among all births: $\frac{1}{4}b \times 100$
0.5	0.0625	12.5
0.4	0.0400	10.0
0.3	0.0225	7.5
0.2	0.01	5.0
0.1	0.0025	2.5

not given birth in the first half of the year. Therefore, a refinement of the estimation of parity transition probabilities and the calculation procedure of parity transitions for the first and the second half of the single age interval will be suggested in sections 6.2 and 7.2.

In Bongaarts' model, each ever-married woman stands for a nuclear family, based on the assumption that no married children live in the parental home. We may call it the nuclear family system. If an ever-married woman and her children live with her parents or her parents-in-law, she stands for a family of more than two generations. Although extended families of more than three generations are rare in contemporary society, three-generation families are not uncommon in Asian cultures and in many other developing countries. Some statistics concerning the relatively important proportion of extended families in China and in a number of other Asian countries, as well as a discussion of the feedback model of Chinese family structure, can be found in section 2.1.

Extending Bongaarts' nuclear family model to a model that accounts for both nuclear and three-generation families is our main objective. (We ignore the rare cases of families in which ever-married siblings live together.) The following three chapters present our extended model.

5

System Identification of the Family Status Life Table

As the reference person in the family, we select the ever-married senior female. Brass calls the reference person a "marker." If we know the characteristics or family status of markers, we can describe the type and size of families. Which characteristics of the markers should we keep track of, and how can we infer the structure and size of families from the characteristics of markers in nuclear family systems and in general family systems including nuclear families and three-generation families? These matters will be discussed in this chapter. The model to be built is a female-dominant model. Theoretically speaking, the male-dominant model can be built in the same way, but the data for male-dominant models are usually questionable.

Bongaarts' nuclear family system assumes that adult children necessarily leave the parental home at the time of marriage. However, reality in China, other Asian countries, and many other developing countries is not as simple as this. Some children may leave the parental home to set up a nuclear family before or after marriage. Some children may not leave the parents' home at all. Parents and their married children and grandchildren form three-generation families or other types of extended families.

How can we model a general family status system in which the members from different generations interact in such a complex way? Brass's concept of a marker provides a good starting point. We also suggest making the female the marker, not only because she marries earlier and lives longer than her husband but also because the parity-specific fertility data are much more easily obtained for females than for males and because, following divorce, young children usually live with their mother.

We may imagine a girl born as a nonmarker. When she grows up, she may or may not leave her parental home. Leaving the parental home may occur before or after marriage. When she leaves her parents to set up an independent family, she becomes a marker. If she lives with her surviving mother or mother-in-law, she is not a marker. If a marker dies, her position as marker will be given to a daughter-in-law who lives at home. If she has no daughter-in-law living at home, her marker position will be taken over by an adult daughter (over 18 years old) living at home when she dies. If she has neither a daughter-in-law living at home nor an adult daughter living at home, the remaining family members (if any) will be attached to another female marker, through remarriage of the father or by joining the relative's family.

Both markers and nonmarkers may get married and give birth; their children may die or leave the home; they may divorce or become widowed, remarry and so on. They may also change their marker status from time to time: a nonmarker may become a marker by setting up an independent family or through the death of her mother or mother-in-law; a marker may become a nonmarker by rejoining her mother or mother-in-law. Four demographic processes operate throughout a woman's life: marital, parity, maternal, and marker status changes.

Clearly, each marker stands for a family. The marital and maternal status of markers can be used to help determine their family size. The number of ever-married nonmarkers with at least one surviving child is equivalent to the number of three-generation families, since a nonmarker has to live with her mother or mother-in-law. Different types of three-generation families can be distinguished by different combinations of grandmothers' (marker) and mothers' (ever-married nonmarker) marital status (figure 5.1). The family size can be determined by the marital status of the grandmother (marker) and mother (nonmarker) and the maternal status of the mother.

Given the status identification for the family system discussed above, it is theoretically possible for a woman to have any combination of marital, marker, parity, and maternal states. For instance, she may be a currently married marker of parity 3 with 2 children living at home; or she may be a widowed nonmarker of parity 2 with 1 child living at home, and so on. We may denote the number of marital, marker, parity, and maternal states as M, K, P, and C, respectively. Since the number of surviving children living at home is always less than or equal to the parity for any woman at any time, the theoretical total number of possible combinations of those states is

$$T = MK \sum_{p=0}^{P} (p + 1).$$

At any moment of life, a woman occupies a state of one of those T combinations. We may call the combination the composite state and denote it as i ($i = 1, 2, \ldots, T$). Let $1_i(x)$ ($i = 1, 2, \ldots, T$) denote the number of cohort members of exact age x in composite state i. Let $P_{ij}(x)$ ($i, j = 1, 2, \ldots, T$) denote the probability that a cohort member in composite state i at exact age x will survive and be in composite state j at exact age $x + 1$. Thus

Nuclear Families

Husband-wife   Lone mother

Three-Generation Families

Husband-wife with both grandparents   Husband-wife with one grandmother

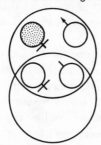   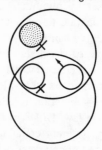

Lone mother with both grandparents   Lone mother with one grandmother

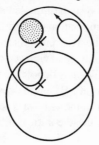   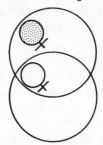

Others

Husband-wife without children   Lone female without children

marker =

Figure 5.1. A general family status system including nuclear families and three-generation families (female-dominant model)

$$l_j(x + 1) = \sum_{i=1}^{T} l_i(x)P_{ij}(x). \qquad (5.1)$$

We may also write equation (5.1) using matrix notation:

$$\mathbf{l}(x + 1) = \mathbf{P}(x)\mathbf{l}(x), \qquad (5.2)$$

where

$$\mathbf{l}(x) = [l_1(x), l_2(x), \ldots, l_T(x)]',$$

$$\mathbf{P}(x) = \begin{bmatrix} P_{11}(x) & P_{21}(x) & \ldots & P_{T1}(x) \\ P_{12}(x) & P_{22}(x) & \ldots & P_{T2}(x) \\ \cdot & \cdot & & \cdot \\ \cdot & \cdot & & \cdot \\ \cdot & \cdot & & \cdot \\ P_{1T}(x) & P_{2T}(x) & \ldots & P_{TT}(x) \end{bmatrix}.$$

If $\mathbf{P}(x)$, which is a T^2 matrix, could be properly estimated, the calculation of $\mathbf{l}(x)$ would be straightforward. Unfortunately, the estimation of $\mathbf{P}(x)$ is usually not practical when the total number of states distinguished is large, which is the case in the family status life table analysis. For instance, if one is interested in four marital states, two marker states, nine parity and maternal states, the total number of states distinguished is

$$T = (4)(2) \sum_{p=0}^{8} (p + 1) = 360.$$

The total number of cells in the transition matrix is thus $(360)(360) = 129,600$, and we have one such large matrix for each age. Although there are many zero cells in the matrices, the number of nonzero cells to be estimated is still much too large. Since so many categories have been distinguished, the

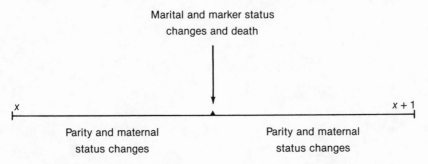

Figure 5.2. Parity, maternal, and marital and marker status changes between ages x and $x + 1$ in a general family status system.

number of observed events for some categories to estimate the transition probabilities is too small even if the sample size is relatively large. Therefore, the estimation of such large transition probability matrices $\mathbf{P}(x)$ is not practical.

In Bongaarts' nuclear family model, he also distinguished a large number of states. He overcame the difficulty by assuming that particular events take place at particular points in time between ages x and $x + 1$. Here, we adopt Bongaarts' approach with a few refinements to calculate the family life history of the life table cohort.

In our model, we assume that marital and marker status changes and deaths occur in the middle of the age interval and that maternal status changes occur throughout the first and the second halves of the age interval (see figure 5.2). This assumption allows us to estimate marital, marker, parity, and maternal status transition probabilities separately, which greatly reduces the complexity and data requirements.

6

Transition Probabilities

The system identification in the previous chapter determined what states are distinguished and the strategy of modeling the transitions of those states. The critical question now is how to estimate the transition probabilities between the states.

Section 6.1 deals with parity transition probabilities. Section 6.2 presents a procedure for estimating marital-marker status transition probabilities. The estimation of maternal status change is discussed in section 6.3.

6.1. Parity Transition Probabilities

The age-specific probabilities of parity status change occurring throughout the first and second halves of the interval are "gross" probabilities, that is, in the absence of the mother's mortality since it had already been taken into account in the middle of the interval.

Let $f_p(x, m)$ denote the occurrence/exposure rates of the pth birth by age x and marital status m of the mother, which is defined as the number of pth births by women aged x to $x + 1$, with marital status m divided by the person-years lived in parity $p - 1$ and marital status m of women aged x to $x + 1$. The probability that a woman of parity $p - 1$ and marital status m at exact age x will be in parity p at exact age $x + 1$ in the absence of mortality and marital change, $b_p(x, m)$, can be estimated in a familiar manner with the assumption of a uniform distribution of births between ages x and $x + 1$ (analogous to the estimation of death probabilities from death rates):

$$b_p(x, m) = \frac{f_p(x, m)}{1 + \frac{1}{2}f_p(x, m)} \qquad (p = 1, 2, 3, \ldots, N). \qquad (6.1)$$

As shown in figure 5.2, we are going to calculate the parity status change in the first half and in the second half of the age interval, respectively, so that the corresponding formulas are needed. It should be stated that the following derivation is based on the assumption that no multiple parity transitions take place within a single age interval. There are at least two reasons for making this assumption. First, the multiple parity transitions are very rare, and second, birth rates are usually defined as the number of births divided by the number of women at risk. Multiple births and multiple deliveries in a single year have already counted in the number of births, which is the numerator of the birth rates to be used.

Define $_\frac{1}{2}b_p(x, m)$ and $_\frac{1}{2}b_p(x + \frac{1}{2}, m)$ as the probabilities of giving a pth birth between exact ages x and $x + \frac{1}{2}$ and between exact ages $x + \frac{1}{2}$ and $x + 1$, respectively, in the absence of mortality. Define W as the number of women of parity $p - 1$ at exact age x. Assuming the uniform distribution of births in a year, the number of pth births to these W women in the first half of the year is equal to those that occur in the second half of the year; both are $\frac{1}{2}Wb_p(x, m)$. Therefore, the probability of giving a pth birth in the first half of the year is

$$_\frac{1}{2}b_p(x, m) = Wb_p(x, m)/(2W) = b_p(x, m)/2. \tag{6.2}$$

There are $W - \frac{1}{2}Wb_p(x, m)$ women of parity $p - 1$ in the middle of the year at risk of giving a pth birth. (Since we assume that no multiple births occur in a single age interval, we must assume that the women who were of parity $p - 2$ at the beginning of the age interval but who give a $(p - 1)$th birth in the first half of the interval are not at risk of giving a pth birth in the middle of the interval.) The probability of giving a pth birth in the second half of the year is:

$$_\frac{1}{2}b_p(x + \frac{1}{2}, m) = \frac{1}{2}Wb_p(x, m)/[W - \frac{1}{2}Wb_p(x, m)]$$
$$= b_p(x, m)/[2 - b_p(x, m)] \tag{6.3}$$

Note that the data $f_p(x, m)$ are for a one-year age interval, but the calculation of parity transitions between exact age x and $x + 1$ is divided into two steps by formulas (6.2) and (6.3). Fortunately, however, the parity distribution at the end of the age interval calculated by $_\frac{1}{2}b_p(x, m)$ and $_\frac{1}{2}b_p(x + \frac{1}{2}, m)$ with two steps is the same as the parity distribution calculated by one step only, using $b_p(x, m)$ estimated by formula (6.1). This equivalence can be demonstrated as follows: first, combining two steps, the probability of parity progression is

$$_\frac{1}{2}b_p(x, m) + [1 - _\frac{1}{2}b_p(x, m)]_\frac{1}{2}b_p(x + \frac{1}{2}, m) =$$
$$\frac{1}{2}b_p(x, m) + \frac{[1 - \frac{1}{2}b_p(x, m)]b_p(x, m)}{2 - b_p(x, m)} = b_p(x, m).$$

Second, the probability of no parity progression is

$$[1 - \tfrac{1}{2}b_p(x,m)][1 - \tfrac{1}{2}b_p(x + \tfrac{1}{2}, m)]=$$
$$[1 - \frac{b_p(x,m)}{2}][1 - \frac{b_p(x,m)}{2 - b_p(x,m)}] = 1 - b_p(x,m).$$

This supports our two-step approach for calculating parity transitions.

6.2. Marital-Marker Status Transition Probabilities

6.2.1. The three-step estimation procedure

The marker status change is closely related to the marital status change since the time at marriage and a few years after marriage are the most likely moments for children to leave the parental home. Therefore, we suggest the estimation of transition probabilities for the marital-marker composite states. If four marital statuses are distinguished, the composite marital-marker states are:

1. never-married marker
2. never-married nonmarker
3. currently married marker
4. currently married nonmarker
5. widowed marker
6. widowed nonmarker
7. divorced marker
8. divorced nonmarker

The total number of composite marital-marker states is 8. The transition probabilities of the composite marital-marker states can be arranged as an 8×8 matrix.

We propose a three-step procedure for estimating transition probabilities of composite marital-marker states. The first step is the estimation of the marital status transition probabilities. The second step is the estimation of the marker status transition probabilities *conditional on* the marital status change. The third step is the multiplication of the two probabilities to obtain the transition probabilities of the composite states. For example, if we estimated the probability that a 20-year-old nonmarker girl lives to age 21 and marries between ages 20 and 21 as being 0.25, and the probability of becoming a marker due to leaving the parental home between ages 20 and 21, conditional on getting married in the same age interval, as 0.2, then the probability that a never-married nonmarker at exact age 20 will be a currently married marker at the exact age 21 is $0.25 \times 0.2 = 0.05$. The probability that she is a currently married nonmarker at exact age 21 is $0.25 \times (1 - 0.2) = 0.2$. Note that $0.05 + 0.2 = 0.25$. The probability of getting married between ages 20 and 21 is decomposed into becoming a married marker and a married nonmarker:

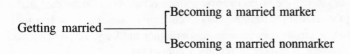

The data needed for estimating marital status transition probabilities are occurrence/exposure rates of first marriage, widowhood, divorce, remarriage, and death. The standard formulas for estimating marital status transition probabilities from the occurrence/exposure rates can be found, for example, in Willekens et al. 1982 or in Appendix 1 of this volume. We will present the estimators of the marker status transition probabilities *conditional on* marital status change in section 6.2.4. Leaving the parental home and death of mother are two main causes of marker status change. We, therefore, discuss these two issues in sections 6.2.2 and 6.2.3 as a preparation for the discussion in section 6.2.4. The procedure for estimating marital-marker composite status transition probabilities can be represented schematically as follows:

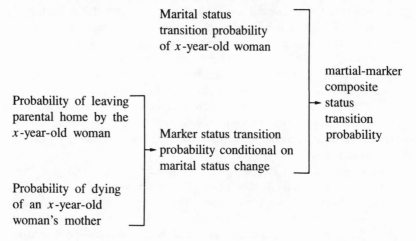

6.2.2. An x-year-old woman's probabilities of leaving the parental home

A baby girl is born as a nonmarker. The marker of the family in which the girl is living is her mother or grandmother (if her grandmother is living with them). We assume that no girl will leave the parental home to set up an independent family before the age of 18. Furthermore, we assume that when a mother dies as a marker, her position of marker will be given to her daughter-in-law living at home or adult daughter living at home (adult is defined conventionally as being over age 18). If a mother dies while she has no daughter-in-law or adult daughter living at home, we assume that the surviving father will remarry soon in order to have someone to take care of the small children. Consequently, the marker position will be taken over by a stepmother. We also assume that orphans will join relatives' families or some collective households or institutions. Therefore, a girl always remains a nonmarker until age 18. After that age, she may become a marker or remain a nonmarker.

Children may leave the parental home before marriage (but after age

18), at marriage, or a number of years after marriage. Note that we do not consider a girl who leaves her own parents to join her husband's parents as "leaving the parental home." Here, leaving the parental home refers to a girl leaving both her own parental home and her husband's parental home to set up an independent family.

The overall proportion leaving the parental home before marriage and its time schedule can be estimated from survey observations. The gross probability of leaving the parental home unmarried can be estimated by a multiple-decrement gross life table (the multiple decrements here are getting married and leaving parental home; "gross" means in the absence of mortality). Let $r(x)$ denote the number of events of leaving the parental home by never-married women between ages x and $x + 1$, and let $t(x)$ denote the number of cohort members of exact age x who are never-married and remain in the parental home, in the absence of mortality (since the deaths of cohort members are taken into account together with marital and marker status changes, and the independence of the events and deaths is assumed). Thus the gross probability of leaving the parental home before marriage can be calculated:

$$O_1(x) = r(x)/t(x). \tag{6.4}$$

The proportion of cohort members leaving the parental home at the time of marriage or after marriage depends on the overall proportion of children ultimately leaving the parental home (determined by the fertility level, or in other words, average number of daughters per family, and the proportion of parents who have married children but do not live with any of them; this will be discussed later) and the time schedule of leaving the parental home.

A survey may provide information on the overall proportion ultimately leaving the parental home after marriage and its time schedule. The time schedule of leaving the parental home can be used directly in calculating probabilities, but the sample observation of the overall proportion depends on the past fertility experience of different cohorts in the sample population. A family status life table often tries to investigate the effects on family size and composition if given regimes of fertility, mortality, and nuptiality prevail. The given regimes are usually period data, which are not consistent with the overall proportion ultimately observed in a survey leaving the parental home, since the observed proportion is the result of the cohorts' experience in the past. Therefore, the observed ultimate proportion leaving the parental home cannot be used for a period family status life table, and we need to estimate the proportion based on the given fertility regime. (Of course, if the family status life table is constructed for a real cohort using cohort data, one can use the observed cohort proportion ultimately leaving the parental home directly.)

Let l denote the proportion ultimately leaving the parental home and s the proportion remaining in the parental home for the cohort members who are living in the parental home at the time of marriage. Obviously, the sum of l and s is equal to 1. The factors which determine the proportion of children ultimately remaining in the parental home (conditional on the parents' survival) are the average number of children per couple given that the couple has at least one child, the desirability of coresidence between parents and married children, and the proportion of parents who are not able to live with a married child because of a shortage of children. Let's take a simple example. Suppose that among 20 elderly couples who have at least one child, the average number of adult children is 1.5; half are boys and half are girls. These 20 elderly couples have 30 children, who can form only 15 younger couples. Assuming that no couples live with more than one of their own married children, 5 couples have a child but are not able to live with any married child due to the fact that the number of younger couples is smaller than the number of elderly couples. The maximum number of elderly couples who can live with a married child is equal to $20 - 5 = 15$. We assume that among those 15 elderly couples, there are 5 elderly couples who do not want to live with a married child or their married children do not want to live with them; since we have assumed that no parents live with more than one of their own married children, the actual number of younger couples who live with their parents is equal to the number of elderly couples who live with one of their married children, that is, $15 - 5 = 10$. Therefore, the overall proportion of children ultimately staying with their parents after marriage is

$$\frac{20 - 5 - 5}{15} = \frac{1 - 0.25 - 0.25}{0.75} = 0.6667.$$

In general, let NRR denote the net reproduction rate. Let n_1 denote the proportion of women who have not had a child during the course of their life; let n_2 denote the proportion of couples who have at least one married child but who do not live with a married child; let n_3 denote the proportion of couples who have at least one child but who are not able to live with a married child due to the shortage of children. According to Coale (1972:18) a good approximation of NRR is given by the product of the gross reproduction rate GRR, which is equal to the total fertility rate TFR times the proportion of girls at birth, and the probability of surviving up to mean age at childbearing $p(m)$. Therefore, $NRR/(1 - n_1)$ is approximately the average number of daughters who survive up to the mean age at childbearing per woman of at least parity 1. Let G stand for $NRR/(1 - n_1)$. Assuming that a married child never lives with both the parents and the parents-in-law at the same time and assuming that a married child does not live with a married brother or a married sister, the number of women living with a married child per woman, $1 - n_2 - n_3$, is equal to the average number of married daughters living with parents-in-law or parents per woman, so that the overall proportion of women who stay with their parents-in-law or parents after marriage is

$$s = (1 - n_2 - n_3)/G \qquad (6.5)$$

where $0 \leq s \leq 1$; $G \geq 0$; $n_1 \geq 0$; $n_2 \geq 0$; $n_3 \geq 0$.

If G (the average number of daughters who survive up to the mean age at childbearing per woman of at least parity 1) is greater than or equal to 1, the proportion of couples who have at least one child but are not able to live with a married child due to the shortage of children in the population is equal to 0, that is, $n_3 = 0$. Then equation (6.5) becomes

$$s = (1 - n_2)/G \qquad (G \geq 1). \qquad (6.6)$$

If $G < 1$, the shortage $n_3 = 1 - G$ (according to the definition of n_2, $n_2 \leq G$). Then equation (6.5) becomes

$$s = (1 - n_2 - 1 + G)/G = (G - n_2)/G \qquad (G < 1). \qquad (6.7)$$

Thus, we need only NRR, n_1, and n_2 in order to estimate s. NRR is commonly available; n_1 is available from census or survey observations and is often very stable; n_2 can be estimated from survey data. The proportion ultimately leaving the parental home after marriage is

$$l = 1 - s. \qquad (6.8)$$

If the proportion of women who leave the parental home before marriage is w, then the proportion of women living with their parents at the time of marriage who ultimately leave the parental home is

$$l = 1 - \frac{1 - n_2}{G(1 - w)} \qquad (G \geq 1 \text{ and } w \leq \frac{G + n_2 - 1}{G}), \qquad (6.9)$$

$$l = 1 - \frac{G - n_2}{G(1 - w)} \qquad (G < 1, n_2 \leq G, \text{ and } w \leq \frac{n_2}{G}). \qquad (6.10)$$

The constraints on n_2 and w, which are of course met in practical application, have been introduced to ensure that the formulas yield logical values for l.

When l is estimated and the time schedule of leaving the parental home after marriage by marriage duration is known, the weighted average probability of leaving the parental home at age x (the weights being the proportions of marriage durations) can be relatively easily estimated.

Let $g(y)$ denote the time schedule of leaving the parental home after marriage at the ever-married duration y (the sum of $g(y)$ over all y is equal to 1), then the products of l and $g(y)$ are the reduced events of leaving the parental home at the ever-married duration y. Applying these reduced events to a synthetic cohort and using the technique of a single-decrement life table, we can compute the column of events of leaving the parental home and the number of persons at risk, that is, ever-married children staying with their parents in the absence of mortality. Thus, the gross probability of leaving the parental home at each ever-married duration y, $k(y)$, can be calculated by dividing the column of events by the column of persons at risk.

Recalling the identification of family states in chapter 5, we have not distinguished marriage duration as an explicit variable. In order to keep the model manageable, we are still not willing to do so. However, the distribution of the ever-married durations at each age is determined by the input first-marriage rates and can be easily estimated from the given first-marriage data.

Define:

$j(x,y)$ = the proportion of x-year-old women with ever-married duration $y = x - a$ among x-year-old ever-married women.

$r(a)$ = the observed reduced events of first marriage, which is defined as the number of first marriages of women aged a to $a + 1$ divided by the total number of women aged a to $a + 1$ in the absence of mortality.

$F(x)$ = cumulative reduced events of first marriage up to age x:

$$F(x) = \sum_{a}^{x} r(a).$$

Hence,

$$j(x,y) = r(a)/F(x). \tag{6.11}$$

Then the probability that an x-year-old ever-married woman living with a parent will leave the parental home between ages x and $x + 1$ is estimated by the weighted average

$$O_2(x) = \sum_{y=0}^{x-15} k(y)j(x,y). \tag{6.12}$$

For women who were newly married during the age interval x to $x + 1$, the probability of leaving the parental home between ages x and $x + 1$ is $k(0)$ since their duration of being ever-married is 0.

6.2.3. Probability of dying of an x-year-old woman's mother

Another important occasion when adult nonmarkers become markers is the death of their mothers or mothers-in-law. To derive the probability of dying of an x-year-old woman's mother or mother-in-law, we first derive the formula for estimating the probability of an x-year-old woman's mother surviving, taken from Goodman, Keyfitz, and Pullum 1974.

If an x-year-old woman was born at age a of her mother, the mother must be $x + a$ years old if still alive. The probability that her mother will survive is $L(x + a)/L(a)$, where $L(x + a)$ and $L(a)$ are standard life table survival functions. The chance that an x-year-old woman chosen at random out of the population being studied was born at age a of her mother is determined by three factors: the cohort size of the mother, the mother's survivorship, and the mother's birth rate at age a. The larger the cohort size of the mother and the greater the probability that these cohort members survive at age a and the higher the birth rate at age a, the greater the chance that an x-year-old woman was born at age a of her mother. Since our family status life table population is of given fixed age-specific fertility and death rates, it can be viewed as a stable population model. (This aspect will be explored in chapter 8.) Hence, the multiplier $\exp[-r(a + \frac{1}{2})]$ accounts for the size of the mother's cohort; $m(a)$ is the birth rate for female babies; r is the growth rate of the stable population. The quantity r can be estimated from given fertility and mortality regimes by a simple approach. It is well known that the relation $\sum_a \exp[-r(a + \frac{1}{2})]L(a)m(a) = 1$ holds in a stable population. Given $L(a)$ and $m(a)$, we can easily estimate r, which satisfies the above relation, by the iterative method.

The probability that a member of the mother's cohort gives birth to a child in the interval a to $a + 1$ is $\exp[-r(a + \frac{1}{2})]L(a)m(a)$. It is also the probability that a child is born between ages a and $a + 1$ of the mother.

The probability that the mother of an x-year-old woman is alive, given that the woman was born at age a of the mother, is $\exp[-r(a + \frac{1}{2})]L(a)m(a)L(x +a)/L(a)$.

Totaling this conditional probability over all possible ages, one obtains the probability of an average x-year-old woman's mother being alive, denoted as $M_1(x)$:

$$M_1(x) = \sum_a \exp[-r(a + \tfrac{1}{2})]L(a)m(a)L(x + a)/L(a)$$

$$= \sum_a \exp[-r(a + \tfrac{1}{2})]m(a)L(x + a). \tag{6.13}$$

Multiplying the probability that an x-year-old woman's mother is alive (conditional on the woman being born at age a of the mother), $\exp[-r(a+ \frac{1}{2})]m(a)L(x + a)$, by the mother's death probability, $d(x + a)$, we obtain the probability that an x-year-old woman's mother will die between the woman's ages x and $x + 1$ (mother's ages $x + a$ and $x + a + 1$), conditional on the fact that the woman was born at age a of the mother. Totaling this probability over all possible ages and dividing by $M_1(x)$, we remove the condition (on the woman born at age a of the mother) and derive the probability that an x-year-old woman's mother will die between the woman's ages x and $x + 1$, given that the woman's mother is alive when the woman reaches age x, denoted as $F_1(x)$:

$$F_1(x) = \sum_a \exp[-r(a + \tfrac{1}{2})]m(a)L(x + a)d(x + a)$$
$$/ \sum_a \exp[-r(a + \tfrac{1}{2})]m(a)L(x + a). \tag{6.14}$$

Equation (6.13) can be easily modified for the purpose of estimating the probability that an average x-year-old woman has a surviving mother of a certain age. For instance, we may be interested in knowing the probability that an x-year-old woman has a surviving mother of age over 65, which can be denoted as $M_1(x, > 65)$. Since the surviving mother in question is over 65 years old and the woman is x years old, she was born when her mother was aged over $65 - x$. Therefore, the formula for estimating the probability that an average x-year-old woman has a surviving mother aged over 65 is

$$M_1(x, > 65) = \sum_{a > 65 - x} \exp[-r(a + \tfrac{1}{2})]m(a)L(x + a). \tag{6.15}$$

Formulas (6.13) and (6.15) can also be modified to estimate the probability that an x-year-old woman has a surviving father. Denote the difference of mean age at marriage for males and females by c. Assuming that the father is alive at the birth of his daughter, the probability of survival of an x-year-old woman's father, conditional on the fact that she was born at age a of her mother, is

$$\exp[-r(a + \tfrac{1}{2})]L(a)m(a)L'(x + a + c)/L'(a + c),$$

where $L'(a + c)$ is the male's probability of surviving up to age $a + c$. Totaling this probability over all possible ages, one obtains the probability that an average x-year-old woman's father is alive, denoted as $M_1'(x)$:

$$M_1'(x) = \sum_a \exp[-r(a + \tfrac{1}{2})]m(a)L(a)L'(x + a + c)$$
$$/L'(a + c). \tag{6.16}$$

The probability that an x-year-old woman has a surviving father aged over 65 is

$$M_1'(x, > 65) = \sum_{a > 65 - x - c} \exp[-r(a + \tfrac{1}{2})]m(a)L(a)L'(x + a + c)$$
$$/L'(a + c). \tag{6.17}$$

The probability that an x-year-old woman has surviving parent(s) (one parent or both parents are alive) is

$$M_1''(x) = 1 - [1 - M_1(x)][1 - M_1'(x)]. \tag{6.18}$$

The probability that an x-year-old woman's parents are both alive is

$$M_1'''(x) = M_1(x)M_1'(x). \tag{6.19}$$

The probability that an x-year-old woman has surviving parent(s) aged over 65 is

$$M_1''(x, > 65) = 1 - [1 - M_1(x, > 65)][1 - M_1'(x, > 65)]. \tag{6.20}$$

The probability that an x-year-old woman has both surviving parents aged over 65 is

$$M_1'''(x, > 65) = M_1(x, > 65)M_1'(x, > 65). \tag{6.21}$$

6.2.4. Marker status transition probabilities conditional on marital status changes

So far, we have derived the formulas for a nonmarker to become a marker either from leaving the parental home—$O_1(x)$, see equation (6.4), and $O_2(x)$, see equation (6.12)—or from the death of the mother—$F_1(x)$, see equation (6.14). Since the marker status change also depends on the marital status change, it is necessary to further derive the marker status transition probability conditional on the marital status change:

a. Never-married to never-married. We made the assumption earlier that an unmarried woman remains a nonmarker up to at least age 18. After this age the probability that a never-married woman becomes a marker at age x conditional on remaining never-married up to age $x + 1$, $C_3(x)$, is the sum of the probability of her mother dying in the age interval, $F_1(x)$, and the probability of leaving the parental home unmarried, $O_1(x)$ (see equation [6.4]) minus the product of $F_1(x)$ and $O_1(x)$ because the death of the mother and leaving the parental home are not mutually exclusive and we assume they are independent; that is,

$$C_3(x) = F_1(x) + O_1(x) - F_1(x)O_1(x). \tag{6.22}$$

b. Never-married to currently married. If a nonmarker woman gets married in the age interval, her marriage duration is 0 in that interval, and her probability of leaving the parental home is denoted as $k(0)$. The probability of her mother dying in the interval is $F_1(x)$. The event of the woman leaving the parental home and the event of the woman's mother's death are not mutually exclusive. As with the case in equation (6.22), we subtract $k(0)F_1(x)$ from the sum of $k(0)$ and $F_1(x)$. Here we do not distinguish between whether the woman lives with her own mother or her husband's surviving mother and we ignore the age difference of her own and her husband's mother. Thus, the probability of transferring from nonmarker to marker conditional on her getting married in the age interval is

$$C_1(x) = k(0) + F_1(x) - k(0)F_1(x). \tag{6.23}$$

c. Never-married to widowed or divorced. It is possible, but very rare, for a never-married girl to get married and widowed or divorced in the same year. These multiple marital status transitions should of course take place through marriage. We therefore assume that the probability that a never-married girl becomes a marker conditional on her becoming widowed or divorced in the same year is the same as that of *b* above, that is, $C_1(x)$.

d. Currently married to currently married. If a nonmarker woman is currently married at the beginning of the age interval and remains so until the end of the interval, the chances for her to become a marker are either by leaving the parental home, which depends on the age and the duration of being ever-married, $O_2(x)$ (see equation [6.12]), or by the death of the mother, $F_1(x)$. Since those two kinds of events are not mutually exclusive and we assume that they are independent, the probability of transferring from nonmarker to marker status conditional on being currently married at the beginning and at the end of the age interval is

$$C_2(x) = O_2(x) + F_1(x) - O_2(x)F_1(x). \tag{6.24}$$

e. Currently married to widowed or divorced. We assume that due to a housing constraint or due to an emotional desire for protection, a new widow or divorcee remains with her parents-in-law or returns to her own parental home if she was living in the home of her parents-in-law immediately before the death of her husband or before divorce. Hence, the probability that a currently married nonmarker will become a marker conditional on her becoming widowed or divorced in the age interval is equal to the probability of her mother's death, $F_1(x)$.

f. For a reason similar to the one in *e*, we assume that the probability that a widowed or divorced nonmarker becomes a marker conditional on the fact that she remains widowed or divorced until the end of the interval is equal to $F_1(x)$.

g. For the sake of simplicity, the probability that a widowed or divorced nonmarker becomes a marker conditional on her getting remarried in the interval is assumed to be equal to the probability that a currently married nonmarker becomes a marker conditional on her remaining currently married, namely, $C_2(x)$. This probability is also applied to the widowed (or divorced) nonmarker who remarries but soon divorces (or becomes widowed) before the end of the interval.

The complements of the probabilities described in a to g are the probabilities that a nonmarker remains a nonmarker until the end of the age interval, conditional on corresponding marital status transitions.

It is not very common for women who have already become markers of independent families to come back to the parental home, possibly with children. For simplicity's sake we assume that the probability of moving from the marker status to the nonmarker status, which may be denoted as $R(x)$, depends only on the age of the markers. This assumption can be easily removed if the phenomenon of "coming back to the parental home" is important and data on this phenomenon in connection with marital status change are available.

6.2.5. Transition probabilities of the composite states

The products of the probabilities of the marital status change and the marker status transition probabilities conditional on the marital status changes are the transition probabilities of composite marital-marker statuses. All the estimators are presented in table 6.1.

6.3. Maternal Status Transition Probabilities

As we discussed in section 4.2 the maternal status (i.e., number of children living at home) change is to be calculated by a partial life table technique. For each exact age x, we carry out the calculation from ages 0 to x. If the cohort members give birth between ages a and $a + 1$, which can be thought of as being concentrated at age $a + \frac{1}{2}$, we multiply the number of these cohort members by the proportion of the cohort members' children surviving and staying in the parental home up to age $x - a - \frac{1}{2}$ (the child born at age $a + \frac{1}{2}$ of the mother will be $x - a - \frac{1}{2}$ years old when the mother reaches age x), so that we obtain the number of cohort members whose maternal status will progress. The cumulative proportion surviving up to age $x - a - \frac{1}{2}$ can be easily obtained from a standard mortality life table. The cumulative proportion staying in the parental home (CPSPH) up to age $x - a - \frac{1}{2}$ conditional on surviving is estimated by a procedure described below. The procedure can be represented schematically as follows:

Table 6.1. Estimators of transition probabilities of marital-marker states

| | | Status at Exact Age X | | | | | | | |
| | | Nonmarker | | | | Marker | | | |
Status at Exact Age X + 1		Never-married	Currently married	Widowed	Divorced	Never-married	Currently married	Widowed	Divorced
Nonmarker	Never-married	$P_{11}(x)(1-C_3(x))$	0	0	0	$P_{11}(x)R(x)$	0	0	0
	Currently married	$P_{12}(x)(1-C_1(x))$	$P_{22}(x)(1-C_2(x))$	$P_{32}(x)(1-C_2(x))$	$P_{42}(x)(1-C_2(x))$	$P_{12}(x)R(x)$	$P_{22}(x)R(x)$	$P_{32}(x)R(x)$	$P_{42}(x)R(x)$
	Widowed	$P_{13}(x)(1-C_1(x))$	$P_{23}(x)(1-F_1(x))$	$P_{33}(x)(1-F_1(x))$	$P_{43}(x)(1-C_2(x))$	$P_{13}(x)R(x)$	$P_{23}(x)R(x)$	$P_{33}(x)R(x)$	$P_{43}(x)R(x)$
	Divorced	$P_{14}(x)(1-C_1(x))$	$P_{24}(x)(1-F_1(x))$	$P_{34}(x)(1-C_2(x))$	$P_{44}(x)(1-F_1(x))$	$P_{14}(x)R(x)$	$P_{24}(x)R(x)$	$P_{34}(x)R(x)$	$P_{44}(x)R(x)$
Marker	Never-married	$P_{11}(x)C_3(x)$	0	0	0	$P_{11}(x)(1-R(x))$	0	0	0
	Currently married	$P_{12}(x)C_1(x)$	$P_{22}(x)C_2(x)$	$P_{32}(x)C_2(x)$	$P_{42}(x)C_2(x)$	$P_{12}(x)(1-R(x))$	$P_{22}(x)(1-R(x))$	$P_{32}(x)(1-R(x))$	$P_{42}(x)(1-R(x))$
	Widowed	$P_{13}(x)C_1(x)$	$P_{23}(x)F_1(x)$	$P_{33}(x)F_1(x)$	$P_{43}(x)C_2(x)$	$P_{13}(x)(1-R(x))$	$P_{23}(x)(1-R(x))$	$P_{33}(x)(1-R(x))$	$P_{43}(x)(1-R(x))$
	Divorced	$P_{14}(x)C_1(x)$	$P_{24}(x)F_1(x)$	$P_{34}(x)C_2(x)$	$P_{44}(x)F_1(x)$	$P_{14}(x)(1-R(x))$	$P_{24}(x)(1-R(x))$	$P_{34}(x)(1-R(x))$	$P_{44}(x)(1-R(x))$

$P_{ij}(x)$ $(i, j = 1, 2, 3, 4)$ = probability that a woman of marital status i at exact age x will be in marital status j at exact age $x + 1$.

$M_1(x)$ = probability of an x-year-old woman having a surviving mother (see equation 6.13).

$F_1(x)$ = probability that an x-year-old woman's mother will die between the woman's age x and $x + 1$ (see equation 6.14).

$k(0)$ = probability of leaving the parental home between the ever-married duration 0 and 1.

$O_1(x)$ = probability of an unmarried woman leaving the parental home between ages x and $x + 1$ (see equation 6.4).

$O_2(x)$ = weighted average probability of an ever-married woman leaving the parental home between the ages x and $x + 1$ (see equation 6.12).

$C_1(x) = k(0) + F_1(x) - K(O)F_1$.

$C_2(x) = O_2(x) + F_1(x) - O_2(x)F_1(x)$.

$C_3(x) = O_1(x) + F_1(x) - O_1(x)F_1(x)$.

$R(x)$ = probability of moving from the marker status to the nonmarker status between ages x and $x + 1$.

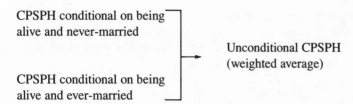

CPSPH conditional on being alive and never-married

CPSPH conditional on being alive and ever-married

Unconditional CPSPH
(weighted average)

6.3.1. Cumulative proportion of children staying in the parental home conditional on being alive and never having married

The cohort members' children may leave the parental home before or after marriage. We have assumed that no never-married girls leave the parental home before age 18. The age-specific probability of children leaving the parental home in a given interval after age 18 but before marriage (in the absence of mortality), $O_1(x)$, is estimated by equation (6.4) explained in section 6.2.2. The calculation of the cumulative proportion of staying in the parental home up to age $x - a - \frac{1}{2}$ conditional on surviving and remaining never-married at age $x - a - \frac{1}{2}$ is then straightforward:

$$c_1'(x - a - \tfrac{1}{2}) = 1 \qquad (x - a - \tfrac{1}{2}) < 18, \tag{6.25}$$

$$c_1'(x - a - \tfrac{1}{2}) = \prod_{y=18}^{x-a-\frac{1}{2}} [1 - O_1(y)] \qquad (x - a - \tfrac{1}{2}) \geq 18. \tag{6.26}$$

6.3.2. Cumulative proportion of children staying in the parental home conditional on being alive and ever-married

The estimation of cohort members' *children's* age-specific probability of leaving the parental home differs from the estimation of the probability of leaving the parental home by the cohort members *themselves,* described in section 6.2.2.

A female cohort member's leaving her parental home to join her husband's parental home is not considered actually leaving the parental home since it does not result in a change of marker status. The likelihood of female cohort members leaving the parental home depends on the average number of *daughters* per family and the desirability of coresidence between parents and married children (see equations [6.9] and [6.10]). However, the maternal status of a cohort member refers precisely to the number of her own children living at home. If any of her children leave home but join their parents-in-law, it is also considered leaving the home, and thus reducing her maternal status. On the other hand, any one of her children's spouses joining her does not increase her maternal status. Therefore, to determine her maternal status we must look at how many *children, whatever the sex,* a cohort member has and the strength of the desire for coresidence on the part of the mother and one of her married children.

The procedure for estimating the proportion of cohort members' children ultimately leaving the parental home is rather simple. First, as in the numerators of equations (6.6) and (6.7), we estimate the overall proportion of parents who live with one of their married children as

$$s' = 1 - n_2 \qquad (G \geq 1), \qquad (6.27)$$

$$s' = G - n_2 \qquad (G < 1). \qquad (6.28)$$

The average number of children who survive up to the mean age at childbearing and stay in the parental home at least up to the time of first marriage per mother is

$$c = \text{TFR}\, p(m)(1 - l_1)/(1 - n_1). \qquad (6.29)$$

Where TFR is the total fertility rate, $p(m)$ is the probability of surviving to mean age m at childbearing, l_1 is the proportion leaving the parental home before marriage, and n_1 is the proportion of women who do not have a live birth during the course of their lives.

In reality (e.g., in Chinese society) most parents may prefer to live with a married son. However, the parity and maternal states in our model do not distinguish sex of children. How can we solve this problem? Let's take a simple example. Assuming that all the elderly couples have one adult son and one adult daughter and 80% of all the elderly couples wish to live with a married son but no one wishes to live with a daughter, the probability that adult sons will live with their own parents is 0.8, and the probability that adult daughters will live with their own parents is 0. If, however, the sex of adult children is unknown, the allocation of the elderly mothers' maternal status can also be properly done. We may give the first child (whatever the sex) of the elderly couple a probability of 0.55 of staying in the parental home after marriage and give the second child the same probability of 0.55, conditional on the first child having moved out. Thus, the proportion of elderly couples living with a married child (or whose maternal status is 1) is $0.55 + (1 - 0.55) \times 0.55 = 0.8$, which is exactly the same result as when the sex of the children is known. This result is also precisely what we want to know in order to investigate the size and generation structure of the family, whereas the sex of children living at home is not important for this particular purpose.

In general, let s' (see equations [6.27] and [6.28]) denote the overall proportion who live with one of their married children, and c denote the average number of children who survive up to the mean age at childbearing and do not move out of the parental home before marriage (see equation [6.29]). We assume that the first child has a probability of l' of staying with the parent after marriage, the second child has a probability of l' conditional on the first child moving out, the third child has the same probability of l' conditional on the first and second child moving out, and so on; then

$$l' + (1 - l')l' + (1 - l')^2 l' + \cdots + (1 - l')^{c-l} l' = s'. \qquad (6.30)$$

For each family, c is of course an integer. For a population, c may be a non-integer. The formula (6.30) is valid when c is either an integer or a non-integer.

With the estimated proportion of cohort members' children ultimately leaving the parental home and a given time schedule of leaving the parental home after marriage by ever-married duration, we can estimate the cumulative proportion of children staying in the cohort members' homes by marriage duration, denoted as $k'(y)$, through a single-decrement life table technique explained in section 6.2.2.

Since we do not keep track of marriage duration of cohort members' children, we once again have to resort to a weighted average with the weights of distribution of marriage durations (see equation [6.12]). As defined in section 6.2.2, let $j(x - a - \frac{1}{2}, y)$ denote the proportion of cohort members' children of $x - a - \frac{1}{2}$ years of age with ever-married duration y; then the weighted average cumulative proportion of cohort members' children staying at the parental home conditional on the children being alive and ever-married at age $x - a - \frac{1}{2}$ is

$$c_2'(x - a - \tfrac{1}{2}) = \sum_y k'(y) j(x - a - \tfrac{1}{2}, y). \qquad (6.31)$$

6.3.3. Unconditional cumulative proportion of children surviving and living in the parental home

We have estimated the cumulative proportion of cohort members' children staying in the parental home conditional on the fact that the children are surviving never-married and surviving ever-married. However, we have not kept track of the marital status of cohort members' children (we do keep track of cohort members' own marital status). We need to estimate the weighted average unconditional cumulative proportion, with the weights being the proportion surviving as never-married, $p_1(x - a - \frac{1}{2})$, and the proportion surviving as ever-married, $p_2(x - a - \frac{1}{2})$. Note that the sum of $p_1(x - a - \frac{1}{2})$ and $p_2(x - a - \frac{1}{2})$ is equal to the cumulative proportion surviving up to age $x - a - \frac{1}{2}$. The quantities $p_1(x - a - \frac{1}{2})$ and $p_2(x - a - \frac{1}{2})$ can be easily obtained by a simple multiple-decrement nuptiality table in which two marital states (never-married and ever-married) and one state of exit (death) are distinguished.[1]

The unconditional cumulative proportion of cohort members' children surviving and living in the parental home up to age $x - a - \frac{1}{2}$ is a weighted average:

$$h_1(x - a - \tfrac{1}{2}) = c'_1(x - a - \tfrac{1}{2})p_1(x - a - \tfrac{1}{2})$$
$$+ c'_2(x - a - \tfrac{1}{2})p_2(x - a - \tfrac{1}{2}). \qquad (6.32)$$

The cumulative proportion of never-married cohort members' children surviving and living in the parental home up to age $x - a - \frac{1}{2}$ is

$$h_2(x - a - \tfrac{1}{2}) = c'_1(x - a - \tfrac{1}{2})p_1(x - a - \tfrac{1}{2}). \qquad (6.33)$$

---

1. At ages that are less than the minimum age at marriage, $p_1(x)$ is identical to the survival probability. The probabilities of surviving up to age $x + \frac{1}{2}$ are approximated as $\frac{1}{2}[p(x) + p(x + 1)]$ where $p(x)$ is the probability of surviving up to age x, which can be obtained from a standard life table. Since most deaths in the first year of life occur during the first few days or the first month, this approximation does not hold for $p(\frac{1}{2})$. Let us assume that two-thirds of all infant deaths (deaths in the first year of life) occur in the first month and the rest occur uniformly over the remaining interval (see Wunsch and Termote 1978:82–84). The death probability is defined as the number of deaths occurring in the age interval 0 to 1, divided by the number of births (individuals at exact age 0). The number of individuals at exact age 0 is the radix of the life table, which can be taken as 1. Therefore, the number of deaths, when the radix is 1, that occur in the first year of life can be approximated as the probability of dying ($_1q_0$) in this interval. Given the assumptions mentioned above, the number of deaths occurring in the first half of the year is equal to

$$(2/3)_1q_0 + (5/11)(_1q_0/3) = (9/11)_1q_0$$

so that $p(\frac{1}{2}) = 1 - (9/11)_1q_0$.

7

Construction of a Family Status Life Table

Our multistate family status life table has four types of status transitions: marital, marker, parity, and maternal status. The transitions occur throughout the cohort member's life. This section discusses a mechanism for constructing a family status life table based on the estimated transition probabilities.

7.1. Assumptions for the Construction of the Life Table

One of the assumptions of a family status life table is the Markovian assumption: status transitions depend on the status occupied at the beginning of the interval but not on the person's past history. More specifically, we assume that in our family status life table model fertility depends on age, parity, and marital status. Mortality depends on age and marital status, and first marriage, widowhood, divorce, and remarriage depend on age and marital status. The marker status change (children stay in or leave the parental home) depends on age, duration of being ever-married, and the average number of siblings.

The Markovian assumption implies another assumption—the homogeneity assumption—namely, people with the same characteristics have the same status transition probabilities. The Markovian assumption and the homogeneity assumption can be lessened by introducing more characteristics of the population studied. For instance, the Markovian and the homogeneity assumptions are less strong for a fertility model that considers age, parity, and maternal status than for a fertility model that takes account of age only. Since our family status life table model accounts for more characteristics of the population under study than most other models in family demography, the Markovian and homogeneity assumptions in our model are less restrictive than in most other models of family demography.

In addition to the Markovian and the homogeneity assumptions, the following assumptions will be introduced:

The distribution of demographic events in one single age interval is uniform.

Persons who die in the age interval have the same demographic rates before death as those who do not die.

Particular events take place at one point in time rather than throughout the year between ages x and $x + 1$.

The parents always live with nonadult children and possibly with only one married child and his (or her) spouse and their unmarried children. No married brothers or sisters live together.

At the time of marriage dissolution, the nonadult children always live with their mother. If the mother dies, they may live with a stepmother or join other relatives.

Multiple births in one single age interval for one woman are counted as single births.

Note that it has been pointed out that the assumption of a constant intensity of the occurrences of events within an age interval has a few theoretical advantages compared with the assumption of a uniform distribution of events, which has long been used by both demographers and scholars from other disciplines (see, e.g., Ledent 1980:554; Hoem and Jensen 1982:157, 160, 194–201; Land and Schoen 1982:136–320; Nour and Suchindran 1984a:325). However, a recent study by Keilman and Gill (1986) found that the difference between the numerical estimates under these two assumptions is about $h^2(\hat{m})^3/12$, where h is the length of the age interval and $\hat{m}$ is the observed rate. When the age interval is 1, the numerical difference is obviously very small even if the observed rates are relatively large.

7.2. Calculation of the Family Life History

As we have discussed in section 4.4 and chapter 5, the construction of the family status life table can be greatly simplified by assuming that particular events take place at one point in time rather than throughout the whole year between the ages x and $x + 1$. More specifically, we assume that changes in marital-marker states as well as deaths take place in the middle of the year and that parity and maternal status changes of ever-married women occur throughout the first half of the year before marital-marker status changes and throughout the second half of the year after marital-marker status changes. The parity and maternal status changes of women who marry for the first time in the age interval and the parity ar.d maternal status changes of women who remain never-married at the end of the age interval are assumed to occur throughout the second half of the age interval. Of course, the newly married women and the women who remain never-married up to the end of the age interval have quite different birth probabilities in the second half of the year. Moreover, we assume that the ever-married women who give birth in the first half of the year would not give birth in the second half of the year; the ever-married women who do not have a delivery in the first half of the year may have a chance to bear a child in the second half of the year.

In fact, we have classified the cohort members into four categories:

1. Remain never-married up to age $a + 1$.
2. Newly married between ages a and $a + 1$.
3. Ever-married at exact age a, giving birth between ages a and $a + \frac{1}{2}$ and assumed not to give birth between ages $a + \frac{1}{2}$ and $a + 1$.
4. Ever-married at exact age a, not giving birth between ages a and $a + \frac{1}{2}$ but may do so between ages $a + \frac{1}{2}$ and $a + 1$.

Fertility differs greatly between the categories, so we will treat them separately.

The introduction of maternal states necessary to determine family size complicates the calculation a bit, because whether or not the children survive and live at home depends on the children's ages, so that the partial life table technique proposed by Bongaarts (1987) is needed. For each age we should compute from the lowest age of the life table up to that age. The calculation's only purpose is to determine the maternal status at that age. For a more detailed discussion of why a partial life table technique is needed, see section 4.2.

To help the reader understand how the family status life table is constructed, we give a simple hypothetical example in table 7.1. Although in this simple hypothetical example only two marital states, two parity states, two maternal states, and only ages 20, 21, and 22 are considered, it does clarify the basic mechanism of the family status life table calculation. Once we understand the calculation procedure of this simple example, it will be much easier to understand the formulas for the construction of a general family status life table.

It is extremely interesting to note that the number of women who make parity progression calculated by our family status life table approach of splitting one whole year interval into two halves (denoted as approach A) is exactly the same as that calculated by the conventional approach of using one whole year interval (denoted as approach B). For example, for age interval (21, 22) in the example in table 7.1, the estimated number of women who make parity progression by approach A and approach B are as follows:

Approach A:
Newly married women: $590M_{12}(21)F = 39$
Ever-married women:
$$320_{\frac{1}{2}}b(21)M_{22}(21) + 320[1 - {}_{\frac{1}{2}}b(21)]M_{22}(21)_{\frac{1}{2}}b(21.5)$$
$$= 62.7 + 62.7 = 125.4.$$

Table 7.1. A simplified example of computation procedure

STATUS DISTINGUISHED	Two marital states: 1, never-married; 2, ever-married Two parity states: parity 0; parity 1 Two maternal states: 0 surviving child; 1 surviving child 1,000 women start to marry from age 20

DATA	(1) Marital status transition probabilities: $M_{11}(20) = 0.59$, $M_{21}(20) = 0$; $M_{11}(21) = 0.65$, $M_{21}(21) = 0$
	               $M_{12}(20) = 0.40$, $M_{22}(20) = 0.99$; $M_{12}(21) = 0.33$, $M_{22}(21) = 0.98$
	(2) Birth probabilities: $b(20) = 0.3$, $\frac{1}{4}b(20) = b(20)/2 = 0.15$, $\frac{1}{2}b(20.5) = b(20)/[2 - b(20)] = 0.176$
	                  $b(21) = 0.4$, $\frac{1}{2}b(21) = b(21)/2 = 0.2$, $\frac{1}{2}b(21.5) = b(21)/[2 - b(21)] = 0.25$
	Newly married women who give birth in the same year as marriage: $F = 0.2$
	(3) Children's probability of surviving: $S(0.5) = 0.96$, $S(1.5) = 0.95$

TASK	To calculate the marital, parity and maternal (number of children surviving) status at age 21, 22
NOTES	B: give birth, $\bar{B}$: do not give birth; C: the child survives up to mother's age; $\bar{C}$: child dies before mother reaches age X

First half of the age interval
FOR AGE 21

Middle of the age interval	Second half of the interval	
Newly married: $1,000M_{12}(20) = 400$	$B: 400F = 80$	$\begin{cases} C: 80S(21 - 20 - 0.5) = 80S(0.5) = 77 \\ \bar{C}: 80(1 - S(0.5)) = 3 \end{cases}$
	$\bar{B}: 400(1 - f) = 320 \longrightarrow$	$\bar{C} \;\;\longrightarrow\;\; 320$
Survive as never-married: $1,000M_{11}(20) = 590$	$\bar{B} \;\;\longrightarrow\;\; \bar{B} \;\;\longrightarrow\;\;$	590
Deaths: $1,000[1 - M_{12}(20) - M_{11}(20)] = 10$		

Calculated status distribution

At age 21	Parity 0		Parity 1	
	0 child	0 child	0 child	1 child
Never-married	590	0	0	0
Ever-married	320	3	3	77

FOR AGE 22: START THE CALCULATION FROM BEGINNING, THAT IS FROM AGE 20 IN THIS CASE

(Age interval 20–21)

Newly married: $1{,}000M_{12}(20) = 400$

B: $400F = 80$
$\quad\{\ C$: $80S(22 - 20 - 0.5) = 80S(1.5) = 76 \longrightarrow 76$
$\quad\{\ \overline{C}$: $80(1 - S(1.5)) = 4$
$\quad\ \ \overline{C} \longrightarrow$

$\overline{B}$: $400(1 - F) = 320 \longrightarrow \overline{C} \longrightarrow 320$

Survive as never-married:
$\quad 1{,}000M_{11}(20) = 590$
Deaths: $1{,}000[1 - M_{12}(20) - M_{11}(20)] = 10$
$\overline{B} \longrightarrow 590$

(Age interval 21–22)

Newly married: $590M_{12}(21) = 195$

B: $195F = 39$
$\quad\{\ C$: $39S(22 - 21 - 0.5) = 39S(0.5) = 37 \longrightarrow 37$
$\quad\{\ \overline{C}$: $39[1 - S(0.5)] = 2$
$\quad\ \ \overline{C} \longrightarrow$

$\overline{B}$: $195(1 - F) = 156 \longrightarrow \overline{C} \longrightarrow 156$

Survive as never-married:
$\quad 590M_{11}(21) = 384$
$\overline{B} \longrightarrow 384$

Ever-married parity 0
B: $320\tfrac{1}{2}b(21) = 64$
$\quad\{\ C$: $64S(0.5) = 61$ survive as ever-married: $61M_{22}(21) = 60 \longrightarrow 60$
$\quad\{\ \overline{C}$: $64(1 - S(0.5)) = 3$ survive as ever married: $3M_{22}(21) = 3 \longrightarrow 3$

$\overline{B}$: $320[1 - \tfrac{1}{2}b(21)] = 256 \longrightarrow \overline{C}$ survive as ever-married: $256M_{22}(21) = 251$

B: $251\tfrac{1}{2}b(21.5) = 63$
$\quad\{\ C$: $63S(22 - 21 - 0.5) = 63S(0.5) = 60 \longrightarrow 60$
$\quad\{\ \overline{C}$: $63[1 - S(0.5)] = 3 \longrightarrow 3$

$\overline{B}$: $251(1 - \tfrac{1}{2}b(21.5)) = 188 \longrightarrow \overline{C} \longrightarrow 188$

Ever-married parity 1
child 0: $4 \to \overline{B} \to \overline{C}$ Survive as ever-married: $4M_{22}(21) = 4 \longrightarrow 4$
child 1: $76 \to \overline{B} \to \overline{C}$ Survive as ever-married: $76M_{22}(21) = 74 \longrightarrow 74$

Deaths: $590[1 - M_{12}(21) - M_{11}(21)]+$
$(61 + 3 + 256 + 4 + 76][1 - M_{22}(21)] = 20$

Calculated status distribution

At age 22	Parity 0		Parity 1	
	0 child	1 child	0 child	1 child
Never-married	348	0	0	0
Ever-married	156 + 188 = 344	2 + 3 + 3 + 4 = 12	37 + 60 + 60 + 74 = 231	0

Approach B (assuming deaths are uniformly distributed and independent of birth):

Newly married women: $590M_{12}(21)F = 39$

Ever-married women: $320b(21)M_{22}(21) = 125.4$

This comparison of approaches A and B shows the validity of our family status life table approach of splitting one whole year interval into two halves.

In general, we define

$m_{nm}^{lk}(a)$ = probability that a woman of marital status n and marker status l at exact age a will be in marital status m and marker status k at exact age $a + 1$, where $m, n = 1, 2, 3, 4$; $k, l = 1, 2$. (The estimators of $m_{nm}^{lk}(a)$ are shown in table 6.1.)

$b_p(a, m)$ = probability that a woman of marital status m and parity $p - 1$ at exact age a will give a birth of order p between ages a and $a + 1$, where $p = 1, 2, \ldots, N$ and $m = 1, 2, 3, 4$ (the estimator of $b_p(a, m)$, see equation [6.1]).

$\frac{1}{2}b_p(a, m)$ = probability that a woman of parity $p - 1$ at exact age a will give a birth of order p between ages a and $a + \frac{1}{2}$ (see equation [6.2]).

$\frac{1}{2}b_p(a + \frac{1}{2}, m)$ = probability that a woman of parity $p - 1$ at exact age $a + \frac{1}{2}$ who does not give birth between exact age x and $x + \frac{1}{2}$ will give a birth of order p between ages $a + \frac{1}{2}$ and $a + 1$ (see equation [6.3]).

$l_{mkpc}(x, a)$ = partial life table population in marital status m, marker status k, parity status p at exact age a, and intermediate maternal status c ($m = 1, 2, 3, 4; k = 1, 2; p = 0, 1, 2, \ldots, N; c = 0, 1, \ldots, p; c \leq p, a \leq x$). The quantity c refers to the number of children born before the mother's age a who will be living at home when the mother reaches exact age x. We note that c does not refer to the mother's maternal status at exact age a because some of the children who survive at home at mother's age a may die or leave the home before the mother reaches age x; c does not refer to the mother's maternal status at exact age x, except when $a = x$, because she may bear an additional child after age a. Therefore, we call c the intermediate maternal status.

For each age x, we need to calculate a partial life table population for ages $a = 0$ to $a = x$. The partial life table population is not our objective. Its sole purpose is to calculate the maternal status at age x. When $a = x$, $l_{mkpc}(x, a)$ is our objective family status life table population of marital status m, marker status k, parity status p, and maternal status c at exact age x. Only when $a = x$, is the maternal status c identical to the maternal status at age x.

In the following notation, $a1$ denotes the beginning of age interval $(a, a + 1)$, $a2$ denotes the middle of the age interval (after the marital-marker status change), $a + 1$, x denotes exact age, and subscripts m, k, p, and c denote marital, marker, parity, and maternal status, respectively.

$n_{mkpc}(x, a1)$, $n_{mkpc}(x, a2)$, and $n_{mkpc}(x, a + 1) - n$ refer to cohort members who were never-married at the beginning of the age interval and who may or may not change their marital, marker, parity, and maternal status when they reach age $a + 1$.

$f_{mkpc}(x, a1)$, $f_{mkpc}(x, a2)$, and $f_{mkpc}(x, a + 1) - f$ refer to cohort members who were ever-married at the beginning of the age interval and who give birth in the first half of the age interval (change their parity status but may or may not change their maternal status) and who do not give birth in the second half of the interval. They may or may not change marital and marker status when they reach age $a + 1$.

$s_{mkpc}(x, a1)$, $s_{mkpc}(x, a2)$, and $s_{mkpc}(x, a + 1) - s$ refer to cohort members who are ever-married at the beginning of the age interval $(a, a + 1)$ and who do not give birth in the first half of the age interval. They may or may not give birth and may or may not change their maternal, marital, and marker status when they reach age $a + 1$.

$h_1(x - a - \frac{1}{2})$ = the unconditional cumulative proportion of cohort members' children surviving and living in the parental home up to age $x - a - \frac{1}{2}$ (see equation [6.32]).

$h_2(x - a - \frac{1}{2})$ = the cumulative proportion of cohort members' children surviving as never-married and living in the parental home up to age $x - a - \frac{1}{2}$ (see equation [6.33]).

F = proportion of women who give birth in the year of first marriage.

The procedure for calculating $l_{mkpc}(x, a + 1)$ from $l_{mkpc}(x, a)$ consists of three steps.

Step 1. Parity and intermediate maternal status transitions in the first half of the age interval. Never-married women are not assumed to give birth in the first half of the age interval.

$$n_{1kpc}(x, a1) = l_{1kpc}(x, a).$$ (7.1)

For ever-married women, $m = 2, 3, 4$. Some of them, $f_{mkpc}(x, a1)$, do give birth in the first half of the age interval and make transitions from one maternal state to another; $f_{mkpc}(x, a1)$ $(m = 2, 3, 4)$ consists of two components. The first component is the number of women who were of marital status m, marker status k, parity status $p - 1$, and intermediate maternal status $c - 1$ at exact age a who bore a child between the ages a and $a + \frac{1}{2}$ and whose newly born child will survive and live at home when the woman reaches age x. The second component is the number of women who were of marital status m, marker status k, parity status $p - 1$, and intermediate maternal status c at exact age a who bore a child between ages a and $a + \frac{1}{2}$ and whose newly born child will die or leave the parental home when the woman reaches age x. Note that the formulas for estimating $s_{mkpc}(x, a + 1)$ $(m = 2, 3, 4)$ and $n_{mkpc}(x, a + 1)$ $(m = 1, 3, 4)$ to be derived below also follow the basic idea of two components and thus have a similar configuration. They look complicated but it is easier to understand them if we keep in mind the idea of two components.

To determine whether a child born at age a of the mother will be living with the mother when the mother reaches age x, we multiply the child's probability of surviving and staying with its parents up to age $x - a - \frac{1}{2}$. To remain consistent with the assumption we have already made clear (namely, that a woman does not live with more than one married son or daughter), we use $h_1(x - a - \frac{1}{2})$ (probability that a child survives and will not move out of the parental home up to age $x - a - \frac{1}{2}$) when the mother gives birth at age a and with intermediate maternal status $c = 0$ (i.e., no child born before age a of the mother and living at home up to the mother's age x). If the mother gives birth at age a with intermediate maternal status c greater than 0 (i.e., at least one child born before age a of the mother and living at home up to age x of the mother), we use $h_2(x - a - \frac{1}{2})$ (probability that a child will survive and live at home as a never-married person up to age $x - a - \frac{1}{2}$) instead of $h_1(x - a - \frac{1}{2})$. The implication of this treatment is that if the mother already has a child who was born before age a and who will be living at home when the mother reaches age x, children born after age a of the mother will stay with the parents up to age $x - a - \frac{1}{2}$ only if those children are never-married and do not leave the parental home before marriage. When $c = 0$,

$$f_{mkp0}(x, a1) = l_{m,k,p-1,0}(x, a)_{\frac{1}{2}}b_p(a, m)[1 - h_1(x - a - \frac{1}{2})].$$ (7.2)

When $c = 1$,

$$f_{mkp1}(x, a1) = l_{m,k,p-1,0}(x, a)_{\frac{1}{2}}b_p(a, m)h_1(x - a - \frac{1}{2})$$
$$+ l_{m,k,p-1,1}(x, a)_{\frac{1}{2}}b_p(a, m)[1 - h_2(x - a - \frac{1}{2})].$$ (7.3)

When $c > 1$,

$$f_{mkpc}(x, a1) = l_{m,k,p-1,c-1}(x, a)\tfrac{1}{2}b_p(a, m)h_2(x - a - \tfrac{1}{2})$$
$$+ l_{m,k,p-1,c}(x, a)\tfrac{1}{2}b_p(a, m)[1 - h_2(x - a - \tfrac{1}{2})]. \quad (7.4)$$

Some ever-married women, $s_{mkpc}(x, a1)$, do not give birth in the first half of the year:

$$s_{mkpc}(x, a1) = l_{mkpc}(x, a)[1 - \tfrac{1}{2}b_{p+1}(a, m)]. \quad (7.5)$$

Step 2. Marital-marker status changes and deaths occur in the middle of the age interval. This step deals with marital and marker states only. Being never-married at age a and being of marital status m ($m = 1, 2, 3, 4$) and marker status k after the marital-marker status change:

$$n_{mkpc}(x, a2) = \sum_{l=1}^{2} m_{1m}^{lk}(a)n_{1lpc}(x, a1). \quad (7.6)$$

Being ever-married at age a, giving birth in the first half of the age interval, and being of marital status m ($m = 2, 3, 4$) and marker status k after the marital-marker status change:

$$f_{mkpc}(x, a2) = \sum_{n=2}^{4} \sum_{l=1}^{2} m_{nm}^{lk}(a)f_{nlpc}(x, a1). \quad (7.7)$$

Being ever-married at age a, not giving birth in the first half of the age interval, and being of marital status m ($m = 2, 3, 4$) and marker status k after the marital-marker status change:

$$s_{mkpc}(x, a2) = \sum_{n=2}^{4} \sum_{l=1}^{2} m_{nm}^{lk}(a)s_{nlpc}(a, a1). \quad (7.8)$$

Step 3. Newly married women and the women who get married and become widowed or divorced in the same year are given a predetermined (observed) probability of giving birth in the same year. For $m = 2, 3, 4$, when $c = 0$,

$$n_{mkp0}(x, a + 1) = n_{mkp0}(x, a2)(1 - F)$$
$$+ n_{m,k,p-1,0}(x, a2)F[1 - h_1(x - a - \tfrac{1}{2})]. \quad (7.9)$$

When $c = 1$,

$$n_{mkp1}(x, a + 1) = n_{mkp1}(x, a2)(1 - F)$$
$$+ n_{m,k,p-1,0}(x, a2)Fh_1(x - a - \tfrac{1}{2})$$

$$+ n_{m,k,p-1,1}(x, a2)F[1 - h_2(x - a - \tfrac{1}{2})]. \qquad (7.10)$$

When $c > 1$,

$$n_{mkpc}(x, a + 1) = n_{mkpc}(x, a2)(1 - F)$$
$$+ n_{m,k,p-1,c-1}(x, a2)Fh_2(x - a - \tfrac{1}{2})$$
$$+ n_{m,k,p-1,c}(x, a2)F[1 - h_2(x - a - \tfrac{1}{2})]. \qquad (7.11)$$

The formulas for estimating $n_{1kpc}(x, a + 1)$ (women who are never-married at age a and $a + 1$) are the same as formulas (7.9) to (7.11) except that $b_p(a, 1)$ is used instead of F.

Women who give birth in the first half of the age interval are assumed not to give birth in the second half of the age interval:

$$f_{mkpc}(x, a + 1) = f_{mkpc}(x, a2). \qquad (7.12)$$

Women who do not give birth in the first half of the age interval may or may not give birth in the second half of the age interval. When $c = 0$,

$$s_{mkp0}(x, a + 1) = s_{mkp0}(x, a2)[1 - \tfrac{1}{2}b_{p+1}(a + \tfrac{1}{2}, m)]$$
$$+ s_{m,k,p-1,0}(x, a2)\tfrac{1}{2}b_p(a + \tfrac{1}{2}, m)[1 - h_1(x - a - \tfrac{1}{2})]. \qquad (7.13)$$

When $c = 1$,

$$s_{mkp1}(x, a + 1) = s_{mkp1}(x, a2)[1 - \tfrac{1}{2}b_{p+1}(a + \tfrac{1}{2}, m)]$$
$$+ s_{m,k,p-1,0}(x, a2)\tfrac{1}{2}b_p(a + \tfrac{1}{2}, m)h_1(x - a - \tfrac{1}{2})$$
$$+ s_{m,k,p-1,1}(x, a2)\tfrac{1}{2}b_p(a + \tfrac{1}{2}, m)[1 - h_2(x - a - \tfrac{1}{2})]. \qquad (7.14)$$

When $c > 1$,

$$s_{mkpc}(x, a + 1) = s_{mkpc}(x, a2)[1 - \tfrac{1}{2}b_{p+1}(a + \tfrac{1}{2}, m)]$$
$$+ s_{m,k,p-1,c-1}(x, a2)\tfrac{1}{2}b_p(a + \tfrac{1}{2}, m)h_2(x - a - \tfrac{1}{2})$$
$$+ s_{m,k,p-1,c}(x, a2)\tfrac{1}{2}b_p(a + \tfrac{1}{2}, m)[1 - h_2(x - a - \tfrac{1}{2})]. \qquad (7.15)$$

Thus,

$$l_{mkpc}(x, a + 1) = n_{mkpc}(x, a + 1)$$
$$+ f_{mkpc}(x, a + 1) + s_{mkpc}(x, a + 1). \qquad (7.16)$$

Repeat step 1 to step 3 from ages $a = 0$ to $a = x - 1$. We obtain the objective life table population with marital-marker, parity, and maternal status distribution at age x, $l_{mkpc}(x)$. When we do it for all ages $x = 0$ to $x = Z$ (highest age), the complete family status life table has been constructed.

7.3. Sojourn Time in Each State

After the life table population $l_{mkpc}(x)$ for $x = 0$ to $x = Z$ has been calculated, the sojourn time in each state can be derived from it without difficulty.

7.3.1. Person-years lived ,

$0 < x < Z$. Based on the linear assumption of the life table function $l_{mkpc}(x)$, the number of expected person-years lived in marital status m, marker status k, parity status p, and maternal status c between ages x and $x + 1$ by a 0-year-old cohort member is estimated by

$$L_{mkpc}(x) = \tfrac{1}{2}[l_{mkpc}(x) + l_{mkpc}(x + 1)]. \tag{7.17}$$

$x = 0$. Formula (7.17) is not valid for $x = 0$, because the linear assumption of the life table function does not hold between ages 0 and 1. Note that no marital, marker, parity, and maternal status transitions occur during the first year of life; therefore, the person-years lived in all states between ages 0 and 1 are equal to 0 except in never-married, nonmarker, parity 0, and maternal status 0, that is, $L_{1,1,0,0}(0)$. The formula for the estimation of $L_{1,1,0,0}(0)$ is the same as formula (A1.11) in Appendix 1.

$x = Z$. We assume that there are no events of first marriage, divorce, or remarriage and that no additional births occur after age Z, the first age of the last, open-ended age-group. To keep things simple, we also ignore any maternal status change after this advanced age. This simplification will not create a significant bias, since the number of maternal status changes after this advanced age compared with the overall population is too small to affect the results.

Since we assume that no marker, parity, or maternal status changes occur after age Z, we can omit the subscripts k, p, and c for person-years lived beyond age Z, for ease of presentation. Therefore, the formulas for calculating the person-years lived in different states are the same as the corresponding formulas in the marital status life table, that is, equations (A1.12) to (A1.15) in Appendix 1.

The number of person-years lived in marital status m, marker status k, parity status p, and maternal status c beyond age x is

$$T_{mkpc}(x) = \sum_{t=x}^{z} L_{mkpc}(t). \tag{7.18}$$

7.3.2. Life expectancy

An x-year-old woman's life expectancy in marital status m, marker status k, parity status p, and maternal status c is

$$e_{mkpc}(x) = T_{mkpc}(x)/l_{....}(x). \qquad (7.19)$$

where

$$l_{....}(x) = \sum_m \sum_k \sum_p \sum_c l_{mkpc}(x).$$

Note that $e_{mkpc}(x)$ together with $l_{mkpc}(x)$ tells us the family life course of a synthetic cohort. For example, if the original cohort size $l_{1,1,0,0}(0) = 100,000$, we can calculate $l_{2,1,1,1}(25) = 5,000$, $l_{4,2,2,1}(30) = 500$, and so on. We know that among those 100,000 cohort members, 5,000 will be married nonmarkers with parity 1 and one surviving child at home when they reach age 25, 500 will be divorced markers with parity 2 and only one surviving child at home when they reach age 30, and so on. If we calculate $e_{2,1,1,1}(0) = 25.5$, $e_{4,2,2,1}(0) = 2.5$, and so on, we know that under the given fertility, mortality, marriage, and divorce regimes, an average newborn girl may expect to live 25.5 years in the married status with parity 1 and one surviving child at home and living with the mother or mother-in-law; she may expect to live 2.5 years in the divorced marker status (without living with the mother or mother-in-law), with parity 2 and one child living at home; and so on.

7.4. Calculation of the Family Status Life Table Population with an Alternative Definition of the Marker and Maternal States

People are sometimes interested in knowing, with given fertility and mortality regimes, which proportion of their lifetime they may expect to have a surviving mother, a surviving mother or father, or both over age 65, or surviving children of whatever age or of a specified age, say, under age 18 (Watkins, Menken, and Bongaarts 1984; Menken 1985). Our family status life table model can answer these kinds of questions through modifications of the definitions of marker and nonmarker states and maternal states. For example, we may define a nonmarker as a woman who has a surviving mother over 65, irrespective of whether the woman lives with her mother or not. A marker means that she has no surviving mother over 65, either due to the fact that her surviving mother is not over 65 or due to the fact that her mother is dead. We may also define the maternal status as the number of surviving children of any age or, say, under the age of 18 irrespective of whether or not the children live at home.

With these definitions of marker and maternal states, what we need to do is to slightly modify a few corresponding formulas and to carry out the calculations without essentially changing the model. When the nonmarker status refers to having a surviving mother over 65, regardless of where she lives, we use formula (7.20) to estimate the proportion of nonmarkers, that is, the proportion of x-year-old women who have a surviving mother (say, over 65):

$$M_1(x, > 60) = \sum_{a>60-x} \exp[-r(a + \tfrac{1}{2})]m(a)L(x + a). \qquad (7.20)$$

When the nonmarker status refers to having a living father (say, over age 65), we use formula (7.21) to estimate the proportion of nonmarkers:

$$M_1'(x, > 65) = \sum_{a>65-x-c} \exp[-r(a + \tfrac{1}{2})]m(a)L(a)L'(x + a + c)$$
$$/L'(a + c). \qquad (7.21)$$

When the nonmarker status refers to having a mother or father or both (say, over age 65) alive, we use formula (7.22) to estimate the proportion of nonmarkers:

$$M_1''(x, > 65) = 1 - [1 - M(x, > 65)][1 - M_1'(x, > 65)]. \qquad (7.22)$$

When the nonmarker status refers to having both parents alive (say, over age 65), we use formula (7.23) to estimate the proportion of nonmarkers:

$$M_1'''(x, > 65) = M_1(x, > 65)M_1'(x, > 65). \qquad (7.23)$$

Assuming independence between the cohort members' status changes and the survivorship of their parents, we may simply first calculate the life table population without the marker status and then multiply the marital, parity, and maternal status distribution at each age x by $M_1(x, > 65)$, $M_1'(x, > 65)$, $M_1''(x, > 65)$, or $M_1'''(x, > 65)$ to determine the nonmarker status (having either an over 65-year-old mother or father, or both parents alive) and marker status (having no over 65-year-old mother or father, or both parents alive).

If we are interested in knowing the survivorship of mothers, whatever their age, the procedure and the formulas are the same, except that the constraint of the summation in the equations is changed as

$$\sum_a \quad \text{instead of} \quad \sum_{a>65-x} \quad \text{or} \quad \sum_{a>65-x-c}.$$

When the maternal status refers to the number of surviving children of any age, regardless of where the children are living, we equate $h_1(x - a - \tfrac{1}{2})$ and $h_2(x - a - \tfrac{1}{2})$ in section 7.2 to the probability of surviving up to age $x - a - \tfrac{1}{2}$.

When the maternal status refers to the number of surviving children of a certain age, regardless of co-residence, we let $h_1(x - a - \frac{1}{2})$ and $h_2(x - a - \frac{1}{2})$ be equal to 0, except when $x - a - \frac{1}{2}$ is within the specified age bracket (e.g., under 18) of the children, in which case $h_1(x - a - \frac{1}{2})$ and $h_2(x - a - \frac{1}{2})$ are set to be equal to the probability of surviving up to age $x - a - \frac{1}{2}$.

Similarly, we can compute the distribution of the number of surviving sons or daughters of a certain age by introducing the sex ratio at birth and the sex-specific probabilities of surviving.

Combining the modified definitions of marker states and maternal states, we can calculate the status of cohort members' responsibilities to dependents. For instance, if we define the nonmarker status as having a surviving mother over 65 and the maternal status as having a number of children under age 18, then a nonmarker with maternal status 2 is a woman with a surviving mother over 65 and two surviving children under 18. The status of having an elderly mother and young children simultaneously is called "overload"; this is an interesting research topic (Menken 1985:479; Watkins, Menken, and Bongaarts 1984).

8
Stable Family Status Life Table Population

This chapter discusses how the cohort (or synthetic cohort) family status life table analysis can be generalized to a stable population analysis.

8.1. Life History Perspective versus Population Perspective

A life table can be approached from two different perspectives. The first views the life table as a description of the life course or life history of members of a real cohort or a fictitious cohort. It is referred to as the life history perspective. The second approach views the life table as a description of a population which is consistent with a set of transition probabilities. It is denoted as the population perspective (Willekens 1987:1). If the number of deaths per unit of time is assumed to be equal to the number of births per unit of time for a very long period, the population is stationary. Fertility is not introduced explicitly into the traditional life table. We may assume that deaths are exactly compensated by births. In the event of a stationary population, an important relation holds: there is a perfect correspondence between the individual life history and the population characteristics (Preston 1982). The life table function $L(x)$ can be thought to be the number of people between ages x and $x + h$ in the stationary population, where h is the age interval.

8.2. Features of the Population Perspective of the Family Status Life Table

The life history perspective holds true for the family status life table. The discussion in chapter 7 adopts a life history perspective. However, the stationary population perspective does not hold for the family status life table, because the underlying fertility and mortality schedules do not necessarily compensate each other.

What are the features of the population perspective of the family status life table? If we assume that the underlying fertility and mortality regimes remain constant for a long period of time, the population under study is stable. If the underlying fertility and mortality regimes change over time, the population is not stable.

Oechsli extended a life table population taking into account nuptiality (first marriage only) and parity to a stable population. The major difference between the distribution of a stationary life table population and the distribution of a stable one is the consequence of population growth. Once the stable situation has been reached, each annual cohort is described by the life tables we have derived, except that each cohort differs from the preceding one by a factor of e^r (Oechsli 1975:239), where r is the rate of natural increase, which can be estimated through the well-known relation

$$\sum_a \exp^{[-r(a+\frac{1}{2})]} L(a)m(a) = 1$$

in the stable population.

The family status life table model can be easily extended to the stable population model using Oechsli's approach. A good approximation of the stable family status life table population is given by

$$K_{mkpc}(x) = \exp[-r(x + \tfrac{1}{2})]L_{mkpc}(x), \tag{8.1}$$

where $K_{mkpc}(x)$ is the number of people in the stable population with marital status m, marker status k, parity status p, and maternal status c and of completed age x; r is the growth rate of the stable population. The life table function is $L_{mkpc}(x)$, denoting the number of person-years lived in marital status m, marker status k, parity status p, and maternal status c between ages x and $x + 1$. Here, nonmarker and marker states refer to living and not living with a mother (or mother-in-law), respectively. The maternal status c here refers to the number of surviving children living at home. With formula (8.1), we are able to calculate a series of stable populations $K_{mkpc}(x)$ based on $L_{mkpc}(x)$ taken from the constructed family status life table and r.

8.3. Number, Size, and Composition of Families in the Stable Population

The family characteristics of a synthetic cohort member are given by the family status life table functions described in chapter 7. The family characteristics of a population cannot be derived from those of a synthetic cohort member, because a population is usually composed of cohorts that vary in size and other characteristics over time. However, once $K_{mkpc}(x)$ of a stable population is estimated by formula (8.1), the family characteristics of the stable population can be deduced.

Nonmarkers, with at least one surviving child at home, necessarily live in three-generation families. Therefore, the number of nonmarkers with at least one surviving child living at home is equal to the number of three-generation families. Since the total number of families is equal to the total number of markers, the number of nuclear families is equal to the total number of markers minus the number of nonmarkers with at least one surviving child living at home. Knowing the total number of three-generation and nuclear families is not sufficient, because we are also interested in the family size and marital status of adult females in the families. Thus we ought to distinguish the markers who stand for nuclear families from the markers who stand for three-generation families. It is clear that the markers with no surviving children living at home stand for nuclear families. But markers with at least one surviving child living at home may stand for a nuclear family if this child does not have any surviving children, and she may stand for a three-generation family if her living-at-home child does have surviving children. The procedure needed to determine who stands for what kind of family is fairly simple. The idea behind it is that one should be old enough to become a grandmother. We assume that parents live with only one of their married children. We may first calculate the number of nonmarkers with at least one surviving child, which is equal to the number of three-generation families in the population:

$$W_1 = \sum_{x=0}^{Z} \sum_{m} \sum_{p} \sum_{c \geq 1} K_{m1pc}(x).$$ (8.2)

Then start from the highest age Z to search for age A, above which the number of markers with at least one surviving child is equal to W_1. To take into account the fact that some old parents of maternal status 1 may live with a never-married child, we multiply $k_{m2p1}(x)$ by the proportion ultimately ever-married (E):

$$\sum_{x=A}^{Z} \sum_{m} \sum_{p \geq 1} EK_{m2p1}(x) + \sum_{x=A}^{Z} \sum_{m} \sum_{p>1} \sum_{c>1} K_{m2pc}(x) = W_1.$$

Therefore, the number of nuclear families is equal to the number of all markers below age A plus the number of markers of age A and over age A with no child living at home or with a never-married child living at home.

For nuclear families, if the marker is currently married, her family size is equal to her maternal status plus 2. If the marker is never-married, widowed, or divorced, her family size is equal to her maternal status plus 1.

For three-generation families, the number of middle-generation members and youngest-generation members (grandchildren) can be determined by the

Table 8.1. Family types in the family status life table population

Family type	Family composition			Family size	Number of families
	Grandparents' generation	Middle generation	Youngest generation		
Nuclear families	Absent	Wife-husband	$c = 1$	3	$\sum\limits_{x=\alpha}^{A-1}\sum\limits_{p=1}^{N} K_{2,2,p,1}(x) + \sum\limits_{x=A}^{z}\sum\limits_{p=1}^{N}(1-E)K_{2,2,p,1}(x)$
			$c > 1$	$2 + c$	$\sum\limits_{x=\alpha}^{A}\sum\limits_{p=1}^{N} K_{2,2,p,c}(x)$
		Widowed mother	$c = 1$	2	$\sum\limits_{x=\alpha}^{A-1}\sum\limits_{p=1}^{N} K_{3,2,p,1}(x) + \sum\limits_{x=A}^{z}\sum\limits_{p=1}^{N}(1-E)K_{3,2,p,1}(x)$
			$c > 1$	$1 + c$	$\sum\limits_{x=\alpha}^{A}\sum\limits_{p=1}^{N} K_{3,2,p,c}(x)$
		Divorced mother	$c = 1$	2	$\sum\limits_{x=\alpha}^{A-1}\sum\limits_{p=1}^{N} K_{4,2,p,1}(x) + \sum\limits_{x=A}^{z}\sum\limits_{p=1}^{N}(1-E)K_{4,2,p,1}(x)$
			$c > 1$	$1 + c$	$\sum\limits_{x=\alpha}^{A}\sum\limits_{p=1}^{N} K_{4,2,p,c}(x)$
		Lone female	Absent	1	$\sum\limits_{x=0}^{z}\sum\limits_{p=0}^{N}\sum\limits_{m=3}^{4} K_{m,2,p,0}(x) + K_{1,2,p,0}(x)$
		Wife-husband	Absent	2	$\sum\limits_{x=\alpha}^{z}\sum\limits_{p=0}^{N} K_{2,2,p,0}(x)$

Three-generation families				
Only grandmother is present	Wife-husband	$c \geq 1$	$2+2+c$	$[1-C(x+m)]\sum_{x=\alpha}^{Z}\sum_{p=1}^{N}K_{2,1,p,c}(x)$
	Widowed mother	$c \geq 1$	$2+1+c$	$[1-C(x+m)]\sum_{x=\alpha}^{Z}\sum_{p=1}^{N}K_{3,1,p,c}(x)$
	Divorced mother	$c \geq 1$	$2+1+c$	$[1-C(x+m)]\sum_{x=\alpha}^{Z}\sum_{p=1}^{N}K_{4,1,p,c}(x)$
	Never-married mother	$c \geq 1$	$2+1+c$	$[1-C(x+m)]\sum_{x=\alpha}^{Z}\sum_{p=1}^{N}K_{1,1,p,c}(x)$
Both grandparents are present	Wife-husband	$c \geq 1$	$1+2+c$	$C(x+m)\sum_{x=\alpha}^{Z}\sum_{p=1}^{N}K_{2,1,p,c}(x)$
	Widowed mother	$c \geq 1$	$1+1+c$	$C(x+m)\sum_{x=\alpha}^{Z}\sum_{p=1}^{N}K_{3,1,p,c}(x)$
	Divorced mother	$c \geq 1$	$1+1+c$	$C(x+m)\sum_{x=\alpha}^{Z}\sum_{p=1}^{N}K_{4,1,p,c}(x)$
	Never-married mother	$c \geq 1$	$1+1+c$	$C(x+m)\sum_{x=\alpha}^{Z}\sum_{p=0}^{N}K_{1,1,p,c}(x)$

marital status and the maternal status of the nonmarkers who have at least one child living at home. The number of oldest-generation members is either two or one, depending on the marital status of the grandmother, and can be estimated approximately by proportional allocation. We may assume that in three-generation families, the grandmother is, on average, m years older than the mother, where m is the mean age at childbearing. We may calculate the proportion currently married for markers aged $x + m$:

$$c(x + m) = \sum_{p} \sum_{c} K_{2,2,p,c}(x + m)/\sum_{p} \sum_{c} \sum_{m} K_{m,2,p,c}(x + m). \quad (8.3)$$

Therefore, the proportion of three-generation families with an x-year-old mother in which both grandparents are present is $c(x + m)$ and in which only the grandmother is present is $1 - c(x + m)$. The types of families in the stable population are summarized in table 8.1.

Part Three
Application of the Model to
Family Dynamics in China

As we described in the first part of this book, changes in family size and structure in China have been characterized by a remarkable increase in the proportion of nuclear families and a decrease in average family size when we compare 1982, 1964, and 1953 census data with the observations prior to the founding of the People's Republic. In 1930, nuclear families accounted for 51.5%, three-generation families accounted for 40.2%, and families of more than three generations accounted for 8.3% of the total number of families (cited from Ma Xia 1984:51). China's 1982 census shows that the proportion of nuclear families increased to 81.2% (nuclear families in this study include one-person families and other families of less than three generations); three-generation families dropped to 17.2%; families of more than three generations accounted for only 1.6% (SSB 1983b). The average family size was estimated at around 5.3 in the 1930s and 1940s and at 4.30, 4.29, 4.78, and 4.43 in 1953, 1964, 1973, and 1982, respectively.

Although nuclear families have now become the dominant form in China, three-generation families still remain important in Chinese society, with respect to both cultural ideals and social reality (Freedman, Sun, and Weinberger 1978; Freedman, Chang, and Sun 1982). A sample survey of 709 elderly persons (females over 55, males over 60) in Lanchou, a city with about 2.3 million inhabitants, indicated that 63.5% of the respondents perferred to live with a married child (Lin and Bi 1984). This proportion would certainly be much higher in rural areas, since almost all of the elderly living in rural areas depend economically on their children.

Apart from socioeconomic and behavioral factors affecting family size and structure, demographic transitions also influence the family system. For example, if fertility falls, the chance that a young couple forms a nuclear family

99

is reduced if coresidence of parents with one married child is desired. Lower mortality means that, other things being equal, the ability of family members to form a three-generation family has improved. Higher or lower divorce rates and death rates of the other sex increase or decrease the proportion of lone-female or lone-male headed families.

Clearly, the average family size observed in 1982 reflected the fertility and mortality before and after the fertility decline in the 1970s. But the demographic influence of fertility decline on family structure (the proportion of nuclear and extended families) has not yet been shown, since children born after 1970 under lower fertility levels have not yet reached the age of family formation.

A particularly interesting research problem concerning family dynamics in China is to determine the impacts of the tremendous demographic changes after 1970 on family life course and structure. We try to shed light on this important issue by performing illustrative applications of the family status life table model presented in the second part of this book, using data before and after 1970, respectively.

The 1981 and 1950–70 data and estimations used in this application are described in chapter 9. We prepared two major different sets of inputs: observed or estimated demographic rates for 1981 and average rates for 1950–70. Chapter 10 presents the life courses of members of synthetic cohorts. They have been derived from two sets of family status life tables before and after the fertility decline (1981 and 1950–70). Chapter 11 gives what would have been the family size and structure in the stable populations if the 1950–70 and 1981 demographic regimes had remained constant. A comparison and interpretation of the 1950–70 and 1981 simulations are also given in chapters 10 and 11.

As discussed in chapter 3, Chinese rural total fertility rates have, since 1966, been about 2 times as high as those in the urban areas. Rural and urban mortality and nuptiality also differ considerably. The large diversity of fertility and nuptiality behavior between Chinese rural and urban areas may be attributed not only to differences in socioeconomic development levels but to differences in population policy. In the countryside, the birth-planning policy is much more relaxed than in the urban areas (Zeng 1988). Given the large differences in socioeconomic development between the countryside and the city in China, the diversity of rural and urban demographic conditions is likely to continue for a long time. The rapid process of population aging in China, especially in the cities, has resulted from extremely low fertility (far below the replacement level since 1974), and the demographic, social, and political implications attract much attention. Therefore, demographic studies looking into the future should necessarily take into account the differences in demographic characteristics and future trends between the countryside and the city. The important questions are: What are the implications of the remarkable demographic differences between the Chinese countryside and the city for changes in the family? Especially, what are the implications of extremely low fertility in the cities for people's family life course? To answer these questions, we performed another application of the family status life table model using 1986 rural and city data. Chapter 12 presents the results based on these simulations.

9

Data and Estimations Used for the
1981 and 1950–70 Simulations

Based on the methodology presented in the second part of this study, the family status life table can be constructed using the following data: (1) age-specific and marital-status-specific death rates; (2) age-specific occurrence/exposure rates of first marriage, widowhood, divorce, and remarriage; (3) age- and parity-specific occurrence/exposure rates of birth (if there is no parity birth control in the study population, the age-specific, rather than the age- and parity-specific, occurrence/exposure rates of births can be used); (4) proportion leaving parental home before marriage, and its age schedule; (5) proportion of parents who have married children but do not live with any of them and the schedule of children leaving the parental home by duration in the ever-married state. All the needed age-specific rates and probabilities are single-age-specific between the lowest and the highest age at childbearing (15 and 49, say) and five-year-age-specific for other ages, with the exception of ages 0–1 and 1–5.

9.1. Death Rates

The death rates are derived from China's 1982 census data (Jiang, Zhang, and Zhu 1984). For the period 1950–70, we adapt two intercensus life tables estimated by Coale (1984:67). We give the proper weights to the 1953–64 life table (0.647) and the 1964–82 life table (0.353) to obtain a set of weighted average death rates for the years 1950–70. The single-age-specific death rates between ages 15 and 49 are derived by linear interpolation. The marital-status-specific death rates are not available for this study; we therefore assume that the death rates are the same for all marital states. Since divorce rates are very low in China and widows and divorcees remarry quickly if they are not too old, we expect that assuming the same death rate for all marital states will not create significant errors.

9.2. Occurrence/Exposure Rates for First Marriage

China's 1982 one-per-thousand fertility survey published female single-age-specific reduced events of first marriage[1] (some authors call it a frequency distribution or rates of the second kind) for calendar years 1940–81. What we need are the occurrence/exposure rates, which are defined as the number of first marriages divided by the number of person-years lived in the never-married status in the age interval.

The number of person-years lived in the never-married status in an age interval can be approximated as the number of never-married women of that age in the middle of the year. Since the denominators of reduced first marriage and the denominators of the proportion never-married are the same when mortality and external migration are disregarded, which is often the case for retrospective fertility survey data, the occurrence/exposure rate of first marriage is equal to the age-specific reduced first marriage rate divided by the proportion never-married in the middle of the year. We took the age-specific proportion never-married to be 1 minus Coale's age-specific, period estimate of the proportion of women ever married (Coale 1984:table A.4). The estimates of occurrence/exposure rates for 1981 and the average occurrence/exposure rates for 1950–70 are plausible except after age 30, when so few women remain unmarried and so few marriages occur. To reduce the noise, we estimate the occurrence/exposure rates over age 30 by extrapolation.

9.3. Widowhood Rates

Widowhood rates can be estimated from the differences between the average age at first marriage for grooms and brides and the mortality rates for married males. On the basis of China's 1982 census data, it was estimated that the difference between age at first marriage for males and females was 2.69 years (Li Rongshi 1985:28). For the sake of convenience, we approximate the difference in age at first marriage in 1981 and 1950–70 as 2.5 years instead of 2.69 years. If we assume that mortality is equal in all marital states, the male death rate $d(x + 2.5)$—which is estimated by the average of $d(x)$ and $d(x + 5)$ or the average of $d(x + 2)$ and $d(x + 3)$—can be said to represent the female widowhood rate.

---

1. A reduced event is defined as the ratio of the number of events in an interval to the number of persons having experienced the event-origin. For instance, if e_i events occurred in interval i (i can be age or year) to N persons born in a given year, the reduced event at i is e_i/N (Wunsch and Termote 1978:14–15).

9.4. Divorce Rates

Following a similar methodology for constructing model life tables and using the age-specific divorce rates of 48 countries listed in the *United Nations Demographic Yearbook 1968*, Krishnan and Kayani (1976) constructed model divorce tables with 13 levels, defined as the number of divorces per 1,000 married couples in a given year. The estimated divorce level of Chinese women (i.e., the number of divorces per 1,000 married couples) was about 1 in 1981 and 2 in 1950–70 (see section 2.2.4). From Krishnan and Kayani's model divorce table, we derived age-specific occurrence/exposure divorce rates of level 1 for 1981 and of level 2 for 1950–70.

9.5. Remarriage Rates

In China, published age-specific remarriage rates by previous marital status had not become available when this study was completed. We did have data on the proportion widowed and divorced from the 1982 census, on the divorce levels in the past 30 years estimated from the published number of divorces between 1950 and 1981 (Li Ning 1985), on life expectancy at birth in the past 50 years using well-established indirect estimation techniques based on 1982 census data (Brass 1984),[2] and on first-marriage rates for the years 1950–81 or for cohorts whose members were 15–49 years old in 1982. In Appendix 2, we propose an indirect estimation procedure to derive remarriage rates by previous marital status using these data.

---

2. Brass estimated mortality levels in China over the past 50 years based on 1982 census data using well-established indirect estimation techniques. His estimations (1984:19) are shown in the following tabulation.

Year	e_0	Year	e_0
1930–44	28	1970	58
1954	44	1975	62
1959	42	1980	65
1965	54		

Bannister and Preston (1981:106) found that one of the regional patterns, the "South Asian pattern" of the United Nations Model Life Tables for Developing Countries, is remarkably similar above the age of 10 to the age pattern of mortality recorded by China's 1972–75 Nationwide Cancer Epidemiology Survey. The author also found that the age pattern of life tables based on the 1982 census data is more similar to the South Asian pattern than to other patterns. We therefore adapt Brass's estimate of e_0 from the 1940s to 1980 and the U.N. South Asian model life tables to estimate widowhood rates (male adult death rates taking into account differences in age at marriage between males and females) from 1948 to 1970.

9.6. Age- and Parity-Specific Occurrence/Exposure Birth Rates

China's one-per-thousand fertility survey published single-age-specific and parity-specific reduced events of birth, which are defined as the ratio of the number of births classified by parity and the age of the mother to the total number of women of the corresponding age. The period parity progressive ratios based upon a synthetic cohort life table using the survey data were published very recently (Feeney and Yu 1987; Ma Yingtong and Wang 1985). However, what we need is the age- and parity-specific occurrence/exposure birth rates, which take the exposure into account. The numerators of the occurrence/exposure rates are the same as those of the reduced birth rates, namely, the number of births classified by parity (p) and age of the mother. The denominators of the occurrence/exposure rates differ from those of the reduced rates; they are not the total number of women of a given age but the number of person-years lived in parity $p - 1$ by women of the corresponding age. These required age- and parity-specific occurrence/exposure birth rates were not available for this study. We therefore estimate 1981 age- and parity-specific occurrence/exposure birth rates by a two-step procedure using available data.

Step 1. Estimation of preliminary birth rates. Multiplying the age-specific proportional distribution of the number of surviving children of women from the one-per-thousand fertility survey by age-specific ratios of the number of women classified by number of children ever born to the number of women classified by number of children surviving from the 1982 census, we obtain the single-age-specific proportional distribution of parity at the survey time (mid-1982). Assuming that the age- and parity-specific reduced events of birth from mid-1981 to mid-1982 are the same as those throughout 1981, and combining them with the age- and parity-specific proportional distribution in the middle of 1982, we estimated the age- and parity-specific proportional distribution in mid-1981. Dividing the observed single-age-specific and parity-specific reduced events of birth by the estimated single-age-specific parity distribution, we obtained the estimates of single-age- and parity-specific occurrence/exposure rates of birth except for first birth. Because the estimated proportion of women with parity 0 includes never-married women, we divide the rates of first birth by the proportion ever-married to estimate the occurrence/exposure rates of first birth for ever-married women. We do not have the same problem for birth rates of orders higher than 1 because the numbers of never-married women with parity 1 or higher are negligible.

Step 2. Improvement of the estimated rates. The age- and parity-specific birth rates in 1981 derived from step 1 need to be further improved because they were not estimated from the same survey data source. This step is to adjust the estimates in step 1 using the published period parity progression ratios (Feeney, Yu, and Tuan 1985). Applying the estimated age- and parity-specific occurrence/exposure rates of birth and first marriage to a synthetic cohort, we obtain a set of parity progression ratios. Comparing these ratios with the published period parity progression ratios, which are also based upon a synthetic cohort life table using age- and parity-specific occurrence/exposure birth rates from the survey (but the occurrence/exposure birth rates used have not been published), we proportionally reduce (if the estimated ratio is higher than the published one) or increase (if the estimated ratio is lower than the published one) the age- and parity-specific occurrence/exposure rates of birth estimated in the first step. This procedure is repeated until there are no further improvements. We finally obtain a set of age- and parity-specific occurrence/exposure birth rates that produce, in combination with nuptiality rates, the parity progression ratios that are exactly the same as the published period parity progression ratios. Although the timing of parity-specific fertility may only be an approximation due to the indirect estimation procedure, the estimated total fertility level and implied final parity distribution are fully consistent with the published ones.

Using the single-age-specific and parity-specific occurrence/exposure rates of birth for 1981 as a basic schedule, we shift all the curves of birth rates with different birth order to the left by three years because the mean age at first marriage in 1950–70 is about three years lower than that in 1981. Then we follow the procedure described in step 2 and estimate a set of single-age-specific and parity-specific occurrence/exposure rates of birth, which produce precisely the mean age of the first marriage schedule and period average parity progression ratios for 1950–70, which are approximated from the 1982 census observation of the parity distribution of women aged 50–59 because the fertility experience of this age-group stands for the fertility level in 1950–70.

9.7. Proportion Ultimately Leaving the Parental Home

The estimator of the proportion of women ultimately leaving the parental home is given by equations (6.9) and (6.10). The required data on the total fertility rate, mean age at childbearing, proportion of baby girls among all births, and the probability of surviving from birth up to the mean age at childbearing can be directly obtained from the observed data described in the previous sections. The proportion of women who do not give birth to a live child during their lifetime has been derived from census data.

For reasons discussed in section 2.1.4, we assume that the proportion of parents who have married children but do not live with any of them, n_2, remains stable from the mid-1950s to 1981. Another important reason for assuming the stability of n_2 is to ascertain the pure effect of the remarkable changes of demographic variables such as nuptiality, fertility, and mortality from 1950–70 to 1981 on family size and structure.

According to a survey of 709 elderly persons (males over 60, females over 55) in Lanchou, 36.5% of the respondents did not want to live with their married children (Lin and Bi 1984). We therefore assume that n_2 is 36.5 among the urban population.

In rural areas, about 97.5% of the elderly are economically dependent on their children (Yun 1985:106). This clearly indicates that a great majority of elderly parents live with a married child. We assume that in rural areas the elderly parents who have married children but do not live with any of them accounted for 15%.

Using the proportions of the rural and the urban populations in 1981 and 1950–70 (SSB 1984b:81), we estimate the weighted averages n_2 for the whole country in 1981 and 1950–70. Thus we can estimate the proportion ultimately leaving the parental home for 1981 and 1950–70 using equations (6.9) and (6.10).

For both periods, we adapt a time schedule of leaving the parental home by marriage duration, derived from the data of China's In-Depth Fertility Surveys. We assume that 5% of all cohort members who survive at least up to age 18 leave the parental home before marriage but after age 18, for both 1981 and 1950–70. A time schedule is also assumed. It should be noted that the arbitrary assumed proportion of those leaving the parental home before marriage but after age 18 and its time schedule may not be accurate, but it is unlikely that the estimate creates significant errors because the proportion is so small and because the period between age 18 and marriage is not long.

10
Life Course Analysis
1981 and 1950–70 Compared

As we discussed in chapters 7 and 8, a family status life table can be approached from two different perspectives. The first views the family status life table as a description of the life course, or life history, of members of a cohort. We call this approach a life course analysis of a cohort. The second approach views the family status life table as a description of a stable population in which the input fertility, mortality, and nuptiality regimes prevail. We may call it a stable population analysis of the family. This chapter presents findings from a life course perspective, and the next chapter deals with the stable population perspective.

Although the picture of the family life course presented in this chapter is not true for any real birth cohort, the results do answer a set of interesting "what if" questions: What would a fictitious cohort member's family life history have looked like if the demographic conditions in 1981 had persisted throughout her life? What would her family life history have looked like if her family had experienced the average demographic conditions in the period 1950–70? How do the family life histories under 1981 and under 1950–70 conditions differ? What can we learn from those differences? In sections 10.1, 10.2, and 10.3 we present the findings of a life course analysis with respect to marital status, childbearing, and adulthood as a daughter and as a mother.

10.1. Marital Status

10.1.1. Population-based measures

This section gives measures of marital status at age x by the status at birth (age 0) of the cohort members. Since all the cohort members can only be in the never-married state at age 0, the life expectancies calculated by the initial status at birth refer to an average member of the entire population studied. We therefore call it a "population-based measure of life expectancy."

Table 10.1. Percentage of women at selected ages by marital status according to family status life tables, China

Age	Period	Never married	Currently married	Currently widowed	Currently divorced	Total
20	1981	82.3	17.6	0.0	0.1	100.0
	1950–70	40.1	59.1	0.4	0.4	100.0
25	1981	11.0	88.2	0.2	0.5	100.0
	1950–70	6.3	91.4	1.4	1.0	100.0
30	1981	0.6	98.1	0.5	0.8	100.0
	1950–70	1.2	95.6	2.1	1.1	100.0
35	1981	0.4	98.2	0.8	0.6	100.0
	1950–70	0.4	95.2	3.4	0.9	100.0
50	1981	0.3	93.8	5.5	0.3	100.0
	1950–70	0.3	82.8	16.3	0.5	100.0
65	1981	0.4	69.4	29.8	0.5	100.0
	1950–70	0.3	43.0	56.0	0.7	100.0
80	1981	0.4	16.9	82.1	0.6	100.0
	1950–70	0.3	2.0	96.9	0.8	100.0

Universal marriage. It is well known that marriage is universal in China (see, e.g., Coale 1984; Zeng, Vaupel, and Yashin 1985). However, period policies or other socioeconomic factors affect the timing of first marriages and may sometimes result in an extremely low total period first marriage rate (TPFMR) (e.g., 0.707 in 1965) or an extremely high TPFMR (e.g., 1.19 in 1962 and 1.30 in 1981). When we transform the observed reduced events of first marriage into occurrence/exposure rates which take the population at risk into account, and if we integrate these rates into life tables, reasonable intensities of first marriage of synthetic cohorts for different periods result. For both family status life tables of 1981 and 1950–70, the proportions never-married at age 35 are all less than 0.5%. In other words, more than 99.5% of Chinese women get married before the age of 35. The intensity of first marriage is almost equal to 1 (see table 10.1).

The effects of increasing age at marriage on marital status distribution. Table 10.1 shows the remarkable effects of increasing age at marriage on marital status distribution. By age 20, 82.3% of Chinese women remained single according to the 1981 family status life table; according to the 1950–70 table the proportion was only 40.1%.

A girl who survives to age 15 is expected to live in the never-married

Table 10.2. Expected length of time spent in different marital statuses after birthday x according to family status life tables, China

Age (x)	Period	Total e_x	%	Never married e_x	%	Currently married e_x	%	Currently widowed e_x	%	Currently divorced e_x	%
0	1950–70	51.0	100	16.5	32.3	27.1	53.1	7.2	14.1	0.3	0.5
	1981	69.3	100	21.1	30.5	39.5	57.0	8.5	12.3	0.3	0.4
15	1950–70	48.2	100	4.9	10.2	33.9	70.3	9.1	18.8	0.3	0.7
	1981	58.5	100	7.3	12.4	41.9	71.7	9.0	15.4	0.3	0.5
25	1950–70	39.6	100	0.3	0.7	29.8	75.1	9.3	23.5	0.3	0.8
	1981	49.1	100	0.3	0.6	39.4	80.3	9.1	18.6	0.3	0.5
35	1950–70	31.6	100	0.1	0.3	21.7	68.6	9.6	30.4	0.2	0.7
	1981	39.8	100	0.1	0.4	30.3	76.0	9.2	23.2	0.2	0.5
50	1950–70	20.4	100	0.1	0.3	10.4	50.8	9.8	48.3	0.1	0.6
	1981	26.3	100	0.1	0.4	16.8	63.8	9.3	35.3	0.1	0.5
65	1950–70	10.6	100	0.1	0.3	2.4	22.4	8.1	76.5	0.1	0.8
	1981	14.6	100	0.1	0.4	5.8	40.1	8.6	58.9	0.1	0.6

status for 7.3 years under the 1981 rates as opposed to 4.9 years according to the 1950–70 rates. According to the 1981 family status life table, a girl who survives to age 15 could expect to spend about 49% more time as an unmarried woman compared with the 1950–70 schedule; the difference is obviously due to the increased mean age at marriage, given that marriage is universal in both periods (see table 10.2 and figure 10.1).

The effects of declining mortality on marital status distribution. Given the stable remarriage rates, the proportion widowed is higher at all ages according to the 1950–70 schedule than in 1981, due to higher mortality in 1950–70 (see table 10.1). A girl who survives to age 15 could expect to live 15.8% of the rest of her life in the widowed status under the 1981 rates, but 19.8% under the 1950–70 conditions. Under the 1981 conditions, a girl who survives to age 15 could expect to spend 8.3 years more with a husband than under the 1950–70 conditions, although on average she marries 3 years later (table 10.2). This change has been brought about by a tremendous decline in mortality, given the low divorce rate in all periods.

Stable marriages. According to the 1981 and 1950–70 family status life tables, the proportion of divorced women is below 1% at all ages. A girl surviving to age 15 could expect to live 0.29 years (0.50%) of the rest of her life in the divorced state according to the 1981 rates. A 15-year-old girl could expect to live 0.36 years (0.75%) of the rest of her life in the divorced state according to the 1950–70 rates. The percentages of marriages ending in divorce are 4% and 6% according to the 1981 and 1950–70 rates, respectively.

Figure 10.1. Expected length of time spent in different marital statuses after birthday 15 according to family status life tables, China

It is clear that the divorce rates are very low for both periods. The reason for the higher rate in the period 1950–70 is given in section 2.2.4.

Comparison with selected Western countries. Table 10.3 shows very large and interesting differences in the patterns of nuptiality between China and three selected Western countries: the United States (white and black) (1975–80), Belgium (1977), and the Netherlands (1976–80). Parallel measures have been drawn from Espenshade 1985 for the United States, Wijewickrema and Alii (1983) for Belgium, and CBS 1984 for the Netherlands.

In China, marriage is much more stable than in the West. The length of time spent in the divorced state of American white and black (1975–80), Belgian (1977), and Dutch (1976–80) females was about 25, 32, 9, and 14 times as long as that of Chinese females. In China, the number of years women spend in the married state is remarkably higher than in the West.

The proportions of American, Belgian, and Dutch women who are still never-married at age 50 are about 10, 19, and 35 times as high as that of Chinese women (Krishnamoorthy 1979; Wijewickrema and Alii 1983; CBS 1984). This is probably due to the fact that marriage is much more important in Chinese society than in the West, and that cohabitation without marriage has become increasingly popular in the West in the past decade.

10.1.2. Measures based on marital status

Sometimes people are very much interested in investigating how life expectancy at age x varies among people who are in different statuses at an age other than 0, without referring to the person's initial status at age 0. For instance, the time spent in the married state by widowed people of age 20, say, is obviously

Table 10.3. Female life expectancy at birth (and percentage) decomposed by marital status in selected countries according to the life tables

Marital status (i)	China 1950–70		China 1981		U.S.A. (white) 1975–80		U.S.A. (black) 1975–80		Belgium 1977		The Netherlands 1976–80	
	$e_i(0)$	%	$e_i(0)$	%	$e_i(0)$	%	$e_i(0)$	%	$e_i(0)$	%	$e_i(0)$	%
Never married	16.5	32.3	21.1	30.5	26.0	33.8	34.5	47.1	25.1	33.8	30.2	38.6
Currently married	26.6	52.2	39.2	56.6	34.5	44.9	22.1	30.2	39.5	53.1	35.2	45.0
Widowed	7.6	15.0	8.7	12.5	8.9	11.6	7.2	9.8	7.1	9.5	8.8	11.2
Divorced	0.3	0.6	0.3	0.4	7.5	9.8	9.5	12.9	2.7	3.6	4.1	5.2
Total	51.0	100	69.3	100	76.8	100	73.4	100	74.4	100	78.4	100

Sources: U.S.A., Espenshade 1985; Belgium, Wijewickrema and Alii 1983; The Netherlands, CBS 1984.

Table 10.4. Percentage distribution of female life expectancy at age 20 by marital status at age 20 in selected countries

Marital status	Country and period	Marital status at age 20			
		Never married	Currently married	Widowed	Divorced
Never married	China, 1950–70	6.9	—	—	—
	China, 1981	5.7	—	—	—
	Belgium, 1977	14.8	—	—	—
	The Netherlands, 1976–80	21.7	—	—	—
Currently married	China, 1950–70	70.5	77.0	69.6	71.0
	China, 1981	76.6	82.1	75.8	77.1
	Belgium, 1977	68.3	81.3	58.3	73.3
	The Netherlands, 1976–80	56.9	73.8	30.5	52.1
Widowed	China, 1950–70	21.9	22.2	29.6	22.1
	China, 1981	17.2	17.3	23.7	17.3
	Belgium, 1977	13.4	14.6	38.8	14.3
	The Netherlands, 1976–80	14.7	17.2	66.3	15.8
Divorced	China, 1950–70	0.7	0.8	0.7	7.0
	China, 1981	0.5	0.6	0.5	5.7
	Belgium, 1977	3.3	4.1	2.9	12.2
	The Netherlands, 1976–80	6.6	9.0	3.2	32.0
Total	China, 1950–70	100.0	100.0	100.0	100.0
	China, 1981	100.0	100.0	100.0	100.0
	Belgium, 1977	100.0	100.0	100.0	100.0
	The Netherlands, 1976–80	100.0	100.0	100.0	100.0

Sources: Belgium, Wijewickrema and Alii 1983; The Netherlands, CBS 1984.

shorter than that of married people of the same age. How big this difference is and how widowed people differ from divorced people depend on how popular remarriage is and on the extent to which remarriage by widows differs from remarriage by divorcees. Calculating an individual's life expectancy in various marital statuses by marital status of that individual at a given age (greater than the minimum age at marriage) is therefore very useful when exploring those differences. We call it a "marital-status-based measure of life expectancy."

Table 10.4 shows an interesting difference in status-based life expectancy between women who are in different marital states at age 20. The proportion of life spent in the married state of a 20-year-old widow is about 90% of that of a 20-year-old married woman. The proportion of life spent in the married state of women who are divorced at age 20 is closer to that of women who are married at age 20. It shows again that remarriage, especially among divorcees, is quite common in contemporary China. The proportion of future life spent in the widowed state is significantly higher for a widowed 20-year-old woman than for any other woman of age 20. Similarly, the proportion of future life spent in the divorced state is much higher for a divorced 20-year-old woman than for any other woman of the same age. This is understandable since widows and divorcees need some time to choose a new spouse and to prepare for remarriage.

Table 10.4 also compares the Chinese female's marital-status-based life expectancies at age 20 with parallel measures for Belgian and Dutch females. A never-married 20-year-old Belgian or Dutch woman may expect to remain unmarried for a longer period of time. This is, to a large extent, due to the fact that a woman in the West is more likely to delay marriage, opt for cohabitation rather than marriage, or both.

A widowed or divorced 20-year-old Belgian or Dutch woman is expected to spend a much larger share of the rest of her life in the widowed or divorced state than her Chinese counterpart. Women in the West who lose their husbands due to widowhood or divorce have a great chance of remaining widowed or divorced because they are likely to be economically independent (through employment or social security benefits) and they may be influenced by the trend toward greater individualism and thus prefer to live alone. A young Chinese widow or divorcee mainly relies on remarriage to solve the difficulties of loneliness or economic constraint.

Another interesting question is, how many years can a 55-year-old (retirement age for women in China) currently married female expect to spend in the married or widowed state during the rest of her life? How do these figures differ for a 55-year-old widow? Table 10.5 provides the answers to these questions.

Under the 1950–70 rates, a 55-year-old currently married woman is expected to spend 56.8% and 42.8% of the rest of her life in the currently married state and the widowed state, respectively. The fractions of life spent in the currently married and widowed states for a currently married 55-year-old woman under the 1981 rates are 64.0% and 35.7%, which differs considerably from the 1950–70 situation. Both period life tables show that a 55-year-old widow would expect to spend more than 97% of the rest of her life in widowhood.

10.2. Childbearing

10.2.1. Parity distribution

Figure 10.2 compares the parity distributions according to the 1981 and 1950–70 family status life tables. For 1981, only 6.6% of 20-year-old women have

Table 10.5. Percentage distribution of female life expectancy at age 55 by marital status at age 55, China

Marital status	Period	Never married	Currently married	Widowed	Divorced
			Marital status at age 55		
Never	1950–70	100.0	—	—	—
married	1981	100.0	—	—	—
Currently	1950–70	—	56.8	2.3	12.5
married	1981	—	64.0	2.7	14.6
Widowed	1950–70	—	42.8	97.7	9.9
	1981	—	35.7	97.3	8.7
Divorced	1950–70	—	0.4	0	77.6
	1981	—	0.3	0	76.8
Total	1950–70	100.0	100.0	100.0	100.0
	1981	100.0	100.0	100.0	100.0

given birth to a child, and very few women (0.05%) have given birth to more than one child by age 20. These figures are 24.2% and 6.2%, respectively, for 1950–70. This is obviously due to early marriage before 1970 and the increased age at marriage in 1981.

At age 50, the end of the childbearing life span, 13.9% would have given birth to only one child, 37.2% to two children, 26.8% to three children, 13.0% to four children, and only 7.8% to more than four children if a cohort experienced the 1981 nuptiality and fertility conditions. However, under the 1950–70 nuptiality and fertility conditions, the picture would be totally different: 3.9% would have given birth to only one child, 5.2% to two children, 7.7% to three children, 12.6% to four children, and the vast majority—67.3%—to more than four children; 22.4% of all 50-year-old women would have had eight or more deliveries (see figure 10.3).

It is very clear that childbearing behavior has changed remarkably. The expected time spent in parity 2 constitutes the largest (31.1%) percentage of a woman's life after age 15; 17.0% of her life is spent in parity 1, 20.8% in parity 3, and only 4.8% in parity 5 or higher according to the 1981 rates. However, under the 1950–70 conditions, a woman would spend 45.0% of her life in parity 5 or higher and about 7.4% and 7.0% in parity 1 and parity 2, respectively.

The analysis shows that the proportion of women who never give birth is 1.44% under the 1981 rates and 3.36% under the 1950–70 rates. These figures are consistent with the China census and survey observations (e.g., the In-

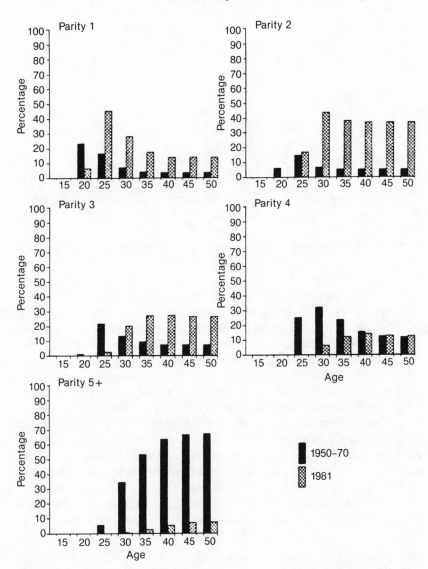

Figure 10.2. Percentage distribution by parity and by age according to family status life tables, China

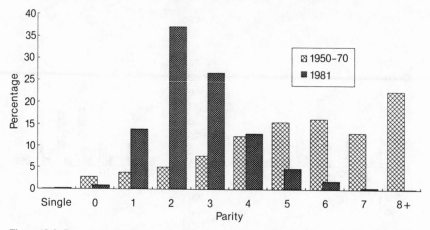

Figure 10.3. Percentage distribution of women at age 50 by parity according to family status life tables, China

Depth Fertility Surveys conducted in 1985 show that the proportions of women aged 45–49 who have never given birth to a child are 1.6%, 0.8%, and 2.9% in Hebei and Shaanxi provinces and Shanghai Municipality, respectively; see SSB 1986:22). According to a widely used standard pattern of sterility estimated by Henry (1965), the proportion of sterility is about 3% at age 20 and 5% at age 25. If Henry's estimates are true for the Chinese population, the percentage of childless women revealed by the original data and the life tables are underestimated for 1981. However, we did not adjust the observed data for three reasons. First, we believe that some primarily sterile women who have adopted a child may declare a birth instead of an adoption since they do not want the child to know that it has been adopted. Second, the purpose of this study is to investigate the family structure rather than fecundity or sterility. We are interested in knowing how many children a woman actually has rather than in knowing whether or not she is the children's biological mother. Third, the error introduced by such possible misdeclarations is most likely too small to affect the results of overall fertility.

10.2.2. Potential for further fertility reduction

The indicators mentioned above reveal the following changes and trends. (1) The fertility patterns of Chinese females have altered considerably since 1970. The changing fertility patterns are characterized by a remarkable decline in the number of births of higher parity and an increase in the age at marriage and at childbearing. (2) If the 1981 birth level and pattern persist, 52.5% of Chinese women will, at the end of their childbearing period, be of parity 2 or less than 2 (13.9% will be of parity 1); 47.5% will be of parity 3 or higher. Although 47.5% is almost half the percentage found in 1950–70, it shows that a further reduction of fertility can be achieved by reducing the proportion of births of order 3 or higher. If one would bring down the proportion of women of parity higher than 3 at age 50 to 0, if the proportion of women of parity 3 is reduced until it is equal to that of parity 1 (13.9%), and if the proportions of women of parity 0 and parity 1 at age 50 remain unchanged, then the total fertility rate will be reduced to 2. Therefore, more attention should be given to reducing birth rates of order 3 or higher, as emphasized by Chinese demographers.

Another important instrument by which Chinese fertility and population growth can be further slowed down is to increase the mean age at childbearing and the spacing of children (Bongaarts and Greenhalgh 1985:602–6). As Lesthaeghe predicted in a study on nuptiality policies over 15 years ago (he took the Chinese case as a very important example in his paper), the increased mean age at first marriage has played a prominent role in slowing down population growth (Lesthaeghe 1973). China's one-per-thousand fertility survey shows clearly that an increase in the mean age at marriage has lowered the period fertility (see e.g., Coale 1984).

The current mean age at marriage is already relatively high in urban areas and some socioeconomically advanced rural areas. It is neither realistic nor reasonable to ask young people to get married at a very late age. But early marriage is still not uncommon in many rural areas. The 1981 family status life table shows that 17.8% of the life table cohort members are married before age 20 if 1981 conditions prevail. The In-Depth Fertility Surveys conducted in 1985 show that in Shaanxi Province almost one-fifth of the young women get married before the legal marriage age. The age at marriage reported as being best by 30% of the Shaanxi women is lower than the legal age (SSB 1986:17–18). Hence, a further increase in the mean age at childbearing may be achieved through reinforcing publicity for late marriage, particularly in rural areas, and monitoring the interval between first marriage and first birth and subsequent birth intervals.

10.2.3. Number of children ever born versus number of children surviving and policy implications

The parity distributions at each age reflect the timing and level of fertility. However, because of mortality, the number of children ever born is not equal to the number of surviving children. Figure 10.4 shows how the declined mortality from 1950–70 to 1981 affects the number of surviving children. The improvement is very impressive. For instance, if the fertility schedule and mortality observed in 1950–70 were experienced by a cohort, 17.1% of the 35-year-old women who had given birth to only one child would have no surviving child. This figure would be 5.4% if the cohort members experienced fertility

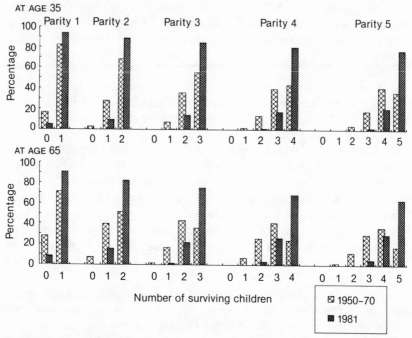

Figure 10.4. Percentage distribution by parity and number of surviving children at ages 35 and 65 according to family status life tables, China

and mortality as observed in 1981. With the 1950–70 regimes, 2.8% of all 35-year-old women of parity 2 would have no surviving children. This figure is 0.3% if the 1981 regimes apply. Age 35 is not the end of the reproductive life span. Those who have given birth to only one or two children and whose only child or both children have died could have another child if they so desired and are still able to do so.

Let's now look at the 65-year-old women who need someone to look after them. If the cohort members experienced the fertility and mortality regimes observed in 1950–70, 28.3% of those who have given birth to only one child and 7.8% of those who have given birth to two children would have no surviving children when they reach age 65. If they experienced the fertility and mortality rates observed in 1981, at this age the percentage of childless women who have given birth to only one child would be 9.2%, and those who have given birth to two children would be 0.8%.

The above results are based on the assumption that fertility depends on parity, marital status, and age but not on the number of surviving children. This may overestimate the proportion of women who have no surviving children because the fertile women who lost their children may have a greater probability of bearing an additional baby than the average woman of the same parity and age. Nevertheless, these results demonstrate to some extent the relationship between mortality and number of surviving children. This is important in societies in which the elderly depend on their children, such as in the rural areas of China. If mortality is high, a substantial proportion of women who have each given birth to only one child would have no surviving children in old age. (If the child dies at a young age of the mother, the mother may try to have another baby. If the child dies when the mother is in her late thirties or forties or older, the mother's chance to bear another baby may be very small or even 0.) Although some women may adopt a child, it is still a heavy socioeconomic burden for society, since many couples do not wish to adopt a child after having lost their own child, or alternatively, there may not be enough children for adoption. However, if the mortality level is low, the situation is much better. Comparing the implications of the 1981 and 1950–70 demographic conditions, figure 10.4 shows the improvement in survivorship of children due to declining mortality.

At present, mortality levels in China vary considerably from one region to another. The difference between the highest and the lowest life expectancies found in all provinces and municipalities of China is about 10 years (Jiang, Zhang, and Zhu 1984:7). These differences are undoubtedly much larger between the remote areas and the southeastern coastal areas. Therefore, different birth-planning policies are required for different localities. In other words, the policy advocating one child per couple in areas in which mortality is high cannot be strictly adhered to as this would create unfavorable socioeconomic situations where substantial proportions of couples would have no surviving children to care for them in old age.

10.3. Adulthood as a Daughter and as a Mother

Every society defines, by custom as well as by law, what parents should do for their children, what they can expect from their children, and what children can expect from their parents (Menken 1985:475; Watkins, Menken, and Bongaarts 1984:4). In all societies, parents have the obligation to rear their children until their children become economically independent. Adult children, on the other hand, have the obligation to take care of their elderly parents either economically or emotionally. In rural China, which accounts for about four-fifths of the total Chinese population, almost all elderly parents are economically dependent on their children. Even among the urban population, where the pension system has been introduced, filiation is still one of the cornerstones of society, and a great majority of the elderly enjoy living with one of their married children. Both in rural and urban areas, married children who do not live with their parents maintain very strong ties—either economic or emotional—with

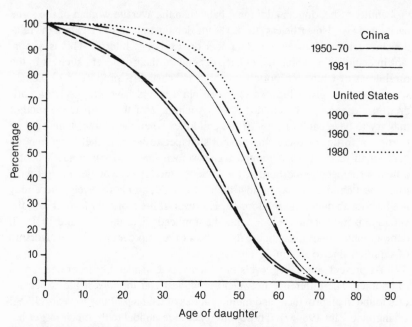

Figure 10.5. Percentage distribution of women with surviving mother according to family status life tables, China and the United States
Source: For the United States, see Menken 1985:477.

their parents (see, e.g., Liu Yin 1985:10). Therefore, it would be extremely interesting to find answers to the following questions: Given the fertility and mortality regimes, what is the proportion of women who are likely to have surviving parent(s) and how many surviving children will a woman have? How long will she be obliged to care for her elderly parent(s) over 65, and how many children under age 18 or 5 will she have to care for? The following sections provide the answers to these questions.

10.3.1. Adulthood as a daughter

Figure 10.5 shows the percentage distribution of women who have a surviving biological mother. Under the 1981 mortality and fertility conditions, 0.7% of all girls aged 5 and 4.8% of all women aged 20 have lost their biological mothers. These figures are much higher if the 1950–70·mortality and fertility conditions prevail: 2.6% and 15.7%, respectively. At ages 35 and 50, the proportions of women who have a surviving biological mother are about 83% and 49%, respectively, if they experienced the 1981 regimes. Under the 1950–70 regimes, about 60% and 23% have obligations toward a surviving mother when they reach age 35 and age 50, respectively. The 1981 demographic conditions

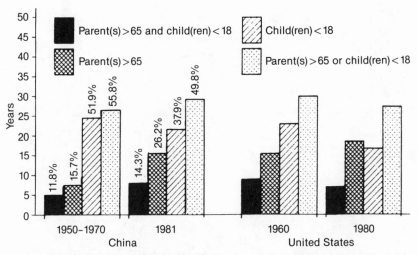

Figure 10.6. Expected years of adult life (beyond age 15) spent as a daughter according to family status life tables, China and the United States

Note: The percentages given are obtained by dividing the expected adult years as a daughter by the total life expectancy at age 15.

raise the adult cohort members' obligation toward a surviving mother, simply as a result of the prolongation of the life span in China.

As a daughter, a woman not only has the obligation to care for her surviving mother but also for her surviving father. By combining the survivorship of mother and father, we calculate the cohort member's adult years as a daughter of at least one surviving parent and both surviving parents. Under the 1981 rates, a girl who survives to age 15 would spend about 10.2 years more with at least one surviving parent than under the 1950–70 rates. A 15-year-old girl would expect to spend about 10.5 years more with both parents alive for the rest of her life under the 1981 rates than under the 1950–70 rates (see figure 10.6). In order to compare the relative obligations as a daughter under 1950–70 and 1981 rates, the percentages of lifetime beyond age 15 spent with surviving parent(s) older than 65 are shown in figure 10.6. The figure demonstrates clearly that under the 1981 rates an average adult woman will spend a larger fraction of her lifetime with a responsibility toward her parent(s) than under the 1950–70 rates.

For comparison, we also present the percentage distribution with a surviving mother from the 1900, 1960, and 1980 U.S. family status life tables (figure 10.5) and the expected adult years as a daughter from the 1960 and 1980 U.S. family status life tables (figure 10.6) (Menken 1985:477–78). In figure 10.5 the 1981 curve for China is a bit lower than the 1960 U.S. curve. The 1950–

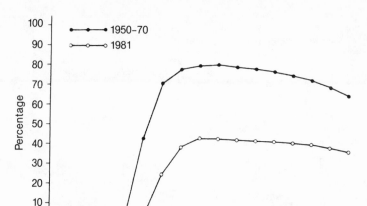

Figure 10.7. Percentage distribution of women with at least three surviving children according to family status life tables, China

70 curve for China almost coincides with the 1900 U.S. curve. This means that approximately the same achievement was reached in a period of 60 years (1900–60) in the United States as in a period of about 20 years in China (1950–70 to 1981). Notestein pointed out in 1969: "Today, the death rates in the newly developing countries are declining from three to five times the speed with which they moved through the similar levels in Europe's 19th century" (1969:352). Our findings confirm the argument Notestein put forward over 20 years ago.

10.3.2. Adulthood as a mother

The fertility decline in China reduces the adult woman's burden by reducing the number of children she has to care for. Figure 10.7 depicts the sharp decline in the percentage of women with at least three surviving children from 1950–70 to 1981. If the 1950–70 fertility level had not been checked, about 80% of women aged 40–50 years would have had at least three surviving children. Small children and teenagers need food, clothing, and an educational investment. Young adult children have to be prepared for marriage and childbearing, which, in Chinese society, has traditionally been an important duty of parents. The fact that so many middle-aged adults have a very heavy burden of child rearing is also felt by society. By contrast, the fraction of women aged 40–50 years with at least three surviving children would be reduced to about half of that found under the 1950–70 rates if the 1981 conditions were to prevail.

10.3.3. Adulthood as both a daughter and a mother

We will now look at the combination of a woman's responsibility to a surviving mother and to surviving children. If the 1981 regimes were to prevail, 31.9%

of the 35-year-old women would have a surviving mother and three or more surviving children; 6.6% would have no surviving mother but three or more surviving children. These figures would be 46.3% and 31.0%, respectively, if the cohort followed the 1950–70 demographic conditions (see table 10.6). For women, the burden of bearing a large number of children has obviously been alleviated by reducing fertility since 1970.

10.3.4. Responsibility for dependents

So far, we have discussed the distribution of surviving parents and the number of surviving children, disregarding the parents' and children's ages. This is not sufficient for the purpose of studying the demographic implications on the cohort members' responsibility to the dependents, since only elderly parents (say, over 65 years) and young children (under 18 years old) need particular care. Therefore, we look at the expectation of life at age 15 as a daughter of elderly parent(s), as a mother with children under 18 years old, and as a combination of the two, that is, as a daughter of elderly parents and a mother of young children. In other words, we look at a 15-year-old girl and ask the following question: in her remaining lifetime, how many years will she spend, on average, as a daughter of elderly parents or as a mother of young children?

The time spent with at least one parent over 65 increased from 7.6 years under the 1950–70 rates to 15.3 years under the 1981 rates (this figure was about 16 years under the 1960 U.S. rates and 19 years under the 1980 U.S. rates). Obviously, we experience the deaths of our parents at ever later ages: they are with us longer and longer. Our own children will have us with them even longer. Since the years spent with at least one elderly parent have increased significantly, the burden on adult children has become much heavier.

For cohort members who survive to age 15, figure 10.8a shows the average number of years spent as mothers with children of different ages. The numbers of years spent with at least one child of age less than 5 and with at least one child of age less than 18 are higher under the 1950–70 rates than under the 1981 conditions. This is the result of the high fertility in 1950–70: women started to bear children at an earlier age and stopped at a later age. However, the number of years spent with living child(ren) of whatever age under the 1950–70 conditions is significantly smaller than in 1981. This is due to the fact that mothers lived for shorter periods of time in 1950–70 than in 1981, given the very low childlessness in both periods.

Comparing the Chinese case with parallel measures in the United States, we found that although the mortality level in the United States in 1980 was significantly lower than that in China in 1981 (U.S. female $e_0 = 78.1$ in 1980 and Chinese female $e_0 = 69.3$ in 1981), the number of years spent with at least one surviving child by a Chinese woman in 1981 was about 7 years longer than that of American women in 1980. This is because a much smaller proportion of women become mothers in the United States (about 75%; Menken

Table 10.6. Percentage distribution of women as daughters and as mothers by number of surviving children according to family status life tables, China

| Age | Period | With surviving biological mother and surviving children | | | | | | | Without surviving biological mother but with children | | | | | | | |
| | | | Number of surviving children | | | | | | | Number of surviving children | | | | | | |
		Total	0	1	2	3	4	5+	Total	0	1	2	3	4	5+	Total
5	1981	99.26	99.26	0	0	0	0	0	0.74	0.74	0	0	0	0	0	100.0
	1950–70	97.39	97.39	0	0	0	0	0	2.61	2.61	0	0	0	0	0	100.0
20	1981	95.19	89.03	6.12	0.05	0	0	0	4.81	4.50	0.31	0	0	0	0	100.0
	1950–70	84.32	60.77	19.26	3.95	0.32	0	0	15.69	11.31	3.58	0.73	0.06	0	0	100.0
35	1981	82.90	2.25	17.14	31.65	21.14	8.87	1.85	17.10	0.46	3.54	6.53	4.36	1.83	0.38	100.0
	1950–70	59.89	2.61	3.91	7.07	12.43	14.48	19.38	40.12	1.75	2.62	4.74	8.33	9.70	12.99	100.0
50	1981	49.03	1.26	8.81	18.30	12.12	5.47	3.07	50.98	1.31	9.16	19.03	12.60	5.69	3.19	100.0
	1950–70	22.72	1.04	1.44	2.28	3.36	4.15	10.45	77.28	3.55	4.88	7.74	11.44	14.11	35.55	100.0
65	1981	6.59	0.20	1.28	2.46	1.58	0.70	0.38	93.41	2.85	18.11	34.80	22.37	9.86	5.42	100.0
	1950–70	1.62	0.08	0.12	0.20	0.28	0.32	0.62	98.38	5.10	7.54	12.12	16.86	19.10	37.66	100.0

1985:476) than in China (about 98%; taken from China's 1982 census observation as well as from our model output).

The years spent with at least one surviving child may be used as an indicator of a woman's responsibility to the subsequent generation. A better indicator would also take into account the number of surviving children. For instance, given that the 1981 fertility level is about 45% of that in 1950–70, the number of years spent with at least one surviving child—whatever the age—according to the 1981 table is 8 years more than in 1950–70. One may thus be misled by only comparing years spent with at least one surviving child in two different periods.

Therefore, we must also look at the fractions of time spent with different numbers of surviving children, which is presented in figure 10.8b (Menken's 1985 paper does not give the measures of the number of children). Under the 1950–70 rates, a cohort member surviving to age 15 is likely to spend about 25.1 years with at least one child under 18 years old (50% of which would be spent with more than two children) and about 12 years with at least one child under 5 (9% of which would be spent with more than two children). The figures based on the 1981 demographic conditions are about 22 years with at least one child under 18 years of age (22% of which would be spent with more than two children) and about 8 years with at least one child under 5 (only 2% of which with more than two children). Having more than two children under 18 or under 5 at the same time is really a heavy burden for any family. This unfavorable situation had fortunately improved in 1981 as compared to 1950–70.

The years with responsibilities to an elderly parent or parents (over 65) and young children (under 18) simultaneously have been called the years of overload (Menken 1985:479). The number of years of overload, disregarding the number of young children, is lower under the 1950–70 rates than under the 1981 conditions due to the higher mortality level found in 1950–70 (see figure 10.9b). Of the overload years, under the 1950–70 rates, the fraction of time spent with more than two young children is, however, 1.6 times as high as that under the 1981 rates. The smaller fraction of time spent with a very heavy overload (with one or both parents over 65 and more than two children under 18) under the 1981 conditions is, of course, the result of the remarkable fertility decline after 1970.

In figures 10.8a, 10.8b, 10.9a, and 10.9b, we also present the percentages obtained by dividing the corresponding adult years of responsibility to dependents by the total life expectancy at age 15. After this standardization, the results also show clearly the burden from old parents would be significantly increased and the burden from young children would be remarkably reduced if a woman experienced 1981 rates compared with the 1950–70 rates. This has, as we discussed before, resulted from the prolongation of the life span and the tremendous fertility decline since 1970.

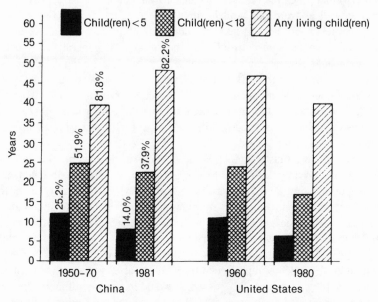

Figure 10.8a. Expected years of adult life (beyond age 15) spent as a mother according to family status life tables, China and the United States

Note: The percentages given are obtained by dividing the expected adult years as a mother by the total life expectancy at age 15.

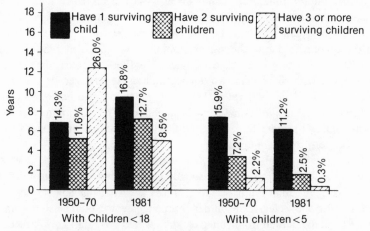

Figure 10.8b. Expected years of adult life spent as a mother by number of surviving children according to family status life tables, China

Note: The percentages given are obtained by dividing the expected adult years as a mother with different numbers of surviving children by the total life expectancy at age 15.

128

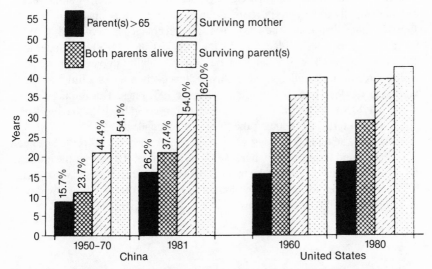

Figure 10.9a. Expected years of adult life (beyond age 15) spent with responsibility for dependents according to family status life tables, China and the United States

Note: The percentages given are obtained by dividing the expected adult years of responsibility for dependents by the total life expectancy at age 15.

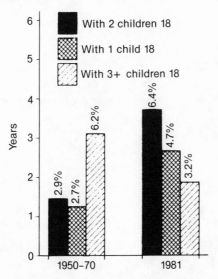

Figure 10.9b. Expected years of adult life (beyond age 15) spent with responsibility for parent(s) over 65 and for children under 18 according to family status life tables, China.

Note: The percentages given are obtained by dividing the expected adult years of responsibility for dependents with different numbers of surviving children by the total life expectancy at age 15.

It is interesting to note that although the absolute number of adult years of responsibility to parent(s) over 65 or children under 18 is smaller under the 1950–70 rates than under the 1981 rates, its percentage share of total life expectancy beyond age 15 is larger under the 1950–70 rates (56%) than under the 1981 rates (50%). The percentage share of responsibility to parent(s) over 65 and to three or more children under 18 simultaneously is about 2 times as high under the 1950–70 rates as that found under the 1981 rates. This finding shows that the 1981 demographic conditions were more favorable than the 1950–70 conditions in terms of reducing the burden of dependents.

In sum, the number of years of responsibility to dependents is the balance of mortality and fertility. The longer the life expectation, the heavier the burden from older parents; the larger the number of children surviving per woman, the heavier the burden from young children. The family status life table provides a nice instrument for measuring this responsibility to dependents.

11

Family Size and Structure of 1950–70 and 1981 Life Table Populations

How do changing fertility and mortality affect family size, family type, and family composition? This interesting research question has received considerable attention from demographers in the past (see, e.g., Coale 1965; Burch 1970; Ryder 1974; Goodman, Keyfitz, and Pullum 1974; LeBras 1978; Krishnamoorthy 1980; Martin and Culter 1983; Brass 1983; Bongaarts 1983; Watkins, Menken, and Bongaarts 1984; Menken 1985).

Most of these model simulations gave the average size of different family types based on the assumption of stability of demographic conditions. Although real demographic conditions are never perfectly stable or stationary, the model output does help one obtain a better understanding of the topic. First, the implications of a set of period demographic rates are clearly shown. By comparing the different implications of different rates one can better understand how changes of demographic rates affect family size and family structure. Second, by imputing the observed rates to a life table model, we can obtain some very useful summary measures which are more impressive and interpretable. The purpose of the life table model in the context of a stationary or stable population is neither to assume that the population in question would remain stationary or stable nor to predict the future for this population. It is only a good tool to pick out the implications of observed rates and to translate the massive rates into a number of more impressive and interpretable measures.

Our new simulations give us more insights by demonstrating not only the average family size but also the frequency distribution by family size, type, and composition. This chapter presents the findings.

We have recognized that the cross-sectional observations of family size and structure at one point in time are generally not equal to the life table output using period rates as input, because the period cross-sectional observation consists of many cohorts' past experiences and the period life table output is "what would be" if a synthetic cohort experienced the observed period rates.

Nevertheless, we compare the family size, type, and its distribution from the 1981 and 1950–70 family status life tables together with parallel measures from the 1982 census, whenever available. The purpose of this treatment is to facilitate some kind of check: to see whether the model output is plausible and to gain better understanding through comparison.

The profiles of the 1950–70 and the 1981 family status life tables do not reflect the real family structure in those two periods since the Chinese population in 1950–70 and 1981 was not stable at all. Again, however, comparing what would be if 1950–70 conditions remained stable with what would be if 1981 conditions remained stable, we can gain a better understanding of how demographic change brings about changes in family structure.

In short, we are neither assuming that the 1950–70 and 1981 rates will remain constant nor predicting the future of the Chinese family size and structure. What we are doing is trying to use the tool of a family status life table to ascertain the effects of tremendous changes in demographic rates on family size and structure. At the same time, we are trying to gain insight into how Chinese family size and structure will evolve.

11.1. Family Size

11.1.1. Comparison between the 1982 census observations and the 1950–70 life table output

The observed average family sizes were 4.78 in 1973 and 4.43 in 1982. The average family size from the 1950–70 life table is 4.90, and from the 1981 life table model, 4.37 (see table 11.1). The fractions of one-, two-, and five-person families from the 1950–70 family status life table models are more or less close to those found in the 1982 census observation. The proportion of three-person families from the 1950–70 family status life table is significantly smaller, whereas the proportions of families of more than five persons are significantly higher than those of the 1982 census (see figure 11.1). This model output seems to be plausible simply because fertility greatly declined from 1970 to 1982. Young couples in 1982 have a much smaller number of children compared with the situation in 1950–70. The proportions of three- and four-person families in the 1982 census have significantly increased since more young couples who are not living with parents have only one or two children. The census observation on the proportion of families of more than five persons is significantly smaller than that from the model output under 1950–70 conditions because those young couples who are living with parents also have fewer children.

11.1.2. Comparison between the 1981 and 1950–70 life table outputs

The average family size under the 1981 rates is 4.37: a decrease of 11% compared with the 1950–70 rates. Is this surprising? Why is the family size reduced

Table 11.1. Average family sizes from the 1982 census and the model outputs

Type	Source		Average size
Total	1950–70	simulation	4.90
	1981	simulation	4.37
	1982	census	4.43
Nuclear family	1950–70	simulation	4.41
	1981	simulation	3.19
	1982	census	NA
Three-generation family	1950–70	simulation	6.17
	1981	simulation	5.60
	1982	census	NA

NA: not available.

by 11% whereas the 1981 fertility was reduced by more than half compared with 1950–70? The explanation is as follows. First, decreased mortality has played an important role. The longer life span gives everyone, including children and older parents, a higher probability of surviving, which partially compensates for the effects of the decline in fertility on average family size. Second, as we will see later on, the proportion of three-generation families will increase with the fertility decline if the desirability of coresidence between parents and married children remains unchanged. The size of three-generation families is generally larger than that of nuclear families. The increased fraction of three-generation families also partially compensates the effects of the fertility decline on average family size. This argument is supported if we look at the average size of nuclear families and three-generation families separately. The average size of nuclear families is 3.19 under the 1981 rates, compared with 4.41 under the 1950–70 rates: a decrease of 27.7%. The average size of three-generation families under the 1981 rates is 5.60, compared with 6.17 under the 1950–70 rates, a decrease of 9.2%.

11.2. Family Types: Nuclear Families versus Three-Generation Families

11.2.1. Comparison between the 1982 census observations and the 1950–70 life table output

The proportions of nuclear families (including one-person families) and three-generation families (including more than three-generation families) are 81.1% and 18.9%, respectively, from the 1982 census. These figures are 72.2% and 27.7% from the 1950–70 family status life table output and 51.3% and 48.8% from the 1981 family status life table output (see table 11.2). The fact that the 1982 census observation on the proportion of nuclear families does not differ very much from what it would be if the 1950–70 rates were to prevail is

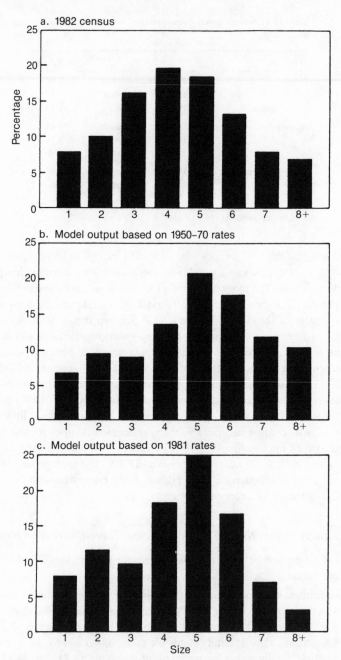

Figure 11.1. Percentage distribution of family sizes in 1982 in China (census observation) and outputs of 1950–70 and 1981 simulations

Table 11.2. Percentage distribution of family types by marital status according to the model outputs

Family type	Year	One female	Husband-wife	Widowed mother	Divorced mother	Total
Nuclear family	1950–70	6.9	62.1	2.7	0.5	72.2
	1981	8.0	42.5	0.6	0.2	51.3
With lone grandmother	1950–70	—	11.8	0.8	0.1	12.7
	1981	—	13.5	0.8	0.1	14.4
With both grandparents	1950–70	—	14.6	0.3	0.1	15.0
	1981	—	33.7	0.5	0.2	34.4
Total	1950–70	6.9	88.5	3.8	0.7	100.0
	1981	8.0	89.7	1.9	0.5	100.0

not surprising. Given that no (or very few) married siblings live together, the proportion of nuclear families mainly depends on the number of adult children per older couple and on the strength of the desire of older couples and one of their married children to live together. In other words, the smaller number of adult children per couple and the greater the desirability of coresidence, the lower the proportion of nuclear families. Up to 1982, the average number of adult children per older couple was the result of high fertility before 1970, since the reduced number of newborn children after 1970 have not yet reached adulthood. Therefore, the availability of adult children per middle-aged or elderly couple in 1982 was not reduced by reduced fertility whereas reduced mortality may have allowed more children to survive up to adulthood and consequently to form more nuclear families, so that the 1982 census observation on the proportion of nuclear families was close to, but somewhat higher than, that of the 1950–70 family status life table.

11.2.2. Comparison between the 1981 and 1950–70 life table outputs

The proportion of nuclear families under the 1981 rates is 51.3%, and under the 1950–70 rates, it is 72.2%. The demographic change (mainly the fertility decline) would bring down the proportion of nuclear families by about 20 percentage points. This striking result may be understood from a simple hypothetical example (see figure 11.2). Suppose there are 4 old couples in a population and that each of those 4 couples has 6 sons and 6 daughters. The children of those 4 couples get married to each other and form 12 young couples. We assume that 3 out of 4 old couples live with 1 young couple and the other young couples move out of the parental home to set up independent families. Thus, there are 13 families in the population, and 10 are nuclear families, that is, 77% (mode A in figure 11.2). However, if each of the 4 couples has 1 son and 1 daughter, there will be 4 young couples. Three young couples live with the husband's (or

Mode A High fertility

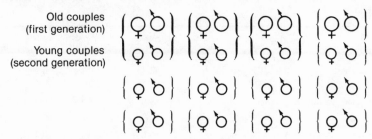

Proportion of nuclear families: 10/13=77%

Mode B Low fertility; propensity for coresidence same as in mode A

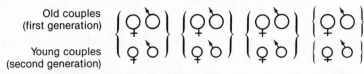

Proportion of nuclear families: 2/5=40%

Mode C Low fertility; propensity for coresidence reduced by 33%

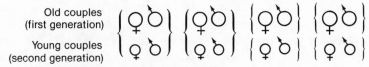

Proportion of nuclear families: 4/6=67%

Mode D Very low fertility; propensity for coresidence same as in mode C

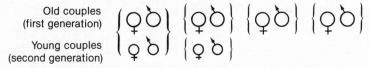

Proportion of nuclear families: 4/5=80%

Figure 11.2. A simple illustration of changes in proportion of nuclear families caused by a decline in fertility

wife's) parents; the other one does not. The nuclear family will account for 40% (mode B in figure 11.2). In mode C each of the 4 couples has 2 children (1 boy and 1 girl). Instead of 3 out of 4, we assume only 2 out of 4 old parents are living with a young couple (in other words, the propensity of coresidence between parents and married children is reduced by 33%). The proportion of nuclear families would be 67%, which is still lower than in mode A (high fertility and the higher propensity of coresidence). Clearly, the tremendously reduced fertility will bring down the proportion of nuclear families.

This argument does not hold, however, when fertility falls below replacement level, as shown in mode D, where each old couple has only 1 child and thus there are only 2 young couples in the system; if 1 out of 2 young couples (50%) live with their parents, the proportion of nuclear families will be 80%; the proportion of nuclear families is obviously increased compared with the situation represented by mode C.

11.3. Family Types by Marital Status

Table 11.2 shows the percentage distribution of families by type as well as by the marital status of the mother for the implied stable populations in which the demographic regimes of 1981 and 1950–70 prevail. Several observations can be drawn from table 11.2.

One-female families account for a small proportion in both implied stable populations since few women leave the parental home to set up an independent family before marriage and there are few childless widowed or divorced lone women. Note that the proportion of one-female families in 1981 is somewhat higher than that under the 1950–70 rates. This is consistent with the remarkably increased mean age at marriage in 1981, because if she marries late, a woman has a longer period during which she is exposed to the risk of moving out of the parental home before marriage.

Nuclear families with a widowed or divorced mother constitute 0.8% under the 1981 rates and 3.2% under the 1950–70 rates. Three-generation families with a widowed or divorced mother account for 1.6% under the 1981 rates and 1.3% under the 1950–70 rates. The proportion of families with at least one widowed or divorced woman (either mother or grandmother) is 15% under the 1981 rates and 15.9% under the 1950–70 rates. Clearly, "incomplete families" have always accounted for a small proportion of the total.

The great majority of families are so-called complete families of husband and wife (plus children and/or one or both grandparents). Families with at least one couple (i.e., either a middle-generation couple or grandparents or both) constitute 90.4% under the 1981 rates and 89.4% under the 1950–70 rates. Families with a middle-generation couple (grandparent(s) may be either present or absent) account for 89.7% under the 1981 rates and 88.5% under the 1950–70 rates. This surprisingly small difference is consistent with the very slight difference in the ratios of currently married to ever-married women from ages 20–45 in 1982 and in the Chinese farm population in 1930, as found by Coale (1984:55; see also table 2.10 and section 2.2.4 of this volume). It implies that among women under age 45, the higher incidence of widowhood in 1950–70, which was the main cause of "incomplete families" for those women, must have been offset by high rates of remarriage.

Note that the proportion of three-generation families with two couples (parents and grandparents) under 1981 conditions is 33.7%, which is more than twice as high as that under the 1950–70 rates (14.6%). This is mainly due to the greater proportion of three-generation families under the 1981 rates and partly due to the longer life span of grandparents.

In short, our findings show that the majority of Chinese families are "complete families" of the husband-wife type and that this feature has remained stable.

11.4. How Will the Size and Structure of the Chinese Family Evolve?

Two prospects are usually described in the popular media: Chinese family size will continue to fall and the proportion of nuclear families will continue to increase. We, however, think the second prospect may not be true since the dramatic fertility decline after 1970 reduces the new generation's chance to move out of the parental home if the traditional preference of most parents to live with one of their married children does not change dramatically.

This section explores this problem by analyzing related output from implied stable populations under the 1950–70 rates and under the 1981 rates as well as a number of extra simulations. A comment concerning the foreseeable evolution of family structure will also be presented. For ease of presentation, we abbreviate hereafter "the desirability of parents and one of their married children to live together" as "the desirability of coresidence."

11.4.1. What have we learned from the model outputs under the 1950–70 and 1981 rates?

The model output illustrates quantitatively the trend of Chinese family structure: if the desirability of coresidence does not change, the average family size will decrease by about 11% under the 1981 rates compared with the 1950–70 rates, and the proportion of nuclear families will decrease significantly (about 20 percentage points) under the 1981 rates compared with the 1950–70 rates because children with fewer siblings will have less chance to move out of the parental home.

Of course, what this exercise tells us is only what would be if the 1981 conditions remain constant compared with what would be if the 1950–70 conditions remain constant. Note that the average family size and proportion of nuclear families resulting from the implied stable populations are not predictions at all, because the demographic rates will not remain constant. Nevertheless, the exercise does tell us that the effect of the dramatically reduced fertility on reducing the proportion of nuclear families will be substantial.

On the other hand, socioeconomic development will reduce the desirability of coresidence, operating therefore in the opposite direction to the reduced fertility. Whether the real proportion of nuclear families will increase or decrease depends on which of those two factors will be stronger. To explore the effects on family size and structure of changing these two factors, we performed a number of extra simulations, which are presented in the next section.

11.4.2. Some extra simulations

With strong and efficient population policies and family-planning programs as well as continued modernization, fertility is likely to be further reduced in China. Rapid economic development will decrease the desirability of coresidence. Based on these considerations, we assumed the values of the parameters for the extra simulations presented in table 11.3. We summarize the main outcome of simulations I to VIII in table 11.4 and table 11.5, comparing the effects of TFR, e_0, and n_2 (total fertility rate, female life expectancy at birth, and proportion of parents who have married children but do not live with any of them).

Table 11.4 and figure 11.3 show that the average family size decreases as fertility decreases. If n_2 remains the same as that estimated for 1981, the average family size decreased very little, from 4.37 to 4.36, when TFR decreased from 2.63 to 2.21 and e_0 increased to 74. The reason why there is such little change in family size in this case is that the effect of reduced fertility (from TFR = 2.63 to 2.21) is almost compensated by the decreased proportion of nuclear families (this will be discussed below) and the increasing life expectancy. If n_2 and e_0 remain unchanged, a further decrease of TFR would result in a sharper decrease in average family size. The average family size decreased as n_2 increased when e_0 and TFR remain unchanged.

As one may expect, table 11.5 and figure 11.4 show that the proportion of nuclear families increased with decreased desirability of coresidence if other things remain unchanged. On the other hand, table 11.5 and figure 11.4 demonstrate some extremely interesting trends of family structure with changing fertility. Let us look at three rows in table 11.5. If n_2 remains constant and the fertility is above replacement level, the proportion of nuclear families decreases with decreasing fertility; this was explained in section 11.2. However, a further reduction in the birth rate after fertility reaches the replacement level will increase the proportion of nuclear families. For example, when $n_2 = 0.35$ and $e_0 = 74$, the proportion of nuclear families increases by about 10 percentage points if total fertility rates decrease from 2.21 to 1.8. Why? The reason is fairly simple. When the number of members of the children's generation is smaller than that of the parent's generation, some of the parents have to live away from their married children even if they do not wish to do so, because of the shortage of children in the population. This is, of course, based on the as-

Table 11.3. Parameters used in simulations

Parameter	1950–70	1981	I	I'	II	II'	III	IV	IV'	V	V'	VI	VII	VII'	VIII	VIII'
1. Expectation of life:																
Females at birth (e_0)	51.0	69.3	74.0	74.0	74.0	74.0	69.3	74.0	74.0	74.0	74.0	69.3	74.0	74.0	74.0	74.0
Males at birth (e'_0)	49.1	66.3	70.0	70.0	70.0	70.0	66.3	70.0	70.0	70.0	70.0	66.3	70.0	70.0	70.0	70.0
2. Total fertility rate (TFR)	5.78	2.63	2.21	2.21	1.80	1.80	2.63	2.21	2.21	1.80	1.80	2.63	2.21	2.21	1.80	1.80
3. Mean age at childbearing ($\bar{m}$)			27	29	27	29	27	27	29	27	29	27	27	29	27	29
4. Intrinsic growth rate of the implied stable population (per thousand)	25.3	5.8	0.0	0.0	−7.6	−7.6	5.8	0.0	0.0	−7.6	−7.6	5.8	0.0	0.0	−7.6	−7.6
5. Proportion of parents who have married children but do not live with any of them:																
Urban	0.365	0.365	0.365	0.365	0.365	0.365	0.500	0.500	0.500	0.500	0.500	0.650	0.650	0.650	0.65	0.65
Rural	0.150	0.150	0.150	0.150	0.150	0.150	0.270	0.270	0.270	0.270	0.270	0.400	0.400	0.400	0.40	0.40
Whole (n_2)	0.181	0.195	0.195	0.195	0.195	0.195	0.350	0.350	0.350	0.350	0.350	0.500	0.500	0.500	0.50	0.50
(Proportion of urban population)	0.142	0.208	0.208	0.208	0.208	0.208	0.350	0.350	0.350	0.350	0.350	0.400	0.400	0.400	0.400	0.40
6. Proportion of children who leave parental home before marriage	0.05	0.05	0.05	0.05	0.05	0.05	0.10	0.10	0.10	0.10	0.10	0.15	0.15	0.15	0.15	0.15
7. Mean age at marriage ($\bar{m}$)	22.8	22.8	22.8	24.8	22.8	24.8	22.8	22.8	24.8	22.8	24.8	22.8	22.8	24.8	22.8	24.8
8. Divorce level (annual no. of divorces per 1,000 married couples, denoted as D)	2	1	1	5	1	5	1	1	5	1	5	1	1	5	1	5
9. Remarriage rates assumed to remain the same																

Table 11.4. Average family sizes under various levels of fertility, mortality, and desirability of coresidence according to the model output

	$e_0 = 69.3$	$e_0 = 74.0$	
	TFR = 2.63	TFR = 2.21	TFR = 1.80
$n_2 = 0.195$	4.37 (1981)	4.36 (II)	3.65 (VI)
		4.21 (I')	3.51 (II')
$n_2 = 0.350$	4.01 (III)	3.87 (IV)	3.28 (V)
		3.73 (IV')	3.21 (V')
$n_2 = 0.500$	3.69 (VI)	3.55 (VII)	2.97 (VIII)
		3.46 (VII')	2.94 (VIII')

Note: The simulation identifications are given in parentheses; for other parameters used, see table 11.3.

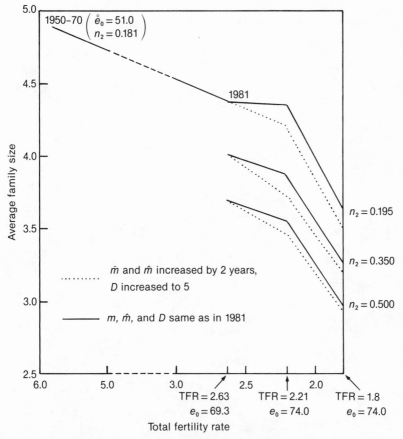

Figure 11.3. Average family sizes under various levels of fertility, mortality, and desirability of coresidence according to the model output

Table 11.5. Percentage of nuclear families (including one-person families) under various levels of fertility, mortality, and desirability of coresidence according to the model output

	$e_0 = 69.3$	$e_0 = 74.0$	
	TFR = 2.63	TFR = 2.21	TFR = 1.80
$n_2 = 0.195$	51.25 (I)	40.92 (I)	56.07 (II)
		47.21 (I')	62.02 (II')
$n_2 = 0.350$	64.01 (III)	59.97 (IV)	68.84 (V)
		65.63 (IV')	72.93 (V')
$n_2 = 0.500$	74.69 (VI)	70.49 (VII)	79.68 (VIII)
		74.57 (VII')	82.01 (VIII')

Note: The simulation identifications are given in parentheses; for other parameters used, see table 11.3.

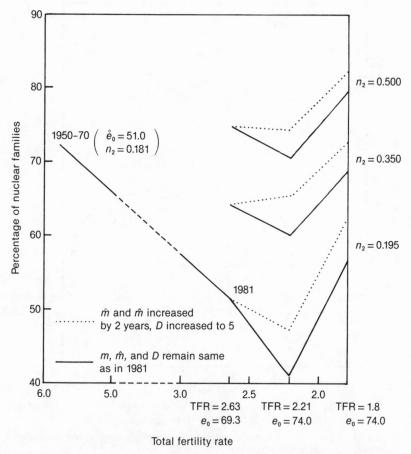

Figure 11.4. Percentage of nuclear families (including one-person families) under various levels of fertility, mortality, and desirability of coresidence according to the model output

sumption that no married children simultaneously live with their parents and parents-in-law, an arrangement that seldom occurs in Chinese society. This finding can also be demonstrated mathematically.[1]

As we stated at the beginning of this chapter, the simulations are not pro-

1. Let's recall equations (6.9) and (6.10):

$$l = 1 - \frac{1 - n_2}{G(1 - w)} \qquad (G \geq 1 \text{ and } w \leq \frac{G + n_2 - 1}{G}); \tag{6.9}$$

$$l = 1 - \frac{G - n_2}{G(1 - w)} \qquad (G < 1, n_2 \leq G, \text{ and } w \leq \frac{N_2}{G}); \tag{6.10}$$

where l is the proportion ultimately leaving the parental home; n_2 is the proportion of parents who have married children but do not live with any of them; w is the proportion of children leaving the parental home before marriage; G is the average number of daughters who survive up to the mean age at childbearing per woman of at least parity 1.

Let n_1 denote the proportion of women who do not give any live births during their whole life. The average number of daughters who survive up to the mean age at childbearing per woman is approximately equal to the net reproduction rate (NRR), so that $G = NRR/(1 - n_1)$, and equations (6.9) and (6.10) become

$$l = 1 - \frac{1 - n_2}{NRR(1 - w)/(1 - n_1)} \qquad (NRR \geq (1 - n_1)) \tag{N1}$$

$$l = 1 - \frac{NRR/(1 - n_1) - n_2}{NRR(1 - w)/(1 - n_1)}$$

$$= 1 - \frac{1}{1 - w} + \frac{n_2(1 - n_1)}{NRR(1 - w)} \qquad (NRR < (1 - n_1)) \tag{N2}$$

In both equations (N1) and (N2), if NRR, n_1, and w remain constant, l will increase (or decrease) with an increase (or decrease) of n_2; in other words, if everything else remains unchanged, the proportion of nuclear families will increase (or decrease) with an increase or decrease in the proportion of parents who have married children but do not live with any of them.

If n_2, n_1, and w remain constant but NRR changes, what will happen to l? The partial differential of l' in terms of NRR when $NRR \geq (1 - n_1)$ is

$$a = \frac{[(1 - n_2)(1 - n_1)]/(1 - w)}{NRR^2}. \tag{N3}$$

Since n_2, n_1, and w can never be greater than 1, a is always positive. It means that when $NRR \geq (1 - n_1)$, l is positively related to NRR. The partial differential of l in terms of NRR when $NRR < (1 - n_1)$ is

$$b = -\frac{[n_2(1 - n_1)/(1 - w)]}{NRR^2}. \tag{N4}$$

The quantity b is always negative so that when $NRR < (1 - n_1)$, l is negatively related to NRR. Thus, we have mathematically proved the conclusion stated in the text: namely, when the fertility is above, or at, the replacement level, the proportion of nuclear families decreases with a decrease in fertility if everything else remains unchanged. On the other hand, when fertility is below the replacement level $NRR < (1 - n_1)$, the proportion of nuclear families increases with a further reduction of fertility.

jections. Nevertheless, they do show how the Chinese family size and structure will change with changing fertility, nuptiality, divorce, mortality, and the desirability of coresidence. Thus a number of observations can be drawn from these simulations.

1. Chinese family size will steadily decrease with the expected decrease in fertility and the desirability of coresidence and with the gradual increase in age at marriage and the divorce level.

2. If the desirability of coresidence does not decrease dramatically, the proportion of nuclear families will decrease when the children born in the 1970s reach the family formation stage, since people of the new generation, who have a reduced number of siblings, will have a smaller chance of moving out of the parental home to form an independent nuclear family. However, when fertility is below the replacement level, a further reduction of TFR will increase the proportion of nuclear families. On the other hand, the gradually increasing mean age at marriage and the divorce level may partly compensate for the effects of the dramatic fertility decline on the decreasing proportion of nuclear families.

3. If the desirability of coresidence decreases rapidly, the effects of decreasing fertility (as long as it remains above replacement level) on the decreasing proportion of nuclear families will be compensated for to a large extent, or even wholly.

4. The change in fertility and the desirability of coresidence can occur simultaneously. But the fertility change, unlike the changing desirability of coresidence, cannot affect the proportion of nuclear families immediately after the change (it does affect family size immediately) because the reduced or increased number of children per couple mainly influences the proportion of nuclear families by reducing or increasing the children's opportunity of leaving the parental home when the children grow up. Therefore, the delayed effects of changing fertility should be taken into account.

11.5. A Sensitive Analysis: Contributions of Changes in Fertility, Mortality, and Nuptiality

What is the contribution of fertility decline alone and of mortality decline alone to the changes in family size between the 1950–70 and 1981 simulations? To answer these questions, we perform two other simulations. One uses 1981 fertility rates but assumes all other inputs to be the same as in the 1950–70 simulation. The average family size from this simulation is 3.97. In other words, the fertility decline alone would reduce the average family size by 19%, in contrast to a reduction of 11% when fertility decline, mortality decline, and changes of marital pattern are considered. Another simulation, using 1981 mortality rates but assuming all other inputs to be the same as in the 1950–70 simulation, shows that mortality decline alone would increase the average family size by 12%.

The fact that the proportion of nuclear families in the 1981 simulation (51.3%) was reduced by 20 percentage points compared with the 1950–70 simulation (72.2%) resulted from the combined effects of fertility decline and mortality reduction. What is the contribution of fertility decline alone? The simulation using 1981 fertility rates but assuming all other inputs to be the same as for 1950–70 gives the proportion of nuclear families as 55.0%. Thus, the fertility decline between 1950–70 and 1981 alone would reduce the proportion of nuclear families by 17.2%.

Note that simulations I to VIII assume the nuptiality and divorce patterns to be constant, as in 1981. This is obviously not the case in reality. But for the purpose of identifying the effects of a foreseeable further decline in fertility and in the desirability of coresidence, we need to control the variables of nuptiality and divorce. The choice of assuming constant nuptiality and divorce can facilitate this purpose.

Now let's consider how changing nuptiality and divorce patterns will affect family size and structure. We modify the inputs of simulations I, II, IV, V, VII, and VIII by increasing the mean age at marriage ($\overline{m}$) and at childbearing ($\hat{m}$) by two years and increasing the divorce level (D) from 1 to 5, while the values of the other parameters remain the same. We call these modified simulations simulations I', II', IV', V', VII', and VIII'. Some of the results of simulations I', II', IV', V', VII', and VIII' are shown in tables 11.4 and 11.5 and are plotted as dotted lines in figures 11.2 and 11.3. The results show that the average family size decreases by 1%–4% and the proportion of nuclear families increases by 2.2%–6.3% as $\overline{m}$ increases by two years and D increases to 5.

The mean ages at marriage have fluctuated around 22.8 since 1977 (22.6 in 1977, 23.1 in 1979, 22.7 in 1982). It is unlikely that the mean age will increase rapidly in the foreseeable future. The divorce level is also expected to increase only gradually. Therefore, the assumptions concerning the possible increase of m and D in simulations I', II', IV', V', VII', and VIII' (m increased by two years, D increased fivefold) are rather extreme. Even so, their effects on family size and structure are not major. We can thus assume that the most important demographic factors affecting Chinese family size and structure will be the decreasing TFR and n_2, rather than m and D.

11.6. Two Opposing Forces

In this section we comment on the above observations drawn from the simulations. With an efficient family-planning network, improved contraceptive services and education, and changing attitudes toward the desired number of children, more and more couples, especially in urban areas and some economically advanced rural areas, wish to have fewer but better educated children. We may expect fertility to continue to fall. We may also expect the mean age at marriage and the divorce level to gradually increase with the process of modernization. Rapid socioeconomic development will gradually reduce the desirability of co-residence. Therefore, the Chinese family size will steadily decrease with the expected decrease in fertility and in the desirability of coresidence.

Will the desirability of coresidence decrease dramatically so that the effect of the remarkable fertility decline will be completely compensated? Our answer is no. To illustrate why we suspect this is unlikely to occur in the near future, we will list and compare two different categories of socioeconomic factors that operate in opposite directions.

The factors that accelerate the decrease in the desirability of coresidence are as follows:

1. Rapid economic development and improvements in education will increase people's demand for a broadening of cultural experience. The growing availability of the mass media (e.g., telephones and television sets) and transportation (e.g., automobiles) will ease communication between family members even if they are not living in the same house or in the same area. With the adoption of a modern life-style, the gap between the young generation and the old generation regarding family life-styles will gradually increase. This change will decrease the desirability of coresidence.

2. Severe housing constraints in the urban areas will be gradually relieved by widespread housing construction, which will allow more young people to live away from their parents.

3. With the relaxation of restrictive policies on migration, the scale of rural-urban and urban-urban migration will become larger. In fact, the Chinese government has permitted, and even encouraged, peasants to go to the towns or cities to invest in shops or enterprises, although the government promotes so-called Li Tu Bu Li Xiang (the transfer from farming to industrial or commercial activities without moving away from the village). The migrants are usually young people. Their elderly parents will either stay in the original place or join the migrants after they have settled down in the new place. Separation (maybe temporary) of some family members is expected, if migration gathers force.

4. With the process of urbanization, the proportion of old people in urban areas who rely on pensions or social security will increase. This will reduce the necessity for elderly parents to live with one of their married children. Of course, a pension cannot be equated with living away from children in China; although the pension system was introduced many years ago for employees working in state or collective enterprises in the urban areas, a considerable majority of elderly urban parents (most of them are entitled to a pension) live with a married child.

Table 11.6. Comparison of family size and structure between better-off
specialized families and ordinary families in rural areas

		Percentage of multigeneration families		
	Average family size	Three generations	More than three generations	Total
Better-off specialized households	6.07	35.15	2.48	37.63
Ordinary households	4.52	22.26	0.98	23.24

Source: A recent survey of 2,036 peasant households in Sichuan Province; see
Zhao Xishun 1985:26–27.

On the other hand, several other factors will be acting in the opposite
direction to the decreasing desirability of coresidence:

1. As indicated in section 2.1.3, the collective mode of production and income distribution suppressed the profitability of maintaining large multigeneration families in the 1950s, 1960s, and 1970s. However, beginning in the early
1980s, under the responsibility system, peasant families became the production
unit instead of part of a production team (for a brief description of the responsibility system, see section 1.1). According to a recent survey of 2,035 peasant
families in Sichuan Province, the so-called better-off specialized households
have a larger average family size and higher proportion of three- (or more than
three) generation families (see table 11.6).

In the urban areas, the number of privately owned small shops, restau-
rants, hotels, and so on has grown very fast in recent years. Up to the end of
1985, the total number of privately owned industrial and commercial enterprises holding an officially issued license was 10.2 million (*People's Daily*,
June 17, 1986), an increase of 25.5% compared with 1984. The total personnel in these privately owned enterprises was 17.6 million, an increase of
34.8% compared with 1984. The total personnel of privately owned industrial and commercial enterprises has exceeded the total number of employees in the state-owned commercial (not including industry) system by more
than 3 million (*People's Daily*, February 23, 1986). The Chinese government
has obviously allocated an increasingly large role to the private sector in the
country's modernization process.

A private enterprise is usually owned and run by people from the same
family, or else they are close relatives. Given the very low levels of automation
in agricultural and private industrial and commercial production, it is profitable
for peasants and urban privately owned industrial and commercial businesses
to maintain larger families to facilitate division of labor and mutual care in
work and daily life among the family members.

2. It is unlikely that the pension system will spread rapidly throughout the rural areas in the foreseeable future. A great majority of the peasants will still depend economically on their children when they are old.

3. Although there is no officially stated government policy promoting three-generation families, there is clear evidence that the Chinese government is in favor of maintaining the three-generation family as a major family type for the sake of upholding a Chinese cultural tradition and due to the economic savings for the state on old age care. For instance, both the New Marriage Law and the current constitution state explicitly that children have full responsibility for caring for their parents in old age. Another example is that a considerable majority of "model families," which are selected and honored by the locals and the community each year, are three-generation families (Liu Yin 1985).

4. Although, on the one hand, the expected rural-urban or urban-urban migration may result in the division of some families, on the other hand, it may result in an increase in the number of extended families because some young migrants may temporarily live with relatives and because rural-urban migration may aggravate the housing shortages in urban areas.

5. The ethical tradition of respecting and caring for the elderly will continue to play an important role in Chinese life. Psychologically speaking, most elderly Chinese parents will continue to dislike being alone and will prefer to have a warm family environment with a married child and grandchildren living with them (Lin and Bi 1984).

The strength of the factors supporting the continued importance of multi-generational families is demonstrated by the persistence of traditional extended families in the Taiwan province of China. It is well known that Taiwan is now an industrial-commercial society. Most families own motorcycles or cars. Universal mass media (e.g., television) link almost everyone to local and international communication networks. The educational system takes more than 95% of all children to the ninth grade. It might have been expected that such changes would greatly hasten Westernization and nuclearization of the family. However, according to the 1973 and 1980 surveys, while there has been a significant decline in the prevalence of extended family types, about 40% of all ever-married women of childbearing age were living in extended families, and a considerable majority of older parents (80% in 1973, 76% in 1980) were living with a married son. A majority of husbands' parents were living with married sons even in the most modern strata: 72% among the best educated, 68%–71% in the big cities (compared with 87%–89% among those living on farms) (Freedman, Chang, and Sun 1982:405).

Table 11.7 shows indices illustrating Taiwan's rapid economic development and the persistence of the extended family. Rapid economic development has been accompanied by some changes in coresidential patterns. However, these familial changes do not replicate the Western nuclear model, as some

Table 11.7. Indicators of economic development and family structure in Taiwan, selected years

Indicators of economic and educational development	Calendar year			
	1952	1960	1972	1979
GNP index[a]	100	176	580	1006
Total industrial production index	100	243	1658	3835
Percentage of population aged 6 and over who are illiterate	42	27	13	11[b]
Percentage of primary school graduates enrolled in junior high school	34	51	84	96
Automobiles per 1,000 population	1.0	2.0	9.3	25.7[b]
Telephones per 1,000 population	3.9	8.6	38.9	122.6[b]
Television sets per 1,000 households	—	—	670	990[b]

Indicators of family structure	Calendar year	
	1973	1980
Percentage of respondents living in nuclear families	60.0	60.6
Percentage of respondents living in extended families	40.0	39.4
Percentage of respondents living in extended families among those with parents available	54.4	48.7
Percentage of respondents' husbands' parents living alone	19.9	24.2

Sources: The data on economic and educational development are from Council for International Economic Cooperation and Development, *Taiwan Statistical Data Book*. The data on family structure for 1973 and 1980 come from two carefully designed samples representing all ever-married women of childbearing age in Taiwan (the respondents are ever-married women of ages 20–39) (Freedman, Chang, and Sun 1982).

[a] At constant 1976 prices adjusted for gain or loss due to changed terms of trade.

[b] 1978 data.

might have anticipated. It is possible that coresidence patterns might merely be lagging—changing more slowly than other aspects of society. It is also worthwhile to point out that the TFR fell from 5.61 in 1961 to 2.67 in 1979 in Taiwan. The effect of the tremendous fertility decline on proportions of nuclear families was not reflected in the 1980 Taiwan survey, because the cohorts born under reduced fertility, who have a much smaller number of siblings, had not yet reached the family formation stage. But when the children born in the late 1960s and the 1970s grow up, the effects of decreased fertility on the proportion of nuclear families will be in the opposite direction to those of modernization.

To summarize, the actual change in Chinese family structure will be the result of two categories of factors acting in opposite directions. We suspect that the average desirability of coresidence in China is not likely to decrease rapidly; instead, it will first remain more or less stable or decrease slowly, and then decrease steadily. On the other hand, the greatly reduced number of births after 1970 will affect family structure in the coming years: when the children born in the 1970s reach the age of family formation, they will have less chance of leaving the parental home to set up an independent nuclear family because they have a much smaller number of siblings than those who are currently in the process of family formation. Thus the proportion of nuclear families will decrease in the near future, given that the desirability of coresidence is not likely to decrease dramatically. However, if fertility drops to below the replacement level, some elderly parents will not be able to live with any married children even if they wish to do so. When the population born under such an extremely low fertility level reaches the age of family formation. At that time, the decreasing fertility will intensify the effect of the gradual reduction in desirability of coresidence, increasing the proportion of nuclear families.

In short, in the foreseeable future the proportion of nuclear families will first decrease and then increase again. Of course, it is still an open question as to what extent and how quickly the Chinese family structure will change. It certainly deserves further study by both sociologists and demographers.

12

How the Remarkable Demographic Differences between the Chinese Countryside and the City May Affect the Family

12.1. Data for 1986 Countryside and City Simulations [1]

The five-year age-specific death rates, the single-year age- and parity-specific occurrence/exposure birth rates, and the single-year age-specific occurrence/exposure rates of first marriage for the 1986 simulations are from the one-percent population survey conducted by the State Statistical Bureau in 1987. In this very large survey, 10.71 million persons were enumerated, covering all provinces, autonomous regions, and municipalities in mainland China (see section 1.2.4).

According to the published total number of divorces and the estimated total number of couples in 1986, we estimated the crude divorce rate, which was about 2 per thousand couples for rural areas and 3 per thousand couples for the cities. Using these estimated crude divorce rates as the input, we derived the age-specific divorce rates from Krishnan and Kayani's model divorce table (Krishnan and Kayani 1976).

The remarriage rates employed in the 1986 simulations are the same as those estimated and used in the 1981 simulations presented in this book because we believe that the remarriage pattern most likely remained more or less stable from 1981 to 1986. The proportions of parents who have married children but do not live with any of them are estimated at 14.0% for rural areas and 39.9% for the cities based on data from a 1987 national survey among the elderly population with a sample size of 36,755 persons aged 60 and over (CASS 1988).

---

1. Although the State Statistical Bureau classifies the areas into three categories: rural (or countryside), town, and city, we have made primarily two family status life tables for the Chinese countryside and the city using 1986 data, because they serve the purpose of our major concern here—namely, to explore rural-urban differences in the changing family life course and structure by focusing on these two extreme categories.

Table 12.1. Percentage distribution of women at selected ages by marital status according to family status life tables: Comparison between rural areas and cities, China, 1986

Age	Area	Never married	Currently married	Currently widowed	Currently divorced	Total
20	Rural	72.0	27.8	0.0	0.2	100.0
	City	87.9	12.0	0.0	0.0	100.0
25	Rural	6.5	92.4	0.3	0.8	100.0
	City	13.4	85.5	0.2	0.9	100.0
30	Rural	2.1	96.4	0.4	1.1	100.0
	City	2.8	95.7	0.3	1.2	100.0
35	Rural	1.0	97.3	0.9	0.9	100.0
	City	1.2	97.0	0.6	1.2	100.0
50	Rural	0.6	91.5	7.0	0.9	100.0
	City	0.8	92.8	5.2	1.3	100.0
65	Rural	0.6	67.6	31.2	1.0	100.0
	City	0.8	70.0	27.8	1.4	100.0
85	Rural	0.6	4.1	94.1	1.2	100.0
	City	0.8	5.6	92.0	1.7	100.0

12.2. Life Course Analysis: Countryside and City Compared

12.2.1. Marital status

Table 12.1 gives the percentage distribution of marital status at selected ages. Almost everyone gets married before age 35 in China. The proportions remaining never married at age 50 in the countryside and cities are all very small (0.6%–0.8%). The pattern of universal marriage is found in both the rural areas and the cities.

The analysis demonstrates that if a cohort of women followed the 1986 age schedules of first marriage, about 28% of rural females would get married before their 20th birthday, the legal minimum age at marriage. If we use the 1981 age-specific occurrence/exposure rates of first marriage as the input, about 20% of the rural women would be married before age 20. This is an increase of 8 percentage points in five years (1981–86) in the number of marriages of women younger than the minimum legal marriage age. The one-percent population survey conducted in mid-1987 demonstrated that 24.5% of 20-year-old rural women were already married at the time of the survey. This finding coincides with the results of the In-Depth Fertility Surveys con-

Table 12.2. Expected duration spent in different marital statuses after birthday x according to family status life tables: Comparison between rural areas and cities, China, 1986

Age x	Area	Never married	Currently married	Currently widowed	Currently divorced	Total
0	Rural	20.8	39.8	9.6	0.5	70.7
	City	22.4	41.3	9.8	0.7	74.2
15	Rural	6.8	41.9	10.1	0.5	59.2
	City	8.0	42.5	10.1	0.7	61.2
25	Rural	0.5	38.5	10.2	0.5	49.6
	City	0.7	40.0	10.2	0.7	51.5
35	Rural	0.3	29.5	10.3	0.4	40.4
	City	0.3	30.9	10.2	0.6	41.9
50	Rural	0.2	16.4	10.3	0.3	27.1
	City	0.2	17.4	10.2	0.4	28.1
65	Rural	0.1	5.6	9.5	0.2	15.4
	City	0.1	6.2	9.6	0.3	16.1

ducted by the State Statistical Bureau in seven provinces and two municipalities in 1985 and 1987 (SSB 1986, 1988b), as well as with the results of a two-per-thousand fertility and contraceptive survey conducted by the State Family Planning Commission in 1988.

The analysis also tells us that if a cohort of women followed the 1986 rates of first marriage in the cities, about 12% would get married before the legal minimum age at marriage. We believe that most cases of early marriages within city administration areas occurred among the farmers or part-time farmers in the suburban areas of the cities.

The expected amounts of life time spent in the currently married and widowed states in both rural areas and cities are more or less the same (see tables 12.2 and 12.3 and figure 12.1). The effects of later marriage on the expected duration of the married and widowed states in the cities is largely compensated by the longer life span of women living in the cities.

The proportion of divorced women and the expected duration of divorce are very small in both the countryside and the cities, but the divorce rate is somewhat higher in Chinese cities than in the countryside.

It is interesting to note that under 1986 mortality and nuptiality regimes, a 65-year-old woman who is a city resident would expect to live 59.4% of her remaining life as a widow. For the rural women, this figure is 61.5%. This is a

Table 12.3. Percentage distribution of expected length of time spent in different marital statuses according to family status life tables: Comparison between rural areas and cities, China, 1986

Age	Area	Never married	Currently married	Currently widowed	Currently divorced	Total
0	Rural	29.5	56.3	13.6	0.7	100.0
	City	30.2	55.7	13.2	0.9	100.0
15	Rural	11.4	70.8	17.0	0.8	100.0
	City	13.0	69.4	16.5	1.1	100.0
25	Rural	1.1	77.5	20.5	0.9	100.0
	City	1.4	77.7	19.7	1.3	100.0
35	Rural	0.7	73.0	25.4	0.9	100.0
	City	0.7	73.7	24.3	1.3	100.0
50	Rural	0.6	60.3	38.1	1.0	100.0
	City	0.6	61.7	36.3	1.4	100.0
65	Rural	0.6	36.9	61.5	1.1	100.0
	City	0.6	38.4	59.4	1.6	100.0

Figure 12.1. Percentage distribution of expected length of time spent in different marital statuses after birthday 15

Figure 12.2. Percentage distribution of expected length of time spent in different marital statuses after birthday 65

useful index for analyzing the social or family support system in the Chinese city and countryside (see figure 12.2).

12.2.2. Parity and the number of children surviving

Table 12.4 and figure 12.3 compare the parity distribution of women in the rural and city life tables. The figures show that even at the rates applying in 1986, a very small proportion of rural females (8%) will have borne only one child by their 50th birthday; about 47% will have borne two children, and 42% will have borne three or more. Therefore, considerable scope exists for a further reduction of fertility, namely, to reduce the proportion of rural women who bear three or more children.

On the other hand, if a cohort of women followed the city rates in 1986, about 61% of them would have borne only one child at age 50, 24% would have borne two children, and 11% three or more. The fertility level in the cities, as shown in table 12.4, is indeed extremely low and should not be further reduced. The policy implications of the extremely low fertility level in the cities will be discussed in detail in the following sections.

The distributions of women by parity reflect both the level and the timing of fertility. However, the number of children who survive is, of course, smaller than the number of children born. Table 12.5 shows proportions of women according to number of surviving children and marital status. Owing to the much lower fertility, there are more urban women with no surviving children than rural women. This phenomenon is even more severe at older ages. For example, at ages 65, 75, and 85 in the city, 6.7%, 8.4%, and 12.5% of the women (including those who never-married) have no surviving children.

Table 12.4. Percentage distribution of women at selected ages by parity according to family status life tables: Comparison between rural areas and cities, China, 1986

Age	Area	Never married	Parity of ever-married women						Total
			0	1	2	3	4	5+	
20	Rural	72.0	20.0	7.3	0.6	0	0	0	100.0
	City	87.9	8.2	3.9	0.1	0	0	0	100.0
25	Rural	6.5	27.0	40.5	22.8	3.1	0.2	0	100.0
	City	13.4	30.1	49.8	5.9	0.7	0	0	100.0
30	Rural	2.1	7.8	23.9	45.6	16.6	3.5	0.5	100.0
	City	2.8	9.5	66.5	15.3	5.0	0.9	0.1	100.0
35	Rural	1.0	4.3	11.8	49.8	24.1	7.2	1.7	100.0
	City	1.2	4.4	63.0	21.7	7.1	2.2	0.4	100.0
50	Rural	0.6	2.6	7.9	47.2	29.5	9.2	3.0	100.0
	City	0.6	3.1	61.0	24.3	7.9	2.5	0.5	100.0

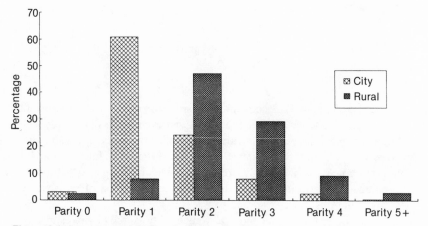

Figure 12.3. Percentage distribution of women at age 50 by parity according to family status life tables, 1986

The percentages of city women who are both childless and widowed are 1.7%, 4.9%, and 11.0% at ages 65, 75, and 85, respectively. There is no doubt at all that the life of an old and childless widow is very difficult in China, where the social support system for the elderly is underdeveloped. The relatively high proportion of childless people among the elderly in the cities is the result of the extremely low fertility (see figure 12.4). Policymakers and society should pay more attention to this phenomenon.

12.2.3. Adult life with responsibility for young children and elderly parents

In rural China, almost all elderly parents are economically dependent on their children. Even in the cities where pension schemes have been introduced, filia-

Table 12.5. Percentage distribution of women by marital status and number of surviving children at selected ages according to family status life tables: Comparison between rural areas and cities, China, 1986

Age	Marital status	Area	No. of surviving children of ever-married women						
			0	1	2	3	4	5+	Total
55	Currently married	Rural	2.8	11.5	40.7	23.1	6.9	1.9	86.8
		City	4.8	54.2	21.0	6.7	2.0	0.4	89.0
	Currently widowed	Rural	0.4	1.6	5.5	3.0	0.9	0.2	11.7
		City	0.5	5.7	2.2	0.7	0.2	0.0	9.3
	Currently divorced	Rural	0.0	0.1	0.4	0.2	0.1	0.0	0.8
		City	0.1	0.7	0.3	0.1	0.0	0.0	1.1
65	Currently married	Rural	2.3	10.0	31.2	17.2	5.1	1.3	67.2
		City	4.3	42.6	16.4	5.1	1.5	0.3	70.2
	Currently widowed	Rural	1.1	4.7	14.5	7.9	2.3	0.6	31.2
		City	1.7	16.9	6.5	2.0	0.6	0.1	27.8
	Currently divorced	Rural	0.0	0.2	0.5	0.3	0.1	0.0	1.0
		City	0.1	0.9	0.3	0.1	0.0	0.0	1.4
75	Currently married	Rural	1.3	5.9	15.2	7.9	2.3	0.5	33.1
		City	2.8	21.5	8.1	2.5	0.7	0.1	35.7
	Currently widowed	Rural	2.7	11.6	29.8	15.5	4.4	1.1	65.1
		City	4.9	37.3	14.1	4.3	1.2	0.2	62.0
	Currently divorced	Rural	0.1	0.2	0.5	0.3	0.1	0.0	1.2
		City	0.1	1.0	0.4	0.1	0.0	0.0	1.7
85	Currently married	Rural	0.2	1.0	2.0	0.8	0.2	0.1	4.1
		City	0.7	3.4	1.2	0.4	0.1	0.0	5.8
	Currently widowed	Rural	5.3	21.8	41.4	19.5	5.1	1.1	94.1
		City	11.0	54.0	19.5	5.7	1.5	0.3	91.9
	Currently divorced	Rural	0.1	0.2	0.5	0.3	0.1	0.0	1.2
		City	0.2	1.0	0.4	0.1	0.0	0.0	1.7

tion remains a cornerstone of society and the great majority of the elderly enjoy living with one of their married children. Even those married children who live apart from their parents maintain strong economic and emotional ties with them. It is therefore of interest to estimate the proportion of women of different ages who have surviving parents, as well as the proportion of women who have surviving children. For how long will a woman be obliged to care

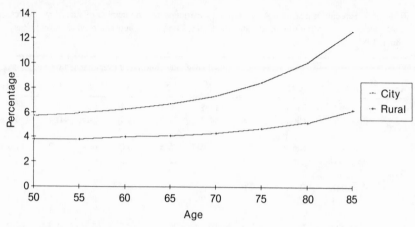

Figure 12.4. Percentage distribution of women of all marital statuses who have no surviving children according to family status life tables, 1986

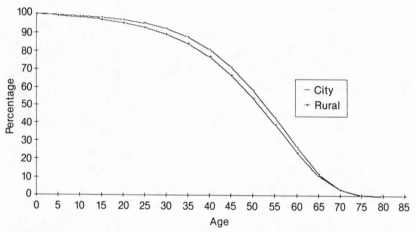

Figure 12.5. Percentage distribution of women having a surviving mother according to family status life tables, 1986

for an elderly parent and how many children of different ages will she have to look after? How are these proportions affected by changes and differences in fertility and mortality in rural areas and cities?

In figure 12.5, we show the proportions of women of different ages whose mothers are still alive. Table 12.6 and figure 12.6 give the expected adult life (beyond age 15) with parents of whatever age. Not surprisingly, the proportions of city women whose mothers are still alive and the time they spend in the

Table 12.6. Expected years of adult life (beyond age 15) with surviving parent(s) according to family status life tables: Comparison between rural areas and cities, China, 1986

	Rural areas	City
Surviving mother	33.0 (55.7%)	34.9 (57.0%)
Surviving parent(s)	37.5 (63.5%)	39.0 (63.8%)
Both parents alive	22.5 (38.0%)	24.4 (39.8%)

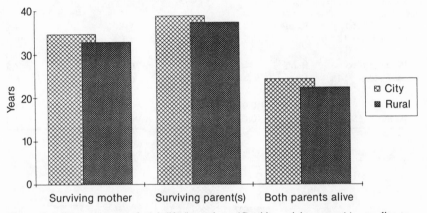

Figure 12.6. Expected years of adult life (beyond age 15) with surviving parent(s) according to family status life tables, 1986

state "having parents alive" are somewhat higher than those of rural women, because of the lower mortality level in the city.

Since only elderly parents (those who have reached age 65) and young children (those who have not yet passed their 18th birthdays) need care, we shall consider how many years a 15-year-old girl may expect to live with a surviving elderly parent or as a mother of young children (see table 12.7 and figure 12.7). The 1986 rates imply that a 15-year-old girl's expected time spent as a mother of young children (< 18 years old) in the cities would be 3.5 years, or 16.7%, less than for their rural counterparts. However, due to the relatively lower mortality levels in the cities, city women spend a longer period of time with elderly parents. The number of years of overload, that is the expected number of years during which a woman has to care for both elderly parent(s) and young children, is smaller in the city than in the countryside, due to the higher rates of fertility (after compensation for higher mortality) in rural areas.

Table 12.7. Expected years of adult life (beyond age 15) spent with responsibility for dependents according to family status life tables: Comparison between rural areas and cities, China, 1986

	Area	Never married	Currently married	Currently widowed	Currently divorced	Total
Parent(s) > 65	Rural	0.1	14.2	1.1	0.1	15.7
	City	0.2	15.7	1.0	0.2	17.1
Children < 18	Rural	—	21.2	0.4	0.2	21.8
	City	—	17.9	0.2	0.2	18.3
Parent(s) > 65	Rural	0.1	28.1	1.4	0.2	29.8
or children < 18	City	0.2	27.7	1.1	0.3	29.3
Parent(s) > 65	Rural	—	7.3	0.2	0.1	7.6
and children < 18	City	—	5.9	0.1	0.1	6.1
Both	Rural	0.0	3.0	0.2	0.03	3.2
parents > 65	City	0.03	3.8	0.2	0.05	4.0

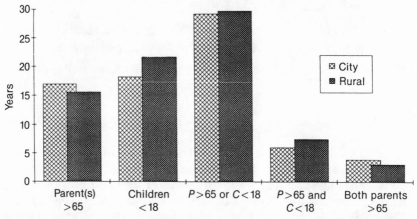

Figure 12.7. Expected years of adult life (beyond age 15) spent with responsibility for dependents according to family status life tables, 1986

12.3. Family Size and Structure of the Life Table Population: Countryside and City Compared

12.3.1. Family size

As mentioned in the Introduction, the output of the family status life table simulations, including the figures of family size and structure presented in this and the following sections, is neither a reflection of the past or the cur-

Table 12.8. Average family size by family type and marital status of mother according to family status life tables: Comparison between rural areas and cities, China, 1986

Family type	Area	Husband-wife	Widowed mother	Divorced mother	Total
Nuclear	Rural	3.48	2.80	3.10	3.47
	City	2.72	2.29	2.33	2.71
Three-generation	Rural	5.53	3.77	4.38	5.46
	City	5.02	3.46	3.65	4.96

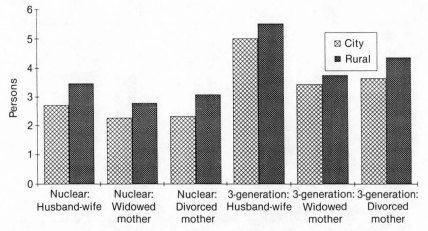

Figure 12.8. Average family size by family type and marital status of mother according to family status life tables, 1986

rent family size and structure nor an accurate projection for the future. The simulations describe the effects on a synthetic cohort experiencing the observed period rates.

The average sizes of families of various types under the city rates are all significantly smaller than their rural counterparts (see table 12.8 and figure 12.8). Two major factors may explain this large difference between the city and the countryside. One is that the city family has far fewer children and the other is that in the city many more elderly prefer to live apart from their children.

12.3.2. Family structure

According to the 1986 family status life tables, the proportion of nuclear families (plus one-person households) is 45.6% under the rural rates versus 76.9% under the city rates. Nuclear families with a widowed or divorced mother con-

Table 12.9. Percentage distribution of family type by marital status of mother (or childless woman) according to family status life tables: Comparison between rural areas and cities, China, 1986

Family type	Area	One-woman	Husband-wife	Widowed mother	Divorced mother	Total
Nuclear	Rural	7.9	37.0	0.5	0.2	45.6
	City	20.5	55.3	0.7	0.3	76.9
Three-generation	Rural	—	52.2	1.8	0.5	54.5
	City	—	22.2	0.6	0.3	23.1
Total	Rural	7.9	89.2	8.4	0.9	100.0
	City	20.5	77.2	20.1	1.3	100.0

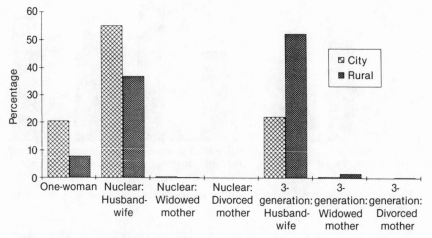

Figure 12.9. Percentage distribution of family types by marital status of mother according to family status life tables, 1986

stitute 0.7% of the total under the rural rates and 1.0% under the city rates. Three-generation families with a widowed or divorced mother account for 2.3% under the rural rates and 0.9% under the city rates (see table 12.9 and figure 12.9). Clearly, "incomplete families" accounted for a small proportion of the total both in the countryside and in the city.

The great majority of families are "complete families," consisting of a husband and a wife (plus children and/or one or two grandparents). Families with a couple and grandparent(s) either present or absent account for 89.2% under the rural rates and 77.2% under the city rates. The proportion of one-woman households under 1986 city rates is 20.5% versus 7.9% under 1986 rural rates. About 90% of the women of one-woman households are aged 60 or over 60, under the city rates. This figure is about 76% under the rural rates.

In the implied stable female population applying the 1986 city rates, the percentage of elderly aged 60 and over is about 36%, of whom about 40% would live alone. The percentage of elderly aged 60 and over under 1986 rural rates is about 18%, of whom only 12% would live alone. The remarkably higher proportion of one-woman households in the city can be explained by socioeconomic and demographic factors. The proportion of elderly who do not wish to live with their children in Chinese cities is much higher than that in the countryside. Furthermore, since the number of members of the children's generation is smaller than that of the parents' generation in Chinese cities, assuming that the current fertility level persists, some parents have to live away from their married children even if they do not wish to do so, because of the shortage of children in the city population.

12.4. Discussion: Policy Implications

As indicated in the previous sections, the observed 1986 demographic rates imply that if a cohort of women followed the 1986 age schedules of first marriage, about 28% of the rural females would get married before their 20th birthday, which is the legal minimum age at marriage. In current Chinese society, especially in rural areas, almost no one uses contraceptives immediately after marriage, so that early marriage certainly results in early childbearing, which is one of the reasons why fertility rates increased in 1986 and 1987. It is therefore very important and imperative that policymakers and society put more effort into publicizing the advantages of late marriage and giving more economic incentives to encourage late marriage and discourage early marriage.

The analysis demonstrates that under the 1986 rates, about 8% of rural women would have borne only one child, 47% would have borne two children, and about 42% would have borne three or more during their entire lives. This means that on average each woman would have more than two and a half children. By contrast, the 1986 rates imply that the majority (61%) of city women would bear only one child during their entire lives, and on average each woman would have about one and a half children, which is indeed extremely low. Many demographers have warned about the quick process of population aging and its socioeconomic implications in China.[2] In this study, we focus on comparing the implications of demographic conditions on the family in the Chinese country-

2. For example, Judith Banister projected that the number of people age 60 and over will increase from 77 million counted in 1982 to about 298 million in 2025 and further to 430 million by the year 2050; even assuming a two-child policy in both urban and rural areas after the turn of the century, the proportion of elderly aged 65 and over will increase to 14% in 2025 and 22% in 2050 (Banister 1989).

side and cities. The tendency for the extremely low urban fertility levels to raise the number of elderly people living alone, due to a shortage of children in the future, has been confirmed quantitatively by our study. As mentioned in the previous section, if the 1986 city fertility rate remained constant for a long time, women aged 60 and above would account for about 36% of the total stable female population. Of those elderly females, about 40% would live alone. A little further calculation tells us that 14.4% of the total female population will be elderly living alone. Clearly, because of the extremely low fertility in Chinese cities, severe future population aging in the urban areas is likely, unless counteracted by rising fertility and immigration of young people from rural areas. To avoid or mitigate the serious problems resulting from aging—such as labor force shortages and the heavy burden of caring for too many elderly—it seems necessary to change the urban birth-planning policy to a two-child policy with birth spacing, and this should be accomplished at the latest by the turn of the century. We should also encourage young rural people to migrate to the small and medium-sized towns and cities. For the rural areas, action should also be taken: on the one hand, to reduce the proportion of births of order 3 and higher and, on the other hand, to gradually adopt a two-child policy with birth spacing before the end of this century.

Conclusions

The overview in Part I of this volume presents a demographic profile of family dynamics in China that includes observed family size and structure and their determinants, such as the level and age patterns of nuptiality, fertility, and mortality. The Chinese family has become a smaller unit and is more likely to be a nuclear family, compared with what it used to be. It is very impressive that fertility and mortality have been remarkably reduced, and marriage has been delayed, compared with the 1950s and 1960s.

In Part III, we applied the family status life table model developed in Part II to observed or estimated Chinese data for 1981 and 1950–70 to investigate how the tremendous change in fertility, marriage, and mortality would affect people's family life course and to ascertain what would be the implications of two completely different sets of demographic rates in 1981 and 1950–70 on changing family size and structure. A rural-urban comparative analysis using the most recent available data of 1986 was also performed. Some more impressive and more interpretable measurements, compared with the conventional measurements in Part I, have been derived through the application of our model.

According to the family status life tables, a girl who survives to age 15 would expect to live 2.4 years more in the never-married status and spend 8 years more in the currently married status during the rest of her life under the 1981 rates than under the 1950–70 rates.

The proportion of 50-year-old women of parity higher than 3 would be 3.9 times as high under the 1950–70 rates as under the 1981 rates. Under the 1950–70 rates, a cohort member surviving to age 15 is likely to spend about 25 years (76.9% of the rest of her life) with at least one surviving child under age 18, 50% of which will be spent with more than two children. A 15-year-old cohort member who experiences 1981 rates would expect to spend 22 years (only 37.9% of the rest of her life) with at least one child under 18 years old, of which only 22% will be spent with more than two. The number and the proportion of years of overload (with simultaneous responsibilities to an elderly

165

parent or parents over 65 and young children under 18) irrespective of the number of young children is somewhat larger under the 1981 rates than under 1950 conditions due to the extended life span in 1981. However, the proportion of a woman's lifetime beyond age 15 spent in the very heavy overload condition (with parent or parents over 65 and more than two children under 18) under the 1950–70 rates is about 2 times as high as that under the 1981 rates because of the much higher fertility in 1950–70.

Clearly, the family status life table is a very good tool for investigating the family life course. However, perhaps the most impressive results of our family status life table model concern family size, number of generations, marital status, and age of female members (or reference person) of the family. The model output shows how decreasing fertility may reduce family size. Another extremely interesting finding of this exercise is that when young people born after the tremendous fertility decline reach the age of family formation, given that certain proportions of parents wish to live with one of their married children, they will have a much smaller chance of forming an independent nuclear family since they have a much smaller number of siblings; thus the proportion of nuclear families will decrease. If, however, fertility continues to fall after reaching the replacement level, this further reduction in the birth rate will raise the proportion of nuclear families. In that case, some parents will find it impossible to live with their married children even if they wish to do so, because of the shortage of children.

The simulations tell us that because of the remarkably decreased fertility, the average family size would be reduced by about 11% and the proportion of nuclear families would be brought down by about 20 percentage points under the 1981 rates compared with what would be found under the 1950–70 rates. Our findings also show that the majority of Chinese families are "complete families" of the husband-wife type and this feature has remained stable.

Based on the insights or better understanding obtained from our model outputs and the sociological considerations, we suspect that fertility and mortality will continue to decline, the mean age at marriage and the divorce level will gradually increase, and the desirability of coresidence between parents and one of their married children will probably first remain stable or decrease slowly and then decrease steadily. Therefore, the average family size will steadily decrease, and the proportion of nuclear families will at first decrease, when children born in the 1970s and the early 1980s grow up, because they will have less chance of moving out of the parental home to form independent nuclear families. After the period of the dominant effect of the tremendous fertility decline of the 1970s and early 1980s, the proportion of nuclear families will again increase due to a decrease in the desirability of coresidence and a further decrease in fertility, possibly below the replacement level. The degree of change and the rate of change deserve further study.

As indicated in the rural-urban comparative analysis using the family status life table (chapter 12), if a cohort of women were to follow the 1986 age schedules of first marriage, about 28% of rural females would get married before their 20th birthday, the legal minimum age at marriage. The analytical results show that, surprisingly, the incidence of illegal early marriage is increasing. It is therefore imperative that policymakers expedite efforts to publicize the advantages of late marriage.

At the rates applying in 1986, a very small proportion of rural females (8%) will have borne only one child by their 50th birthday, about 47% will have borne two children, and 42% will have borne three or more. Therefore, considerable scope exists for a further reduction of fertility, and the family-planning program should be strengthened to reduce the proportion of births of order 3 and higher in rural areas.

The analysis demonstrates that the observed 1986 age- and parity-specific birth rates imply that the majority (61%) of city women would bear only one child during their lifetimes and that 24% and 11% of the women would have two and three children, respectively. Owing to the much lower fertility level, the proportion of elderly women who have no surviving children is significantly higher in the cities than in the countryside. This phenomenon is even more severe at very old ages. For example, at ages 75 and 85 in the cities, 8.4% and 12.5% of the women have no surviving children. The percentages of city women who are both childless and widowed are 4.9% and 11.0% at ages 75 and 85, respectively.

Our study has also shown that the extremely low city fertility levels will increase the proportion of elderly people living alone among the total population due to a shortage of children in the future. If the 1986 city fertility rate remained constant for a long time, the women aged 60 and over would account for 36% of the total stable female population. Among those elderly females, about 40% would live alone.

There is no doubt at all that the life of childless elderly people is very difficult in China, where the social support system for the old is underdeveloped. Unless counteracted by rising fertility and immigration of young people from rural areas, we may expect severe problems in the cities caused by population aging. It seems necessary to gradually adjust the birth-planning policy to a two-child policy with birth spacing by the turn of the century at latest. We should also encourage young rural people to migrate to the small and medium-sized towns and cities.

The impressive and plausible outcome of our model encourages us to have confidence in its strength. As indicated by Bongaarts in his original, innovative work, the family status life table model allows us to estimate the number, size, and structure of families in the life table population. The proportion of women in different family states and the average duration in each state can also be estimated. The model can be used to make detailed analyses of the effects of various proximate determinants (fertility, mortality, marriage, divorce, remarriage, children leaving parental home, and so on) on family composition and on the timing and quantity of life course events. It also yields sound results applicable to population and social policy decisions.

Compared with Bongaarts' original nuclear family status life table model, the major contribution of our extended model is that it accounts for both nuclear families and three-generation families. The three-generation family is an important family type in Asian and Third World societies. To introduce three-generation families into the model, the concept of the *marker,* first put forward by Brass, has been elaborated, and the associated estimation procedures have been suggested. The family status life table has been generalized to a stable population model, which gives the distribution of family types by size, number of generations, and marital status of the female members. The general family status life table model developed in this book is applicable to both developing countries and industrial populations (e.g., S. Wijewickrema applied the model to Belgian data [1987]).

A future research project may be to incorporate a stochastic process and competing risks theories into the family status life table model (Willekens 1988, 1989).

With respect to the application of the model, some more sophisticated techniques to estimate indirectly the occurrence/exposure rates of age- and parity-specific fertility, marital status change, and children leaving the parental home when the direct data are not available also deserve attention in future studies. In the cases in which direct or indirect estimates of the input rates are not available, the demographic model schedules are needed. The program developed by the author for the family status life table analysis has included a few model schedules such as an age- and parity-specific fertility model schedule and nuptiality and divorce model schedules as well as the Coale-Demeny model life tables and United Nations model life tables for developing countries. However, the model schedule of remarriage is not yet available. Further study of existing model schedules of divorce and nuptiality is needed to account for the situation in developing countries.

Yet another important practical extension of the family status life table model (with, of course, a number of methodological innovations) would be the projection of future trends in family size and composition. The current version of our family status life table is a female-dominant, one-sex model. It cannot account for the families in which there are no adult (over 18 years old) female members. This is a reasonable approximation for the purpose of the life table analysis since families lacking an adult female are uncommon. If, however, one wants to extend the family status life table model into a family projection model, some mechanism to resolve the problems of two sexes is necessary. For example, the number of married men should equal the number of married women (Keilman 1985a, 1985c; Imhoff 1988).

In terms of its application to China, we performed comparative analyses along a time dimension (1950–70 compared with 1981) and along a spatial dimension (countryside compared with city). Because China is such a large and heterogeneous country, we may need more comparative studies for different provinces or regions as well as for different ethnic groups.

Appendices
Bibliography
Indexes

Appendix 1. The Mathematics of the Multistate Marital Status Life Table

The marital status system

Define $m_{ij}(x)$ as the occurrence/exposure rate of the transition from state i to j $(i,j = 1, 2, \ldots, N)$ between exact ages x and exact ages $x + h$. The death rate between exact ages x and $x + h$ in state i is denoted by $d_i(x)$. The marital status system can be formulated as shown in figure A1.1 if we distinguish four marital states—never married, currently married, widowed, divorced—and one absorbing state—death.

Estimation of transition probabilities

The first step in constructing a multistate increment/decrement life table is to estimate the transition probabilities. A rich set of papers on the estimation of transition probabilities has been published: for example, Schoen 1975; Rogers and Ledent 1976; Ledent 1980, 1982; Hoem and Funck Jensen 1982; and Willekens 1983, 1987. Here, we discuss only the approach using occurrence/exposure rates.

We may arrange the rates $m_{ij}(x)$ and $d_i(x)$ $(i,j = 1, 2, \ldots, N)$ into matrix form:

$$\mathbf{m}(x) =$$

$$
\begin{bmatrix}
d_1(x) + \sum_{j \neq 1} m_{1j}(x) & -m_{21}(x) & \ldots & -m_{N1}(x) \\
-m_{12}(x) & d_2(x) + \sum_{j \neq 2} m_{2j}(x) & \ldots & -m_{N2}(x) \\
\cdot & \cdot & \ldots & \cdot \\
\cdot & \cdot & \ldots & \cdot \\
\cdot & \cdot & \ldots & \cdot \\
-m_{1N}(x) & -m_{2N}(x) & \ldots & d_N(x) + \sum_{j \neq N} m_{Nj}(x)
\end{bmatrix}
$$

Define $p_{ij}(x)$ as the probability that a cohort member who is in state i at exact age x will be in state j at exact age $x + h$:

$$
\mathbf{p}(x) =
\begin{bmatrix}
p_{11}(x) & p_{21}(x) & \ldots & p_{N1}(x) \\
p_{12}(x) & p_{22}(x) & \ldots & p_{N2}(x) \\
\cdot & \cdot & \ldots & \cdot \\
\cdot & \cdot & \ldots & \cdot \\
\cdot & \cdot & \ldots & \cdot \\
p_{1N}(x) & p_{2N}(x) & \ldots & p_{NN}(x)
\end{bmatrix}
$$

173

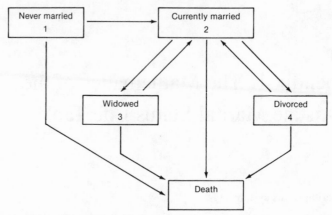

Figure A1.1. The marital status system
Source: Willekens et al. 1982:132.

Denote $_{iy}l_j(x)$ as the number of persons in state i at age y who will be in state j at age x $(x \geq y)$ $(i, j = 1, 2, \ldots, N; y$ could be 0 or any other interested age):

$$_y\mathbf{l}(x) = \begin{bmatrix} _{1y}l_1(x) & _{2y}l_1(x) & \cdots & _{Ny}l_1(x) \\ _{1y}l_2(x) & _{2y}l_2(x) & \cdots & _{Ny}l_2(x) \\ \cdot & \cdot & \cdots & \cdot \\ \cdot & \cdot & \cdots & \cdot \\ \cdot & \cdot & \cdots & \cdot \\ _{1y}l_N(x) & _{2y}l_N(x) & \cdots & _{Ny}l_N(x) \end{bmatrix},$$

$$_y\mathbf{l}(x + h) = \mathbf{p}(x)_y\mathbf{l}(x). \tag{A1.1}$$

If $_y\mathbf{l}(x)$ is nonsingular,

$$\mathbf{P}(x) = _y\mathbf{l}(x + h)_y\mathbf{l}^{-1}(x). \tag{A1.2}$$

Denote $_{iy}L_j(x)$ as the number of person-years lived in state j between ages x and $x + h$ for persons who are in state i at age y. The matrix $_y\mathbf{L}(x)$ has the same configuration as matrix $_y\mathbf{l}(x)$.

$$_y\mathbf{l}(x + h) - _y\mathbf{l}(x) = -\mathbf{m}(x)_y\mathbf{L}(x). \tag{A1.3}$$

Substitute equation (A1.1) into (A1.3):

$$\mathbf{p}(x) = \mathbf{I} - \mathbf{m}(x)_y\mathbf{L}(x)_y\mathbf{l}^{-1}(x), \tag{A1.4}$$

where $\mathbf{I}$ is the identity matrix.

Based on the assumption of a uniform distribution of events between ages x and $x + h$, we may write

$$_y\mathbf{L}(x) = \tfrac{1}{2}h[_y\mathbf{l}(x) + {}_y\mathbf{l}(x + h)].\tag{A1.5}$$

Substitution of equation (A1.5) into equation (A1.4) gives the formula (Rogers and Ledent 1976)

$$\mathbf{p}(x) = [\mathbf{I} + \tfrac{1}{2}h\mathbf{m}(x)]^{-1}[\mathbf{I} - \tfrac{1}{2}h\mathbf{m}(x)].\tag{A1.6}$$

If we assume a constant intensity between ages x and $x + h$, we can derive the formula (see Krishnamoorthy 1979; Willekens 1983; or Nour and Suchindran 1984a)

$$\mathbf{p}(x) = \mathbf{e}^{-h\mathbf{m}(x)}\tag{A1.7}$$

For age interval 0–1, no marital status transition occurs, so that all transition probabilities are equal to 0 except $p_{11}(0)$, which is the probability of surviving up to exact age 1. Note that most infant deaths occur during the first few days after birth due to congenital malformations and diseases of the newly born; deaths are not distributed uniformly over the first year of life. The formula (A1.6) for estimating transition probabilities, which is based on the assumption of a uniform distribution of events, is not valid for the first year of life. We adapt a better approximation for $_1q_0$, the probability of dying before reaching exact age 1 (Wunsch and Termote 1978:93):

$$_1q_0 = 2_1d_0/(2 + 1.82_1d_0),\tag{A1.8}$$

where $_1d_0$ is the death rate between exact ages 0 and 1. Thus,

$$P_{11}(0) = 1 - {}_1q_0,\tag{A1.9}$$

when $P_{ij}(0) = 0$ $(i \neq j)$, $P_{ii}(0) = 0$ $(i \neq 1)$.

Person-years lived

$0 < x < Z$. The last open-ended age-group will be denoted by Z. When x lies between ages 0 and Z, the assumption of a uniform distribution of events between ages x and $x + h$ leads to

$$_y\mathbf{L}(x) = \tfrac{1}{2}h[_y\mathbf{l}(x) + {}_y\mathbf{l}(x + h)].\tag{A1.10}$$

$x = 0$. A better approximation of the number of person-years lived for the first year of age is

$$_0L_1(0) = k''l_0 + k'l_1,\tag{A1.11}$$

$_0L_i(0) = 0$ $(i \neq 1)$ and where l_0 and l_1 are the number of survivors at exact ages 0 and 1, respectively.

When infant mortality is low (i.e., roughly a probability of dying of 100‰ or less), the separation factors are approximately equal to $k' = 3/4$ and $k'' = 1/4$. When infant mortality is high, better separation factors can be obtained by taking $k' = 2/3$ and $k'' = 1/3$ (Wunsch and Termote 1978:81).

$x = Z$. A common procedure for calculating the expectation of life at the first age of the last open-ended age-group is to calculate the reciprocal of the death rate among persons over the age in question. We assume that no events of first marriage, divorce, or remarriage occur after this very advanced age. The number of person-years lived in a currently married status beyond age Z, $L_2(Z)$ is equal to $l_2(Z)$ times the balance of the total life expectancy at age Z of women who are currently married at age Z minus their life expectancy in the widowed status (which can be approximated as the difference between the female total life expectancy at age Z), those who are currently married at age Z, and the male total life expectancy at age $Z + c$ (c being the difference between the mean age at marriage of males and females). The number of person-years lived in the widowed state over age Z, $L_3(Z)$, is equal to the product of $l_3(Z)$ and the life expectancy of a widow at age Z plus the product of $l_2(Z)$ and the life expectancy in the widowed state of women who are currently married at age Z.

Let $d_m(Z)$ denote the death rate among females of age Z and higher in marital status m, and let $d'_m(Z + c)$ denote the death rate among males of age $Z + c$ and higher in marital status m; then

$$L_2(Z) = \left[\frac{1}{d_2(Z)} - \left(\frac{1}{d_2(Z)} - \frac{1}{d'_2(Z + c)} \right) \right] l_2(Z)$$

$$= \frac{1}{d'_2(Z + c)} l_2(Z), \tag{A1.12}$$

$$L_3(Z) = \frac{1}{d_3(Z)} l_3(Z) + \left[\frac{1}{d_2(Z)} - \frac{1}{d'_2(Z + c)} \right] l_2(Z), \tag{A1.13}$$

$$L_1(Z) = \frac{1}{d_1(Z)} l_1(Z), \tag{A1.14}$$

$$L_4(Z) = \frac{1}{d_4(Z)} l_4(Z). \tag{A1.15}$$

Number of events

Given $_y L(x)$, we can easily calculate the life table events. Denote the number of events of the $i - j$ movement occurring between ages x and $x + h$ to the cohort members who are in marital status i at age x and in marital status k at age y as $_{ky}O_{ij}(x)$:

$$_{ky}O_{ij}(x) = {}_{ky}L_i(x)m_{ij}(x). \tag{A1.16}$$

Life expectancy

The sum of $_y L$ matrices over all ages greater than x yields the total number of person-years lived beyond age x:

$$_y T(x) = \sum_{t=x}^{z} {}_y L(t). \tag{A1.17}$$

The life expectancy at age x is

$$_y e(x) = {}_y T(x) {}_y l(x)^{-1*} \tag{A1.18}$$

The quantity $_y l(x) \Sigma_k^*$ is a diagonal matrix with diagonal element $\Sigma_k \, _{iy} l_k(x)$. Its inverse is also a diagonal matrix with the inverse of the diagonal element: $1/\Sigma_k \, _{iy} l_k(x)$. If there are empty state(s) at age y, the corresponding diagonal element(s) of $_y l(x)$ will be 0. The asterisk in formula (A1.18) indicates that we only inverse the non-zero diagonal elements and keep the zero diagonal element(s) as they are. Changing y yields two kinds of life expectancies.

1. *Population-based measure of life expectancy.* This is the life expectancy by initial state of the cohort when $y = 0$ or $y \leq a$, where 0 is the age at birth and a is the minimum age at which the transitions can occur, such as the minimum age at marriage. This measure gives the expectation of life at age x by the initial state of the cohort without reference to the state occupied by the cohort member at age x. Since all the cohort members can only be in the never-married state at age 0 or at any other age that is less than or equal to the minimum age at marriage, the matrix $_y l(x)$ has only one nonzero column and the life expectancies calculated by formula (A1.18) in fact refer to an average member of the entire population studied. We therefore call it a "population-based measure of life expectancy."

2. *Marital status–based measure of life expectancy.* This measure is the life expectancy, by state, at age $y = c$ $(x \geq c > a)$ and enables one to investigate how the life expectancy at age x varies among people who are in a different state at age c without referring to their initial state at age 0 or a. For instance, the time spent in the married state by widowed people of age 20, say, is obviously shorter than that of married people of the same age. How big this difference is and how widowed people differ from divorced people depend on how popular remarriage is and on the extent to which remarriage by widows differs from remarriage by divorcees. Calculation of the life expectancy by marital status of the cohort member at a given age (greater than the minimum age at marriage, e.g., 20) is therefore very useful when exploring these differences.

Note that the family status life table model in this study considers only the population-based measure of life expectancy.

Appendix 2. Estimation of Remarriage Rates

The estimated male life expectancies at birth ($e^{(m)}$) and the divorce level (D) for different periods between years 1947 and 1982 based on the data mentioned in section 9.5 are shown in figure A2.1. The age-specific first-marriage data between 1950 and 1981, which are also *cohort data*, can be found in CPIC (1984, pp. 174–176).

The estimation procedure proposed here basically assumes that remarriage rates have remained constant in the past 35 years (for the reasoning behind this assumption, see section 2.2.4), but it allows for changes in the first-marriage, mortality, and divorce levels. The estimation procedure consists of the follow steps:

a. Predict the proportion of widowed and divorced females for cohorts whose members are 20–24 years old at the time of the census if there had been no remarriages. To do this, we use the same computer program as for the construction of the multi-state marital status life tables, but we set remarriage rates from age 15–24 equal to 0 and death rates of the surviving cohort members equal to 0 because they were living at the time of the census. The other input data are the cohort first-marriage occurrence/ exposure rates, which are derived from published first-marriage data of the 1982 nation-wide fertility survey. Widowhood rates of these cohorts are derived from proper period male life tables taking into account age differences at marriage for males and females. Divorce rates are derived from proper model divorce tables for each period based on the released yearly number of divorces in China.

The execution of the computer program using the above input data shows that, of 100,000 women aged 20–24 who were living at the census time, 108 women (0.108%) would be widowed and 340 women (0.34%) would be divorced if no remarriage had taken place at all. The observed proportions of widowed and divorced at the time of the census are 0.0486% and 0.1648%, respectively. Applying these observed proportions of widowed and divorced to a cohort of 100,000, only 49 and 165 out of 100,000 would actually be widowed and divorced at age 20–24 at the time of the census. We therefore found that the number of remarriages by widows is $108 - 49 = 59$, and by divorcees is $340 - 165 = 175$ between ages 15–20 and 20–24 for these 100,000 cohort members.

The next question is how to estimate person-years lived in the widowed and divorced state. If we had already taken into account both increment (occurrence of widowhood or divorce) and decrement (deaths, remarriages of widows or divorcees), the person-years lived in the widowed or divorced state can be approximated as $0.5h$ times the

178

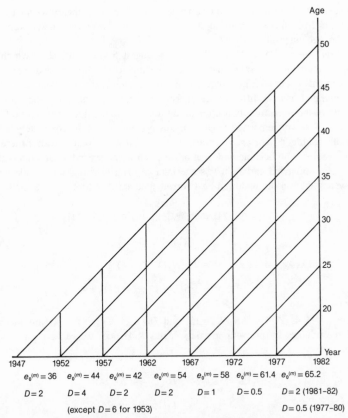

Figure A2.1. Estimated parameters for the indirect estimation of remarriage rates
Sources: $e^{(m)}$ = life expectancy at birth for males; values are taken from Brass 1984. D = divorce level, defined as the number of divorces per 1,000 married couples per year; calculated from the data presented by Li Ning 1985. The data on first marriages for different periods for each cohort are from the one-per-thousand fertility survey (CPIC 1984). The age-specific proportions of widowed and divorced people in mid-1982 are the census figures.

sum of the number of widowed or divorced women at the beginning and end of the age interval based on a linear assumption, where h is the length of the age interval (see, e.g., Willekens et al. 1982:136).

$$L_i(X) = 0.5h[N_i(X) + N_i(X + h)] \qquad (i = 3, 4). \qquad (A2.1)$$

However, the current calculation gives the number of widowed or divorced, $N_i'(X)$ and $N_i'(X + 5)$, if no remarriage occurred in the age interval. Substituting $N_i'(X)$ and $N_i'(X + 5)$ for $N_i(x)$ and $N_i(x + 5)$ in formula (A2.1) overestimates the number of person-years lived in the widowed or divorced state. We must, therefore, subtract the person-years lived in the remarried state by the women who were newly remarried during the age interval.

Since age interval (15–19; 20–24) is the youngest 5-year interval in which first marriage, widowhood, divorce, and remarriage can occur, and since widowhood and divorce can only occur after first marriage, we may assume that widowhood and divorce are concentrated in three-fifths of the interval and that remarriage is concentrated in the middle of the remaining two-fifths of the interval, so that the average duration of remarriage of newly remarried women in this age interval is approximately 1 year. For the other, older 5-year age intervals, we assume it is 1.5 years because there may be some women who became widowed or divorced in the preceding age interval and subsequently remarried earlier in this age interval. The formulas for calculating the person-years lived in the widowed or divorced state are therefore

$$L_i(15\text{–}19; 20\text{–}24) = 2.5[N'_i(15\text{–}19) + N'_i(20\text{–}24)]$$

$$- U_i(15\text{–}19; 20\text{–}24), \tag{A2.2}$$

$$L_i(X, X + 4; Y, Y + 4) = 2.5[N'_i(X, X + 4) + N'_i(Y, Y + 4)]$$

$$- 1.5U_i(X, X + 4; Y, Y + 4). \tag{A2.3}$$

Where $i = 3, 4$, $Y = X + 5$, $X > 15$, and $U_i(X, X + 4; Y, Y + 4)$ are the numbers of remarriages by previous marriage status i. Hence, we can estimate the remarriage rates:

$$V_i(15\text{–}19; 20\text{–}24) = U_i(15\text{–}19; 20\text{–}24)$$

$$/L_i(15\text{–}19; 20\text{–}24), \tag{A2.4}$$

$$V_i(X, X + 4; Y, Y + 4) = U_i(X, X + 4; Y, Y + 4)$$

$$/L_i(X, X + 4; Y, Y + 4). \tag{A2.5}$$

b. Input the estimated widowhood rates and divorce rates and the remarriage rates estimated above for ages 15–19 to 20–24 for a cohort whose members are 25–29 years old at the time of the census (assuming that the 25–29 year cohort had the same remarriage rates between ages 15–19 and 20–24 as the 20–24 year cohort). We estimate the marital status at age 20–24 for the cohort whose members were 25–29 years old at the census. For the age interval (20–24; 25–29) of this cohort, we first estimate, as we did in step *a* for the 20–24 year cohort, the number of widowed or divorced women at age 25–29, assuming no one remarried in the age interval (20–24; 25–29). (Note that the remarriages in the age interval [15–19; 20–24] for this cohort have been accounted for.) Comparing this figure with the census observations of the number of widowed or divorced women for this cohort, one obtains the number of remarriages in the age interval (20–24; 25–29) for this cohort. Thus, the remarriage rate for the age interval (20–24; 25–29) can be estimated.

Table A2.1. Reconstructed and observed proportion remarried

	25–29	30–34	35–39	40–44	45–49
Reconstructed	0.012	0.032	0.048	0.062	0.077
Fertility survey observation	0.016	0.031	0.049	0.073	0.099

Source: The observed proportion remarried was derived from the one-per-thousand fertility survey, SFPC 1984.

c. By repeating the above calculations, we can estimate remarriage rates up to ages 45–49 to 50–54.

d. Since we do not have enough first-marriage data for cohorts whose members are older than 55 and the estimation of mortality levels and divorce levels for very old cohorts is problematic, we apply estimation procedures up to the 50–54 year cohort. The remarriage rates for ages over 50–54 years are derived by extrapolation.

Has indirect estimation given us acceptable remarriage rates? To answer this question, we perform two calculations for each cohort of 5-year age groups from 25 to 49 (the number of remarriages under age 25 is too small to test): (1) We input the cohort age-specific first-marriage rates, widowhood rates, divorce rates, and remarriage rates for each cohort to reconstruct the proportion of widowed and divorced at each age. (2) We input the cohort age-specific first-marriage rates, widowhood rates, and divorce rates but set all remarriage rates equal to 0 for each cohort to obtain the proportion of widowed and divorced at each age if no remarriage has taken place at all. Subtracting the result of (1) from the result of (2) yields the proportion remarried at each age. We compare the reconstructed proportion of remarried women with the proportion of remarried women observed from the 1982 one-per-thousand fertility survey in table A2.1. We found that they are relatively close to each other. We can therefore trust that our estimated remarriage patterns are reasonably acceptable.

Bibliography

Bai Jianhua. 1986. Status of China's urban-rural population *Population Research* (in Chinese), no. 2. pp. 11–14.

Banister, J. 1985. Surprises and confirmations in the results of China's 1982 census. In Conference volume of the 20th conference of the International Union for the Scientific Study of Population. Florence, June, 1985. Vol. 4, pp. 465–78.

Banister, J. 1986. *Urban-rural population projection for China*. Staff paper of Centre for International Research, no. 50. Washington: U.S. Bureau of the Census.

Banister, J. 1990. Implications of the aging of China's population. In *Changing family structure and population aging in China: A comparative approach*, ed. Zena Yi, Zhang Chunyuan and Peng Songjian. Beijing: Peking University Press.

Banister, J., and S. H. Preston. 1981. Mortality in China. *Population and Development Review* 7(1):98–109.

Barclay, G. W., A. J. Coale, M. A. Stoto, and T. J. Trussel. 1976. A reassessment of the demography of traditional China. *Population Index* 42(4):606–35.

Bongaarts, J. 1983. The formal demography of family and households: An overview. *IUSSP Newsletter*, no. 17 (November).

Bongaarts, J. 1987. The projection of family composition over the life course with family status life tables. In Bongaarts, Burch and Wachter 1987.

Bongaarts, J., T. Burch, and K. W. Wachter, eds. 1987. *Family demography: Methods and applications*. Oxford: Oxford University Press.

Bongaarts, J., and S. Greenhalgh. 1985. An alternative to the one-child policy in China. *Population and Development Review* 11(4):585–617.

Brass, W. 1983. The formal demography of the family: An overview of the proximate determinants. In *The family*. Occasional paper 31. London: Office of Population Censuses and Surveys.

Brass, W. 1984. Mortality in China over the past fifty years: Indirect estimates from the 1982 census. Paper presented at the international seminar on China's 1982 population census, March 26–31, Beijing.

Burch, T. K. 1970. Some demographic determinants of average household size: An analytic approach. *Demography* 7(1):61–69.

Burch, T. K. 1979. Households and family demography: A bibliographic essay. *Population Index* 43(2):173–95.

Caldwell, J. M., M. Bracher, G. Santow, and P. Caldwell. 1984. Population trends in China: A perspective provided by the 1982 census. Paper presented at the international seminar on China's 1982 population census. March 26–31, Beijing.

Calot, G. 1985. Quelques suggestions visant à faciliter l'analyse des statistiques démographiques chinoises. In Conference volume of the 20th conference of the International Union for the Scientific Study of Population. Florence, June, 1985. Vol. 4, pp. 479–502.

CASS (Institute of Population Research, China Academy of Social Sciences). 1988. China's 1987 sample survey of elderly population age 60 and above. Special issue of *Population Sciences of China (I)* (in Chinese).

CBS (Central Bureau of Statistics of the Netherlands). 1984. *Over-levingstafels naar burgelijke staat, 1976–1980* (Life tables by marital status, 1976–1980). Voorburg and Heerlen, Netherlands.

Chen, Pi-Chao, and Adrienne Kols. 1982. Population and birth planning in the People's Republic of China. *Population Report*, no. 25.

Chiang, C. L. 1984. *The life table and its applications*. Malabar, Florida: Robert E. Krieger Publishing Co.

Chiang, C. L., and B. J. van den Berg. 1982. A fertility table for the analysis of human reproduction. *Mathematical Biosciences* 62:237–51.

CICRED. 1984. *Demography of the family*. Inter-centre Cooperative Research Programme, project no. 2: final report. Paris: CICRED.

Coale, A. J. 1965. Appendix: Estimates of average size of household. In *Aspects of the analysis of family structure*, ed. A. J. Coale et al. Princeton, N.J.: Princeton University Press.

Coale A. J. 1972. *The growth and structure of human populations: A mathematical investigation*. Princeton, N.J.: Princeton University Press.

Coale, A. J. 1981a. A further note on Chinese population statistics. *Population and Development Review* 7(3):512–18.

Coale, A. J. 1981b. Population trends, population policy and population studies in China. *Population and Development Review* 7(1):85–97.

Coale, A. 1984. *Rapid population change in China, 1952–1982*. Committee on Population and Demography, National Research Council, Report no. 27. Washington, D.C.: National Academy Press.

Coale, A., and Chen Shengli. 1985. Age-specific and duration-specific fertility in the provinces of China, 1940–1982. Paper presented at the international symposium on China's one-per-thousand fertility survey, October 14–18, Beijing.

Concepción, M. B., and Felipe Landa-Jocano. 1974. Demographic factors influencing the family cycle. In *The population debate: Dimensions and perspectives (Papers of the World Population Conference, Bucharest, 1974)*. Vol. 2. New York: United Nations.

CPIC (China Population Information Centre), ed. 1984. *Analysis of China's national one-per-thousand population fertility sampling survey*. Beijing: CPIC.

Dankert, Gabriele, Qian Zhenchao, and Xu Gang. 1989. China in-depth fertility survey phase I: household structure. Unpublished paper.

Dankert, Gabriele, and Hu Yu. 1989. Coresidence with parents: level and trends in six provinces of China. Unpublished paper.

Encyclopedic Yearbook of China. 1982. Beijing: China Great Encyclopedia Publishing House.

Espenshade, T. J. 1985. Marriage trends in America: Estimates, implications and causes. *Population and Development Review* 11(2):193–245.

Feeney, G. 1985. Parity progression projection. In Conference volume of the 20th conference of the International Union for the Scientific Study of Population. Florence, June, 1985. Vol. 4, pp. 125–36.

Feeney, G., and Yu Jingyuan. 1987. Period parity progression measures of fertility in China. *Population Studies* 41(1):77–102.

Fei Xiaotong. 1982. Changes in Chinese family structure. *China Reconstruction*, July 1982, pp. 23–26.

Fei Xiaotong. 1983. Problem of providing for the senile in the changing family structure. *Journal of Peking University (Philosophy and Social Sciences)* (in Chinese), no. 3:6–15.

Freedman, R., Baron Moots, Te-Hsiung Sun, and M. B. Weinberger. 1978. Household composition and extended kinship in Taiwan. *Population Studies* 32(1):65–80.

Freedman, R., Ming-Cheng Chang, and Te-Hsiung Sun. 1982. Household composition, extended kinship and reproduction in Taiwan: 1973–1980. *Population Studies* 36(3):395–411.

Gambill, B. A., and J. W. Vaupel. 1985. The LEXIS program for creating shaded contour maps of demographic surfaces. International Institute for Applied Systems Analysis Working Paper 85–94. Laxenburg, Austria.

Goldstein, S. 1985. Urbanization in China: New insights from the 1982 census. *Papers of the East-West Center Population Institute*, no. 93.

Goldstein, S., and A. Goldstein. 1985. Population mobility in the People's Republic of China. *Papers of the East-West Center Population Institute*, no. 95.

Goodman, L. A., N. Keyfitz, and T. W. Pullum. 1974. Family formation and the frequency of various kinship relationships. *Theoretical Population Biology* 5(1):1–27.

Goodman, L. A., N. Keyfitz, and T. W. Pullum. 1975. Addendum to Family formation and the frequency of various kinship relationships. *Theoretical Population Biology* 8:378–81.

Graunt, J. 1977. National and political observations mentioned in the following index and made upon the bill, of mortality. In Smith D. and N. Keyfitz (eds). *Mathematical Demography: Selected Papers*, New York: Springer-Verlag.

GRFFC (Group of Researchers on Families in Five Cities). 1985. *Families in the cities in China: Survey report and data compilation of the family survey in five cities* (in Chinese). Shandong: Shandong People's Press.

Henry, L. 1965. French statistical research in natural fertility. In *Public Health and Population Change*, ed. M. C. Sheps and J. C. Ridley. Pittsburgh: University of Pittsburgh Press.

Hirosima, K. 1984. A basic demographic condition for living arrangement: Formal demography of parent-child co-residentiality. Paper presented at the seminar on the demography of the latter phases of the family life cycle, September, Berlin.

Hoem, J. 1970. Probabilistic fertility models of the life table type. *Theoretical Population Biology* 1(1):12–38.

Hoem, J., and U. Funck Jensen. 1982. Multi-state life table methodology: A probabilistic critique. In Land and Rogers 1982a.

Hofferth, S. L. 1985. Updating children's life course. *Journal of Marriage and the
Family* 47(1):93–115.

Hu Huanyong. 1982. *A brief survey of China's population geography*. Shanghai: Shanghai Foreign Language Education Press.

Hu Huanyong 1983. *The population densities of China's eight major regions and the relevant population policies*. Shanghai: Shanghai Foreign Language Education Press.

Hu Huanyong and Zhang Shanyu. 1982. *World population geography* (in Chinese).
Shanghai: East China Normal University Press.

Imhoff, E. Van. 1988. A general characterization of consistency algorithms in multidimensional demographic projection models. Manuscript.

Jiang Zheng-hua, Zhang Wei-min, and Zhu Li-wei. 1984. The preliminary study to the
life expectancy at birth for China's population. Paper presented at the international
seminar on China's 1982 population census, March 26–31, Beijing.

Kannisto, V. 1984. Features of the 1982 China census from an international stand-
point. Paper presented at the international seminar on China's 1982 population census, March 26–31, Beijing.

Keilman, N. 1985a. Internal and external consistency in multidimensional population
projection models. *Environment and Planning A* 17:1473–98.

Keilman, N. 1985b. Measuring period first marriage. In Conference volume of the
20th conference of the International Union for the Scientific Study of Population.
Informal session 7. Florence, June, 1985.

Keilman, N. 1985c. Nuptiality models and the two-sex problem in national population
forecasts. *European Journal of Population* 1(2/3):207–35.

Keilman, N. 1986. Dynamic household models. In Keilman, Kuijsten, and Vossen
1986.

Keilman, N., and R. Gill. 1986. On the estimation of multidimensional demographic
models with population registration data. NIDI (Netherland, Interuniversity Demographic Institute) working paper no. 68. Den Haag.

Keilman, N., A. Kuijsten, and A. Vossen, eds. 1988. *Modelling household formation
and dissolution*. Oxford: Oxford University Press.

Keyfitz, N. 1979. Multidimensionality in population analysis. In *Sociological methodology, 1980*, ed. K. F. Schuessler. San Francisco: Jossey-Bass.

Keyfitz, N. 1984. The population of China. *Scientific American* 250(2):22–31.

Keyfitz, N. 1985. *Applied mathematical demography*. 2nd ed. New York: Springer-
Verlag.

Kiernan, K. E. 1985. The departure of children: The timing of leaving home over the life
cycles of parents and children. *CPS Research Paper* (Centre for Population Studies,
London School of Hygiene and Tropical Medicine) 85(3).

Kobayashi, K., and K. Tanaka. 1984. *Population of Japan*. Country Monograph Series,
no. 11, United Nations ESCAP, Bangkok, Thailand, 1984, 140–62.

Krishnamoorthy, S. 1979. Classical approach to increment-decrement life tables: An
application to the study of the marital status of United States female, 1970. *Mathematical Biosciences* 44:139–54.

Krishnamoorthy, S. 1980. Effects of fertility and mortality on extinction of family and number of living children. *Social Biology* 27(1):62–69.

Krishnan, P., and A. K. Kayani. 1976. Model divorce tables. *Genus* 32(1–2):109–26.

Kuijsten, A. C. 1984. Application of household models in studying the family life cycle. Paper presented at the international workshop on Modelling of Household Formation and Dissolution, December 12–14, Voorburg, Netherlands.

Land, K. C., and A. Rogers. 1982a. *Multidimensional mathematical demography*. New York: Academic Press.

Land, K. C., and A. Rogers. 1982b. Multidimensional mathematical demography: an overview. In Land and Rogers 1982a.

Land, K. C., and R. Schoen. 1982. Statistical methods for Markov-generated increment-decrement life tables with polynomial gross flow functions. In Land and Rogers 1982a.

Lavely, R., and Li Bohua. 1985. A tentative survey on family structure in Liaoning, Hebei and Fujian provinces. Paper presented at the international symposium of China's one-per-thousand fertility survey, October 14–18, Beijing.

LeBras, H. 1978. Living forebears in stable populations. In *Statistical studies of historical social structure*, ed. K. E. Wachter, E. A. Hammel, and P. Laslett. New York: Academic Press.

Ledent, J. 1980. Multi-state (increment-decrement) life tables: Movement versus transition perspective. *Environment and Planning A* 12:533–62.

Ledent, J. 1982. Transition probability estimation in increment-decrement life tables using mobility data from a census or a survey. In Land and Rogers 1982a.

Ledent, J., and P. Rees. 1986. Life tables. In Rogers and Willekens 1986.

Lesthaeghe, R. 1973. The feasibility of controlling population growth through nuptiality and nuptiality policies. In Conference volume of the international population conference of the International Union for the Scientific Study of Population, Liège. 9.1.b, pp. 319–41.

Lesthaeghe, R. 1980. On the social control of human reproduction. *Population and Development Review* 6(4):527–48.

Li Bohua and Chi-hsien Tuan. 1985. The Chinese sex ratio at birth (1930–1981). Paper presented at the international symposium on China's one-per-thousand fertility survey. October 14–18, Beijing.

Li Chengrui. 1985a. Evaluation of the results of China's 1982 population census and problems discussed by the IUSSP Florence conference. *Population Research* (in Chinese), no. 6:1–5.

Li Chengrui. 1985b. The reliability of China's 1982 population census data. In Conference volume of the 20th conference of the International Union for the Scientific Study of Population. Florence, June, 1985. Vol. 4, pp. 125–36.

Li Hechang, Song Tingyou, and Li Cheng. 1984. Current fertility state of women of Han and minority nationalities in rural areas. In CPIC 1984.

Li Ning. 1985. How does China deal with divorce? *Beijing Review*, no. 5 (February 4): 18–21.

Li Rongshi. 1985. A tentative analysis of the age at first marriage in China. *Population Research* (in Chinese), no. 1:28–32.

Lin Xiao and Bi Ke. 1984. A sample survey of 709 elderly urban citizens. *Social Science* (in Chinese), no. 6:61–70.

Liu Yin. 1984. A tentative analysis of three-generation families in China: Survey report of "model families" in Beijing. *Sociology Bulletin* (in Chinese), March, pp. 45–50.

Liu Yin. 1985. Development of and changes in urban families in China: A tentative analysis of the family survey of Beijing, Tianjin, Shanghai, Nankin, and Hangchow cities (in Chinese). Paper presented at the second international conference on Modernization and Chinese Culture, November, Hong Kong.

Liu Zheng. 1985a. Overview of formal session 27 on the 1982 census of China. In Conference volume of the 20th conference of the International Union for the Scientific Study of Population. Florence, June, 1985. Vol. 4, pp. 427–28.

Liu Zheng. 1985b. Population age structure and sex ratio in 1982. *Population Research* (in Chinese), no. 6:7–10.

Lu Shuhua. 1984. Social statistical analysis in sampling survey of marriages and families in Beijing. *Journal of Beijing Normal University* (in Chinese), Social Science Edition, no. 5:82–89.

Lutz, W., and G. Feichtinger. 1985. A life table approach to parity progression and marital status transitions. Paper contributed to the 20th conference of the International Union for Scientific Study of Population, Florence, June, 1985.

Ma An. 1984. An evaluation on the quality of the data of the 1982 population census in China. In *A Census of One Billion People*, ed. Li Chengrui et al. Beijing.

Ma Xia. 1984. An analysis on the size of family household and family structure in China. Paper presented at the international seminar on China's 1982 population census, March 26–31, Beijing.

Ma Xia. 1988. Criterion for urban-rural classification and the level of urban development. *Population and Economics* (in Chinese), no. 6:29–33.

Ma Yingtong and Wang Yanzu. 1985. A study on the first marriage and fertility status of Chinese women. Paper presented at the international symposium on China's one-per-thousand fertility survey. October 14–18, Beijing.

Martin, L. G., and S. Culter. 1983. Mortality decline and Japanese family structure. *Population and Development Review* 9(4):633–49.

Menken, J. 1985. Age and fertility: How late can you wait? *Demography* 22(4):469–83.

Notestein, F. 1969. Population growth and economic development. *Population and Development Review* 9(2):345–60.

Nour, E., and C. M. Suchindran. 1984a. The construction of multi-state life tables: Comments on the article by Willekens et al. *Population Studies* 38:325–28.

Nour, E., and C. M. Suchindran. 1984b. The interaction between marital status and childbearing: A multi-state life table approach. Paper presented at the 1984 annual meeting of the Population Association of America, May 3–5, Minneapolis.

Oechsli, F. W. 1975. A population model based on a life table that includes marriage and parity. *Theoretical Population Biology* 7(2):229–45.

OPCS (Office of Population Census and Surveys). 1983. The family. Occasional papers no. 31. London: OPCS.

Page, H. J. 1977. Pattern underlying fertility schedules: A decomposition by both age and marriage duration. *Population Studies* 31(1):85–106.

Pan Yongkang and Pan Nai-gu. 1982. On the urban family and family structure in China. *Tianjin Social Sciences* (in Chinese), no. 3:7–14.

Preston, S. H. 1982. Relations between individual life cycles and population characteristics. *American Sociological Review* 47:253–64.

Priest, G. E. 1985. Private households by number of generations present: New data from the census of Canada. *Canadian Statistical Review* 60(1):6–10.

Priest, G. E., and Pryor, E. T. 1984. Household composition: 1982 census of China. Paper presented at the international seminar on China's 1982 population census, March 26–31, Beijing.

Qian Xinzhong. 1983a. China's population policy: Theory and methods. *Studies in Family Planning* 14(12).

Qian Xinzhong. 1983b. Speech at the Third Asian and Pacific Population Conference: "Population policy and family planning practice". Edited by China Population Information Centre and the State Family Planning Commission, Beijing.

Qiu Shuhua, Wu Shutao, Wang Meizeng. 1984. Birth control of women of reproductive age. In CPIC 1984.

Rodriguez, G., and J. N. Hobcraft. 1980. *Illustrative analysis: Life table analysis of birth intervals in Colombia.* Scientific Reports, no. 16. London: World Fertility Survey.

Rogers, A. 1975. *Introduction to Multi-regional Mathematical Demography.* New York: John Wiley & Sons.

Rogers, A., and J. Ledent. 1976. Increment-decrement tables: A comment. *Demography* 13(2):287–90.

Rogers, A., and F. Willekens, eds. 1986. *Migration and settlement: A multi-regional comparative study.* Dordrecht, Netherlands: Reidel Press.

Ryder, N. B. 1974. Reproductive behaviour and the family life cycle. In *The population debate: Dimensions and perspectives (Papers of the World Population Conference, Bucharest, 1974).* Vol. 2. New York: United Nations.

Ryder, N. B. 1977. Methods in measuring the family life cycle. In Conference proceedings of the international population conference of the International Union for the Scientific Study of Population, Mexico 1977, Liège, pp. 219–26.

Schoen, R. 1975. Constructing increment-decrement life tables. *Demography* 12:313–24.

Schoen, R. 1988. *Modeling Multi-group Populations.* New York: Plenum Press.

Schoen, R., and J. Baj. 1984. Twentieth-century cohort marriage and divorce in England and Wales. *Population Studies* 38(3):439–49.

Schoen, R., and W. Urton. 1979. *Marital status life tables for Sweden: Years 1911–1973 and cohorts born 1885–89 to 1940–44.* Stockholm: National Central Bureau of Statistics, Urval No. 10.

SDSFPC (Statistical Department, State Family Planning Commission). 1989. Report on the major results of the national two-per-thousand fertility and contraceptive survey (in Chinese). Beijing.

SFPC (State Family Planning Commission). 1984. Chart of one-per-thousand population fertility sampling survey in China. Special issue of *Population and Economy.*

Shen Biguang, and Ma Qingping. 1984. Recent marriage and the marriage state of women of Han and minority nationalities in rural areas. In CPIC 1984.

Song Jian, Chi-Hsien Tuan, and Jing-Yuan Yu. 1985. *Population control in China: Theory and applications*. New York: Praeger Press.

Song Yuanjie, Shi Yulin, and Zhan Guichao. 1984. The birth order of women's fertility. In CPIC 1984.

SSB (State Statistical Bureau of China). 1982. *Important data from China's third population census* (in Chinese). Beijing: Statistical Press of China.

SSB. 1983a. *Statistical yearbook of China, 1983*. Hong Kong: Economic Information Agency.

SSB. 1983b. *10 Percent sampling tabulation on the 1982 population census of the People's Republic of China (computer tabulation)* (in Chinese). Beijing: Statistical Press of China.

SSB. 1984a. *China's major statistics—1984* (in Chinese). Beijing: Statistical Press of China.

SSB. 1984b. *Statistical yearbook of China, 1984* (in Chinese). Beijing: Statistical Press of China.

SSB. 1985. Data for servicemen at the 1982 population census. *Population Research* (in Chinese), no. 6:5.

SSB. 1986. *Preliminary report on In-Depth Fertility Surveys in China, phase 1*. Beijing.

SSB. 1988a. China Population Statistics Yearbook, 1988. Beijing: China Prospective Press.

SSB. 1988b. *Preliminary report on the second phase of China's In-Depth-Fertility Surveys*. Beijing.

SSB. 1988c. *Tabulations of China's 1987 1% Population Sample Survey: National Volume* (in Chinese). Beijing.

SSB. 1988d. *Major figures of China's 1987 1% Population Sample Survey*. Beijing: China Statistical Press.

State Family Planning Commission. 1983. *Data collection of China's National One-per-Thousand Population Fertility Sampling Survey* (National volume). Beijing.

Suchindran, C. M., N. K. Namboodiri, and K. West. 1979. Increment-decrement tables for human reproduction. *Journal of Biosocial Sciences* 11(4):443–56.

Tien H. Yuan. 1983. China: Demographic billionaire. *Population Bulletin* 38(2) (special issue).

Vaupel, J. W., B. A. Gambill, and A. I. Yashin. 1985. Contour maps of population surfaces. International Institute for Applied Systems Analysis Working Paper 85-47. Laxenburg, Austria.

Watkins, S. C., J. Menken, and J. Bongaarts. 1984. Continuities and changes in the American family. Paper presented at the 1984 annual meeting of the Social Science History Association, May, California.

Wei Zhangling. 1983. Chinese family problems: Research and trends. *Journal of Marriage and the Family* 45(4):943–48.

Wijewickrema, S. 1987. Family status life table for Belgium: Construction and ensuing simulations. Interuniversity Programme in Demography Working Paper 1987-5. Brussels Free University.

Wijewickrema, S., and Alii 1983. Marital status trends in Belgium (1961–1977): Application of multistate analysis. In *Population and family in the Low Countries*, IV. Voorburg and Heerlen, Netherlands.

Willekens, F. 1979. *Computer program for increment-decrement (multi-state) life table analysis: A user's manual to LIFEINDEC*. WP-79-102. Laxenburg, Austria: International Institute for Applied Systems Analysis.

Willekens, F. 1982. Multidimensional population analysis with incomplete data. In Land and Rogers 1982a.

Willekens, F. J. 1983. Multistate life table analysis of marriage and family. Paper presented at the IUSSP workshop on Family Demography: Methods and Their Applications. December, New York.

Willekens, F. J. 1987. The marital status life table. In Bongaarts, Burch, and Wachter 1987.

Willekens, F. J. 1988. A life course perspective on household dynamics. In Keilman, N., A. Kuijsten and A. Vossen (eds): *Modelling household formation and dissolution*. Oxford: Oxford University Press.

Willekens, F. J. 1989. Life course analysis: Stochastic process models. Manuscript.

Willekens, F. J., and A. Rogers. 1978. Spatial population analysis: Methods and computer programs. International Institute for Applied Systems Analysis Research Report RR-78-18. Laxenburg, Austria.

Willekens, F. J., I. Shah, J. M. Shah, and P. Ramachandran. 1982. Multistate analysis of marital status life tables: Theory and application. *Population Studies* 36(1):129–44.

Wu Cangping. 1985a. Demographic transition in China, inferred from age structure of the 1982 census. In Conference volume of the 20th conference of the International Union for the Scientific Study of Population. Florence, June, 1985. Vol. 4, pp. 453–64.

Wu Cangping. 1985b. A preliminary inquiry into the strategy of China's population development. *Population Research* (in Chinese), no. 5:2–8.

Wunsch, G. J., and M. G. Termote. 1978. *Introduction to demographic analysis, principles and methods*. New York and London: Plenum Press.

Xiao Wencheng, Li Menghua, and Wang Liying. 1983. Changes in the total fertility of women since the 1950s. In CPIC 1984.

Yang Shuzhang and Lancy Dodd. 1985. A statistical analysis of infant mortality in China. Paper presented at the international symposium on China's one-per-thousand fertility survey, October 14–18, Beijing.

Yu, Y. C. 1984. The reliability of China's 1982 population census. Paper presented at the international seminar on China's 1982 population census, March 26–31, Beijing.

Yun Kalin. 1985. Primary research on ways of providing for the aged. *Social Science Front* (in Chinese) 8(1):106–11.

Zeng Yi. 1984. Raising education level and population control in rural areas in China. In *Articles on Population Research*. Vol. 3. East China Normal University Press (in Chinese). Shanghai.

Zeng Yi. 1985a. Het Chinese gezin in demografisch pespectief (A demographic profile of family in China). *Demos* (Netherlands Interuniversity Demographic Institute, Voorburg), no. 4.

Zeng Yi. 1985b. Marriage and marriage dissolution in China: A marital status life table analysis. Paper presented at the 20th General Conference of the International Union of Scientific Study of Population, Florence, June, 1985 and Working Paper No. 57, NIDI, Voorburg.

Zeng Yi. 1986. Changes in family structure in China: A simulation study. *Population and Development Review* 12(4):675–703.

Zeng Yi. 1988. Changing demographic characteristics and the family status of Chinese women. *Population Studies* 42(2):183–203.

Zeng Yi. 1989a. Is China's family planning program tightening up? *Population and Development Review* 15(2):333–37.

Zeng Yi. 1989b. A Policy in Transition. *People* 16(1):20–22.

Zeng Yi. 1989c. Population policy in China: New challenge and strategies. In *An aging world*, ed. J. M. Eekelaar and D. Pearl. Oxford: Oxford University Press.

Zeng Yi and A. Coale. 1990. Age schedules of leaving the parental home. In Zeng, Zhang, and Peng 1990.

Zeng Yi, Zhang Chunyuan, and Peng Shongjian, eds. 1990. *Changing family structure and population aging in China: A comparative approach.* Beijing: Peking University Press.

Zeng Yi and J. Vaupel. 1989. Impact of urbanization and delayed childbearing on population growth and aging in China. *Population and Development Review* 15(3).

Zeng Yi, J. Vaupel, and A. Yashin. 1985. Marriage and fertility in China: A graphical analysis. *Population and Development Review* 11(4):721–36.

Zhao Weigang and Yu Huilin. 1984. Changes in women's ages at first marriage since liberation. In CPIC 1984.

Zhao Xishun. 1985. An analysis of rural family structure and its transition in China (in Chinese). Paper presented at the second international conference on Modernization and Chinese Culture, November, Hong Kong.

Zhao Xuan. 1983. State of women's first marriage in forty-two years from 1940 to 1981. In CPIC 1984.

Zhao Xuan. 1985. Report of a sampling survey (conducted in 1983) on female first marriage and fertility status in 1982. *Population and Economy* (in Chinese), no. 4:27–34.

Name Index

Subject Index